THE DEVELOPMENT OF THE DETECTIVE NOVEL

Charles Dickens

Wilkie Collins

Sheridan Le Fanu

Lord Bulwer-Lytton

Alexandre Dumas

Edgar Allan Poe

THE
DEVELOPMENT
OF THE
DETECTIVE NOVEL

A. E. MURCH M.A.

GREENWOOD PRESS, PUBLISHERS
WESTPORT, CONNECTICUT

The Library of Congress cataloged this book as follows:

Murch, Alma Elizabeth.
    The development of the detective novel ₍by₎ A. E. Murch.
New York, Greenwood Press ₍1968, ᶜ1958₎

    272 p. ports. 23 cm.

    Bibliography : p. 258–269.

    1. Detective and mystery stories—History and criticism.
ɪ. Title.

    PN3448.D4M78   1968b   809.3′872   69–10138

    Library of Congress   ₍3₎

This edition originally published in 1958 by Philosophical
Library Inc., New York

Reprinted with the permission of Peter Owen, Ltd

Reprinted by Greenwood Press,
a division of Williamhouse-Regency Inc.

First Greenwood Reprinting 1968
Second Greenwood Reprinting 1975

Library of Congress Catalog Card Number 69-10138

ISBN 0-8371-0581-1

Printed in the United States of America

CONTENTS

ILLUSTRATIONS

Frontispiece

Charles Dickens
Wilkie Collins
Sheridan Le Fanu
Lord Bulwer-Lytton
Alexandre Dumas
Edgar Allan Poe

Facing page 64

Vidocq
G. K. Chesterton
Mary Roberts Rinehart
Sir Arthur Conan Doyle
A. E. W. Mason
Dorothy Sayers

Facing page 96

Agatha Christie
Michael Innes
Erle Stanley Gardner
Georges Simenon
John Dickson Carr
Margaret Millar

PREFACE

The idea that inspired this book sprang from an informal occasion at Bristol University a few years ago, when the conversation turned to detective fiction and the comment was made that its origins might well be explored more fully than hitherto. My thanks are due to Professor W. McC. Stewart for his encouragement and interest, and to Dr. S. C. Gould, whose stimulating comments have been invaluable to me as the work began to take shape. I am grateful to Mr. Darsie Gillie for information on certain points concerning the judicial system of France, and to Mr. J. Shum Cox and his staff at the Bristol University Library for their helpful co-operation. I should also like to express my appreciation of the special facilities for research extended to me by the London Library, the Bodleian Library and the Taylor Institution of Oxford University.

The staff of the Oxford County Library, and the Public Libraries of Banbury and Leamington Spa, have been very helpful; the trustees of the Estate of Sir Arthur Conan Doyle, and Messrs. John Murray Ltd., have kindly permitted quotations from *Memories and Adventures*; Messrs. Ernest Benn have allowed me to use excerpts from works by M. P. Shiel and John Gawsworth; the National Portrait Gallery has provided portraits of Edward Bulwer-Lytton, Wilkie Collins, Charles Dickens and Gilbert Keith Chesterton; and the picture of Sheridan Le Fanu was supplied by the Hulton Press. I am grateful to Messrs. Victor Gollancz for photographs of Dorothy L. Sayers and Michael Innes; to Messrs. Elliott and Fry for their portrait of A. E. W. Mason; and to Camera Press, Ltd., for their studies of Agatha Christie and John Dickson Carr. Messrs. Heinemann were good enough to send me a portrait of Erle Stanley Gardner; Messrs. Routledge & Kegan Paul, one of Georges Simenon. Through the courtesy of two American publishers, Messrs. Rinehart & Co. Inc., and Random House, Inc., it was fortunately possible to include photographs of Mary Roberts Rinehart and Margaret Millar. To all who have assisted in these various ways, my appreciative thanks.

INTRODUCTION

A very considerable proportion of the popular novels and short
stories written in England, France and America during the last
hundred years are of the type known as Detective Fiction, a type
which has acquired a separate existence largely within that
period.

General studies of the history of fiction have given singularly
little consideration to this variety of popular literature. Specialised discussions of detective fiction did not begin to appear until
the second and third decades of the twentieth century, when the
subject attracted several writers in quick succession. Carolyn
Wells wrote a brief study of *The Technique of the Mystery Story*
(1913)[1] from the stand-point of an American writer, and E. M.
Wrong gave a review of the history and characteristics of English
detective fiction as an Introduction to a collection of short stories,
Crime and Detection (1921).[2] The American author Willard
Huntington Wright, "S. S. Van Dine," also compiled an anthology, *The World's Great Detective Stories* (1927)[3] with an Introduction discussing fiction of this type and its place in literature.
In England, Dorothy L. Sayers, introducing her first anthology
of *Great Short Stories of Detection, Mystery and Horror* (1928)[4]
gave as comprehensive a survey of the subject as could be contained within some thirty pages. Régis Messac, a distinguished
French scholar writing in Montreal, studied certain aspects of
such fiction in his *Le "Detective Novel" et l'influence de la
pensée scientifique,*[5] and some years later another French writer,
François Fosca, published his *Histoire et technique du roman-
policier,*[6] dealing more particularly with developments in the
twentieth century from the French point of view. Neither of
these two French works became available in English translation.

[1] Published at Springfield, Mass., by the *Home Correspondence School.*
[2] World Classics Series, Eng. O.U.P., 1921; New York, O.U.P., 1926.
[3] Published New York, Scribners.
[4] London, Gollancz, 1928. Published in America with the title: *The Omnibus of
Crime,* New York, Payson & Clarke, 1929.
[5] Paris, Champion, 1929.
[6] Paris, Nouvelle revue critique, 1937.

Since that time, several authors[1] have examined the techniques of detective story writing, generally as a guide to new writers in the *genre*, but they have not been concerned to show how or when these details of technique originated, or the way in which the now-familiar patterns were gradually evolved.

In touching upon the history of the detective story, most of these writers begin with the tales of Edgar Allan Poe. After some reference to Wilkie Collins and the French school of Gaboriau, they move on to Conan Doyle, G. K. Chesterton, E. C. Bentley, and so to more recent times. These famous names are important landmarks in the evolution of the *genre*, but the intervals that lie between them, the paths that lead from one to another, have been left virtually unexplored. There were detective themes in fiction before Poe; considerable further developments took place in the popular literature of France and the English-speaking world before Lecoq emerged to rival Dupin, and was in his turn eclipsed by Sherlock Holmes; and in many cases the techniques perfected in the twentieth century have been evolved from experiments first made in the nineteenth. It has therefore seemed worth while to enquire more closely into the evolution of the detective novel, (or the detective story, for the length is immaterial), from the time when analogous themes first appeared in fiction up to the present day, when its popularity seems to have reached its zenith.

This popularity first began to manifest itself in the middle of the nineteenth century, when a new, rapidly increasing reading public developed a preference for novels that offered entertainment and relaxation. Fiction which made a strong appeal to curiosity and a taste for excitement was still considered undesirable by more discriminating readers, but by 1883 this view was largely superseded, and the *Saturday Review* was frankly discussing the general popularity of detective fiction in England.[2]

---

[1] Cf. H. Douglas Thomson, *Masters of Mystery*, London, Collins, 1931.
Howard Haycraft, *Murder for Pleasure*, London, Peter Davies, 1942.
Sutherland Scott, *Blood in Their Ink*, London & New York, Stanley Paul, 1953.
Marie F. Rodell, *Mystery Fiction: Theory and Technique*, London, Hammond & Hammond, 1954.
[2] The *Saturday Review*, May 5th, 1883 (Vol. LV, p. 558).

With the appearance of Sherlock Holmes a few years later a new era dawned, that was to raise English fiction of this type to an important place in the popular literature of the world, and in 1901 G. K. Chesterton, discussing 'the genuine psychological reason for the popularity of detective stories,' said: —

> 'The first essential value of the detective story lies in this, that it is the earliest and only form of popular literature in which is expressed some sense of the poetry of modern life.[1]

From the 1920's onward, a great new growth of detective fiction began to appear and has continued to the present day. Writers have succeeded in creating their own special type of story, designed to appeal to a particular group of readers, and as a consequence new varieties of the *genre* have come into being, portraying all the diversities of modern civilisation. Somerset Maugham, discussing contemporary detective fiction and its literary importance, has said: —

> 'It may well be that when the historians of literature come to discourse upon the fiction produced by the English-speaking peoples in the first half of the twentieth century, they will pass somewhat lightly over the compositions of the 'serious' novelists and turn their attention to the immense and varied achievement of the detective writers.[2]

But to view this achievement in its true perspective, it is necessary to consider not only the developments in the first half of the twentieth century but also those which took place in the nineteenth, when stories of this kind first emerged as a distinct variety of fiction. French novels of similar type must also be included in any comprehensive survey, for these developments in France and the English-speaking countries are very closely associated.

There are, of course, differences between the detective stories produced in France, England and America, for the popular literature of any country has its own individuality, derived from its reflection of national character and contemporary economic

---

[1] ' In Defence of the Detective Story ', *The Defendant*, London, Dent, 1901.
[2] W. Somerset Maugham, ' The Decline and Fall of the Detective Story ', *The Vagrant Mood*, London, Heinemann, 1952, p. 110.

or social conditions. Fiction of this particular type is further affected by differences in the status and organisation of the police; in the judicial systems that have grown up in these countries, and in the attitude of the general public towards such matters. Basically, however, a detective story, whether written in French or English, may be defined as a tale in which the primary interest lies in the methodical discovery, by rational means, of the exact circumstances of a mysterious event or series of events. The story is designed to arouse the reader's curiosity by a puzzling problem which usually, though not always, concerns a crime. Fiction of this type, though not as yet precisely of 'fixed form,' has nevertheless acquired its own methods of plot construction, characteristic techniques of presentation and a code of ethical values peculiar to itself.

The detective story has links with certain other groups of popular fiction, notably the Crime Story and the Mystery Story. Indeed, these three groups are often considered as analogous. Taken all together, however, they represent an immense range, too extensive to be examined in any detail in a single volume, and to avoid confusion it seems advisable to consider what differences lie between them, and so to define more precisely the field we plan to cover.

Tales of crime are as old as civilisation, and constitute a vast literature of their own. It is true that detective fiction has inherited certain features from this group, such as studies of cunning criminals, reconstructions of ingenious crimes, and the *motif* of flight and pursuit, but whereas in the crime story these form the chief interest, in the detective story, if they appear at all, they are subordinate to the writer's primary purpose, which is to puzzle his readers and make them think.

The typical subject of the crime story is theft, carried out with quick-witted dexterity, the rogue's clever tricks being told to amuse the reader and arouse his sympathetic interest in the entertaining rascal, either out of admiration for his adroitness or because some past injustice drove him into dishonest practices. The tales of Robin Hood or Gil Blas; romantic highwaymen such as Dick Turpin, Claude Duval and Jack Sheppard; or the

11

exploits of more recent 'gentleman-adventurers,' are all crime stories, but not detective stories. In detective fiction the reader's sympathy is invariably engaged, if only by inference, on the side of law and order, and the hero is not the criminal, but the detective who is clever enough to catch him. Some detective stories are not concerned with a crime, and in that case the hero's function is simply to discover the truth. In Conan Doyle's *The Yellow Face* Sherlock Holmes was seriously misled, simply because he assumed that a crime had been committed, which was not so. Nevertheless, in spite of such exceptions, in the majority of detective stories the central puzzle does concern a crime, for crime lends itself particularly well to the creation of a dramatic and complicated plot, with an exciting chase and a display of detective acumen by an amateur or a police officer, leading to a sensational conclusion with all the evidence clearly explained and justice triumphant.

Humour and love-making almost invariably play an important part in the crime story, providing the only happy, human side-lights upon the rogue's career and securing the reader's interest. They have no real place in the detective story, for laughter does not mix harmoniously with analytical reasoning, and, as Sherlock Holmes once remarked to Dr. Watson : —

> 'Detection is, or ought to be, an exact science, and should be treated in the same cold and unemotional manner. To tinge it with romanticism produces much the same effect as if you worked a love-story or an elopement into the fifth proposition of Euclid.'

During the twentieth century some writers have disregarded this dictum, and have successfully introduced a love interest, or even humorous interludes into a detective novel. There is always the possibility, however, that such matters will divert attention from the detective theme.

The Mystery Story is also akin to, but not identical with, the detective story. If the mystery is the central problem and is eventually clarified through the efforts of an analytical reasoner, the story obviously comes within our purview; equally obviously we are not concerned with tales in which the mystery remains unexplained or is solved by chance. Le Fanu's *Uncle Silas* is a case in point. In this novel's closing pages a secret mechanism opens a locked room in a manner quite unforeseen and unsuspected, so that a hitherto unsolved murder mystery is at once explained, without the exercise of any detective powers.

Mysteries involving the supernatural are also, in general, outside our province, for they seek to disarm the reader's power of logical thought by arousing fear. Yet, paradoxically, a few detective story writers have found a use for supernatural themes. Very occasionally an author has gone so far as to show his detective grappling with 'other worldly' mysteries. Algernon Blackwood, in *John Silence, Physician Extraordinary*,[1] created a 'psychic doctor,' a kind of Sherlock Holmes of the spirit world, complete with a Watson-like colleague, Mr. Hubbard, and Sydney Horler's investigator, Sebastian Quin, dealt with a somewhat similar problem in *Black Magic*.[2] Such examples, however, are comparatively rare in detective fiction

Far more often the writer excites the reader's apprehensions by hinting at supernatural causes for some terrifying mystery which is eventually proved by the detective to have a perfectly rational explanation, *The Hound of the Baskervilles*[3] is an example of this technique, so is *The Ghost at Massingham Mansions*.[4] Many a reader finds a certain fascination in such themes, and the mystery grips his attention even more closely. But he fully expects that his detective-hero will, in due course, sweep away all ghostly fears and make everything clear.

It is true that many writers of detective fiction have also written stories of the supernatural, but they have generally kept the two varieties separate and distinct, not attempting to blend both in any one story. Poe wrote many terrifying tales of supernatural horror, but allowed no such thoughts to intrude upon the logical dissertations of his detective, Dupin, and later writers

[1] London, Eveleigh Nash, 1908.
[2] *The Screaming Skull*, London, Hodder & Stoughton. A collection of short stories of which *Black Magic* is one.
[3] A. Conan Doyle. First published as a serial in the *Strand Magazine*, August, 1901—April 1902.
[4] Ernest Bramah, *The Eyes of Max Carrados*, London, Grant Richards, 1923. A collection of short stories of which this is one.

have followed Poe's example fairly closely in this particular, as in others. Dorothy L. Sayers has clearly defined the essential difference between these two types of fiction: —

> 'The story of detection and the story of horror form about as strong a contrast as it is possible to imagine. Their aims are, indeed, entirely opposed. The detective story seeks to leave nothing unexplained; the story of horror must always leave us guessing.[1]

We shall follow the lead thus given by writers of detective fiction, and exclude tales of the supernatural as being beyond our scope, decision which has the support of fictional detectives themselves: —

> ' "Do you believe in ghosts, Max?" queried Mr. Carlyle. "Only as ghosts," replied Carrados with decision.'[2]

> ' " Are we to give serious attention to such things?" [demanded Sherlock Holmes, when a similar question arose.] "This Agency stands flat-footed upon the ground, and there it must remain. The world is big enough for us. No ghosts need apply." '[3]

*   *   *

Whether or not we agree with Chesterton that detective fiction expresses 'some sense of the poetry of modern life,' there can be no doubt that it expresses drama, especially the drama of city life, —the crowds of strangers, the ever-present possibility of a chance encounter with crime in a train or bus, the frightening, unexpected things that "could happen to any one" and which therefore are particularly thrilling to those city dwellers whose everyday life is humdrum. The detective story appeals not only to their need for drama but also to their curiosity, even to their

---

[1] D. L. Sayers, Introduction to the Third Series of *Great Short Stories of Detection, Mystery and Horror*, London, Gollancz, 1934. U.S. title: *The Third Omnibus of Crime*, New York, Coward, McCann, 1934.
[2] The opening lines of *The Ghost at Massingham Mansions*, Bramah, *Op. Cit.*
[3] Sir Arthur Conan Doyle, *The Complete Sherlock Holmes Short Stories*, London, Murray, 1928, p. 1179, ' The Sussex Vampire '.

self-esteem. Once an interesting puzzle has absorbed the reader's attention, his mind keeps questing forward until the explanation is within his grasp. He is particularly gratified if he succeeds in solving the problem himself, before being told the answer. Even if he fails to anticipate the solution he may still find, with some satisfaction, that his own general knowledge would have been adequate for the task, if only he had applied it constructively. He thinks "If I had really tried I could have fathomed that," and feels the equal of the detective-hero.

Sometimes the answer to the riddle may depend upon a scientific or pseudo-scientific fact of which he was previously unaware. His enjoyment is then enriched by the acquisition of interesting scraps of information on one or other of the many scientific subjects that can be harmoniously linked with the plot of a detective story, such as chemical tests for various poisons, details of forensic medicine, the systematic examination of material clues, or the work of police laboratories. Scientific discoveries are popularly considered to be based upon analytical reasoning from accurate observation of *minutiae*. Similar methods of deduction are employed by fictional detectives, many of whom are presented to the reader as actual scientists.

*   *   *

Régis Messac, tracing from very early times the connection between scientific thought and certain elements of detective fiction, has suggested that the story of Archimedes' discovery of his famous principle in hydrostatics could well be regarded as a detective novel.[1] A brief consideration of this idea may help to clarify some of the essential features of the modern detective story.

Heiro, King of Syracuse, suspecting he had been robbed, asked his friend Archimedes to find some way of proving whether this was so. Could he discover whether the craftsmen entrusted with

[1] Régis Messac, *op. cit.* p. 54.

gold to make a crown had, or had not, stolen some of that gold and replaced it with an equal weight of silver? Archimedes sought diligently for an answer to this problem without success, until one day, when stepping into an over-full bath, he noticed the water running out. By a brilliant flash of inductive reasoning he realised that the excess of bulk occasioned by the introduction of an alloy could be measured by putting the crown and an equal weight of gold separately into a vessel filled with water, and checking the difference of overflow. He was so overjoyed when this happy thought struck him that he rushed through the streets without his clothes, shouting "Eureka! I have found it!"

Here we have much that is familiar in modern detective fiction; the important client; the tantalizing problem about a crime; the distinguished investigator with a scientific turn of mind; the explanation found by clever deduction from observation, and his triumph announced in dramatic fashion by the investigator himself. There is even that touch of personal eccentricity which so often marks the detective of fiction! But other factors even more characteristic of the genre are missing. It may be true, as Messac suggests, that 'Archimedes worked as a scientific detective, carrying out experiments in his laboratory,' but, if he did, we are told nothing about them. We are never taken into his confidence or allowed to share the stages of his quest, his partial successes, his possible disappointments. But for a lucky accident his reasoning powers might never have found the right starting point. Similar fortunate turns of the wheel of chance may sometimes come to the aid of a fictional detective in the course of his investigations, but a stroke of luck and a flash of insight do not, of themselves, constitute a detective story.

In this tale of Archimedes, the reader does not even know whether, in fact, a crime has been committed at all, for the suspicion remains unconfirmed. Did the suspects really plan and execute an almost 'perfect' crime? What sort of men were they? Were they brought to trial, and, if so, did the scientific 'expert witness' give evidence for the prosecution? What was the verdict? A detective story would give a special place to some, if not all, of these questions, for in this type of fiction the criminal has his own importance, second only to that of the detective, and what happens to the criminal is the measure of the detective's success. We cannot, therefore, agree with Messac and accept this as a detective story in the modern meaning of the term, because it does not conform to the almost fixed pattern that characterises detective fiction, a pattern that has come to be accepted by authors and readers alike.

The purpose of this book is to examine the evolution of this 'fixed form' and its accepted variations, from the opening of the nineteenth century; to trace the sources of its recognisable elements and discover the stages by which it arrived at its present popularity. It will be necessary to consider the work of very many writers, but no attempt will be made to include every example of detective fiction, particularly when discussing recent decades. The intention is to review the most representative novelists in this field, those who first introduced features which later became characteristic, and those who influenced or exemplified prevailing trends. Some effort will be made to interpret the changes and developments against a background of the general social history of the period at which they occurred, for variations in popular taste or economic conditions, new technical or scientific discoveries, are quickly reflected in fiction of this type, and each outstanding fictional detective bears, unmistakably, the mark of his own times. So extensive has been the influence exerted by French, English and American writers of detective stories that it will be essential to regard national differences and similarities in this field, and the degree to which each country has, at different times, played a leading part in shaping a variety of popular literature that in our own day has become largely international in its appeal. Thus we will trace the development of the Detective Novel from its slight but significant beginnings in the early nineteenth century to its present status, and discover some of the reasons for the remarkable growth of this particular branch of popular fiction.

CHAPTER
I

EARLY SOURCES OF CERTAIN FEATURES
OF DETECTIVE FICTION

A number of elements which were to play a part in the formation of detective fiction were already present in the literature of France and England at a much earlier period than the opening of the nineteenth century.

Tales of adventurers or tricksters and dramatic episodes from the careers of popular rogues had, for centuries, entertained the people in song and story. That legendary outlaw, Robin Hood, was a traditional hero of May-day pageants long before Shakespeare's time, and Elizabethan literature was rich in Jest Books recounting the frauds of professional beggars, usually in humorous vein. Dekker, in *The Belman of London: Bringing to Light the most notorious villainies now practised in the Kingdom* (1608), gave English readers some acquaintance with the ingenuity and resource shown by the criminals of their day.

Similar information was available in France in *La Vie Généreuse des Mercelots, Gueuz et Bolmiens,* published at Lyons in 1596. This is the autobiography of a boy who ran away from home and joined fortunes with each of these vagabond tribes in turn, becoming familiar with every type of rascal in France, relating their exploits with broad tolerance and amusing detail.

Such stories, whether based on fact or otherwise, were popular throughout the seventeenth century and into the eighteenth. In England, Chap-books told the adventures of such notorious celebrities as Thomas of Reading, Jack of Newbury or Long Tom, the Carrier, usually phrased to amuse the reader, as in *The XII Merry Jests of the Widow Edythe,* where each 'jest' is an audacious crime. In France, tales of somewhat the same type owed their origin to the picaresque novels of Spain, humorous biographies or autobiographies of quick-witted rascally servants, whose careers with a succession of masters in different walks of life afforded endless opportunities for satire or burlesque. Le Sage's *Gil Blas*, which appeared in four parts between 1715 and 1735, brought this kind of story to far greater perfection in France than it had achieved in Spain, the country of its origin. Gentleman-adventurers were also well-represented, and there is ample evidence to show that tales of every type of ingenious criminal were exceedingly popular, both in France and England.

Detective fiction finds some origin here, and stems, at least in part, from a continuance of this same interest in the exploits of a clever villain. But before tales of roguery could begin to develop in the direction of detective fiction a radical change had to come about in the way the rogue was regarded by the general public, for both types of story reflect the opinion of their own times upon this matter.

In Picaresque novels and similar popular stories the rogue was presented as romantic, amusing and 'sharp,' often to be admired for his bravado and effrontery, his quick-witted avoidance of capture, his skill in escaping the punishment he richly deserved. In detective fiction that is precisely what he is not to be allowed to do, and the reader's sympathy is on the side of the detective whose function is to track the villain down. There are, of course, some detective stories in which the entire interest centres on the puzzle with little or no regard for its moral implications, and the solution of the mystery is purely an exercise in analytical deduction.[1] But when there is an appeal to the reader's emotions, instead of solely to his intellectual faculties, he is led to feel indignation or horror at the crime, enjoyment of the hunt for evidence, and satisfaction when the guilty person is discovered. It is an important point that the Detective Story, in direct contrast to the Crime Story, recognises the activities of the criminal as reprehensible and not to be tolerated, much less regarded with amusement or admiration.

[1] It is interesting to note that in most tales of this type the criminal either remains an unidentified shadow, as in Poe's *Mystery of Marie Roget*, or proves to be non-existent. 'Theft' may be committed innocently by a somnambulist, as in *Maître Cornélius;* or by a man under the influence of a drug, as in *The Moonstone;* 'murder' may be due to accidental or natural causes, as in *Trent's Last Case* and Conan Doyle's *The Crooked Man;* or even to an attack by an animal, as in Poe's *Murders in the Rue Morgue*, or Conan Doyle's *Silver Blaze*.

This significant change came about very slowly and was still going on in the middle of the nineteenth century, but early indications that such a development had begun can be discerned in *The Newgate Calendar*, during the first half of the eighteenth century.

By the end of the seventeenth century the official staff of Newgate prison included a clergyman who was given the title of 'The Ordinary Chaplain,' or, more simply, 'The Ordinary.' One of his perquisites was the right to prepare and publish broadsheets giving the "last words," or "confessions," of celebrated prisoners awaiting execution, together with any details he could gather concerning their life histories and criminal careers. These pamphlets found a ready sale, and one of the first to produce them on a large scale was the Reverend Paul Lorraine, Ordinary of Newgate from 1698 to 1719, who actually petitioned the House of Commons to allow him, tax free, sufficient paper for the publication of such brochures, which suggests that they represented quite a considerable volume of business to him.

A whole series of publications similar in spirit and intention, with such titles as *The Newgate Calendar*, *The Malefactor's Register*, or *The New Newgate and Tyburn Calendar*, were produced not by the Ordinary but by enterprising printers, calling themselves 'The Editors.' Lacking the privileges and sources of information open to the Ordinary, they were forced to draw more freely upon their imagination, often expanding their reports into a sort of running commentary. An interesting point is that the Editors sustained throughout a note of pious exhortation, frequently expressed in rhyme, as, for instance, on the title page of *The Malefactor's Register*[1]: —

> 'The Crimes related here are great and true,
> The Subjects vary, and the Work is New.
> By reading, learn the Way of Sin to shun.
> Be timely taught, and you'll not be undone.'

[1] The Frontispiece is headed ' A mother presenting *The Malefactor's Register* to her son and tenderly entreating him to regard the Instructions therein recorded ', and the accompanying engraving shows a woman bestowing the volume upon a tiny child with her right hand and pointing with her left to a window through which can be seen a corpse dangling from a gibbet!

In their efforts to point a moral and show the errors made by certain notorious criminals, the Editors not only stripped these rogues of any pretensions to romantic glamour, but also occasionally came fairly close to writing passages with some detective interest. For instance, after relating the career, trial and execution, in April, 1739, of Richard Turpin, (for the Editors do not stoop to use the more familiar 'Dick'), they proceed to examine the circumstances that led to his identification, and set out in some detail the apparently trivial matters that brought him to the dock. One fine day, Turpin, riding quite unrecognised through a village, shot a cock 'in the mere wantonness of his heart,' and was taken into custody when the indignant owner complained. The magistrates, quite unaware that their prisoner was the famous highwayman for whom the whole country was searching, allowed him to write to his brother asking for money to pay his fine for killing the cock. Unfortunately for him his brother refused to pay the postage, and the letter was being returned, unopened, when by chance it was seen by the schoolmaster who had taught Turpin to write, and who 'immediately knew his hand,' whereupon the authorities took prompt action to ensure that their prisoner faced more comprehensive charges.

For generations *The Newgate Calendar* served as a popular text-book on the careers of English criminals. Perhaps its most immediate effect was felt in the development of the 'Newgate Novel,' so popular in the eighteenth century. This general title was given to a whole series of semi-fictional, highly-coloured accounts of the adventures of highwaymen and other celebrated tricksters, with admiration for the criminal implied or expressed, as in Fielding's mock-heroic *The History of the Life of the Late Mr. Jonathan Wild the Great* (1743). Such novels were in accord with the spirit of the times, and with the popularity of criminal heroes in contemporary literature. To some extent the Newgate Novel may be regarded as a forerunner of the Detective Novel, in so far as it fostered an interest in exciting tales with a background of criminal exploits. It seems, however, that detective fiction is still more closely linked with *The Newgate Calendar* and similar publications of the same period, for these took a realistic view of the criminal, not regarding him as amusing or romantic but as a villain to be caught and punished; they did, on occasion, collect and set out the evidence leading to his conviction, in somewhat the same way as in detective stories; and they have served many writers of detective fiction as actual sources of material.

*   *   *

Daniel Defoe (c. 1659—1731) has an important place in English literature as one of the earliest novel-writers, if not actually the first to whom that title can legitimately be given. Before his day, such fiction as existed was a kind of offshoot from poetry or from religious teachings, but in the hands of Defoe the novel became an independent art form and acquired an identity of its own. For our present purpose it is particularly important to notice that Defoe originated the type of novel which breaks away from philosophical digressions and sets out to tell a straight-forward tale in a straight-forward way about 'ordinary people,' as distinct from the 'good' or the 'great.'

Defoe's "realism," his manner of presenting a story in the form of an eye-witness's account of exciting events actually taking place, giving the reader 'all the facts' and a vivid word-picture, is especially well-suited to detective fiction, and has often been copied by writers in this field. But there is more than his narrative style to link Defoe with the development of the detective novel. Many of his works reveal the close interest he took in the activities of criminals and the attempts made by the police of his day to bring them to justice. In 1724 he wrote two pamphlets on the notorious Jack Sheppard and his daring escapes from Newgate. He even interviewed Sheppard in gaol and wrote a further sixteen articles about him for *Applebee's Journal,* a periodical with which Defoe was closely associated between 1720 and 1726. He made similar critical studies of other criminals such as Jonathan Wild and the pirate, John Gow, both executed in 1725, and six well-known street thieves, executed in 1726. He published two treatises, in 1728 and 1730 respectively, on *How to Police the Metropolis and Suppress Crimes and other Disorders of the Night.* One or two of his novels actually possess some detective interest, though they do not, of course, contain a detective-hero. Many social changes had to occur before such a figure could exist in fact or fiction.

The first volume of *The Life and Strange, Surprising Adventures of Robinson Crusoe* appeared in April, 1719, followed by the second volume in August of the same year.[1] Whether Defoe drew his material from Dampier's *Voyage round the World* (1697), or based his novel upon the reminiscences of Alexander Selkirk, the ship-wrecked sailor whom Defoe often talked with at Mrs. Daniel's house in Bristol, he certainly presented the story as though it were a day-by-day account of actual occurrences, and it was widely accepted as the genuine diary of an Englishman shipwrecked alone on an uninhabited Pacific island. There is no crime in *Robinson Crusoe* and no detection (unless we include the famous footprint and Crusoe's investigations after he found it) but it is worth noting that the hero solved the vital problem of his own survival by learning from observation and deduction, by displaying the same qualities of intelligence and self-reliance that were later to be manifested by countless detectives of fiction.

There is a striking parallel between Robinson Crusoe and Sherlock Holmes, in that both were regarded by readers of their own period, and later, as actual human beings. They are, indeed, the only characters in English fiction to be accepted in this way. Ernest A. Baker has commented that, during the 1720's, the general public was so convinced that Robinson Crusoe was an existing person and his island an existing place, that "sharps were selling bogus relics of both the man and his non-existent domicile."[2] The same unquestioning acceptance was given to Sherlock Holmes, two hundred years or so later.

Towards the end of *The Fortunate Mistress* (1724) Defoe

---

[1] Both parts were almost at once reprinted in instalment form in *Heathcote's Intelligencer*, perhaps the earliest instance of an adventure story being presented as a serial in a newspaper.

[2] Cf. Ernest A. Baker, *The History of the English Novel*, Witherby, 1929-1935. Vol. 3, p. 172.

introduced a lively detective interest to show how the crimes of the adventuress, Roxana, and her confederate maid-servant were at last discovered and avenged. This part of the novel has all the tense excitement, the same atmosphere of mystery and suspense, frantic flight and relentless pursuit that became characteristic of certain types of detective fiction.

Such themes, however, though they often play an important part in the detective novel, are not exclusive to it. The essential feature peculiar to the detective novel is the prominence it gives to that exercise of the mental faculties which solves a problem by analytical deduction. Stories that depend for their point upon inductive reasoning are far less common than tales of criminals in literature prior to the nineteenth century, and those that do occur are seldom, if ever, concerned with crime. They are simply entertaining anecdotes of natural cunning or intelligent perception, and excellent examples can be found among the fables of almost every country, especially stories showing timid animals interpreting danger signals, or tales illustrating the sagacity of the fox. A whole series appeared in the *Roman de Renard,* and they were popular in England as well as France throughout the Middle Ages. Chaucer embodied some of them in his *Canterbury Tales,* in *The Nun's Priest's Tale* for instance.

A story of more particular importance because of its sustained detective interest was published in Paris in 1719 by the Chevalier de Mailly, with the title *Le Voyage et Les aventures des Trois Princes de Serendip, traduit du Persan.* In the course of their wanderings the three princes, asked whether they have seen a strayed camel, reply that they have not, but they describe the animal so accurately that they are accused of stealing it. They are brought before the Emperor, who enquires how, if they are innocent, they could possibly have known that it was blind in one eye, had lost a tooth, and was lame. They reply that they had noticed that the camel had eaten grass from only one side of the track, though on the other side it grew more thickly; that partly-chewed lumps of grass, the size of a camel's tooth, had fallen to the ground at every pace; and that the traces left in the dust showed that the animal was dragging one leg. Similar instances of deduction from observation occur throughout the story.

Mailly did not invent this embryonic tale of detection, nor did he translate it from the Persian, as his title states. He borrowed it from an Italian work printed at Venice in 1557 by Cristoforo Armeno, *Pereginaggio dei Tre Giovanni Figliuoli del Re di Sarendippo*,[1] and this same story, with minor variations, can be traced in the Arabian *Thousand and One Nights*, even in ancient Greek texts.[2]

Mailly's version, however, gave new life to the tale, and was the source of certain details which Voltaire introduced into *Zadig*, (1750), in his story *Le chien et le cheval*. Zadig was thrown into prison because he accurately described the King's horse and the Queen's pet dog, neither of which he could legitimately have seen. He proved his innocence by explaining how he had deduced every detail from the tracks the animals had left in the damp ground, and the hairs brushed from them by the bushes.

Mailly's work was translated into English in 1726, and Horace Walpole mentions in a letter to a friend that he found it amusing reading. He even coins the delightful word 'Serendipity,' to mean reasoning from observation as the three Princes had done, and adds: —

'As their Highnesses travelled, they were always making discoveries, by accidents and sagacity, of things which they were not in quest of. [. . .] One of the most remarkable [recent] instances of this *accidental sagacity* [. . .] was of My Lord Shaftesbury, who, happening to dine at Lord Chancellor Clarendon's, found out the marriage of the Duke of York and Mrs. Hyde, by the respect with which her mother treated her at table.'[3]

It cannot be doubted that Walpole and his contemporaries could appreciate and make use of similar shrewd deductions from observation, even though such details rarely found their way into the literature of the time. When they did, they had

[1] The papal permit for its publication is dated 1555.
[2] Cf. Messac, *Op. cit.*, pp. 17-46.
[3] To Horace Mann, dated January 28th, 1754. *The Letters of Horace Walpole, Fourth Earl of Orford*, Clarendon Press, 1903, p. 204.

nothing whatever to do with the detection of crime.

"It is easy to guess the trade of an artisan by his knees, his fingers or his shoulders," remarked Dr. Samuel Johnson in 1751,[1] and the French encyclopaedist, Denis Diderot (1715—1784), more than once expressed a similar idea which he called his 'Theory of Conditions,' based upon his own detailed observation of the ways in which people are affected physically by their manner of life and the work they do.

Beaumarchais introduced an interesting example of inductive reasoning in *Le Barbier de Seville* (1775), in the scene when Bartolo deduces from such trifles as a missing sheet of paper, a new pen made inky, and a smudge of ink on Rosine's finger, that she has hastily written a letter during his brief absence. When she denies this, Bartolo argues exactly like a detective and proves his point. Beaumarchais further revealed his aptitude for making similar well-reasoned deductions in a letter he wrote to the Editor of the London *Morning Chronicle*, which appeared in the columns of that paper on May 1st, 1776. Beaumarchais had found a lady's cloak at the Panthéon after a ball, and wished to return it to its rightful, but unknown, owner. A careful scrutiny of the cloak proved to him, (and he gave in full his reasons for arriving at these conclusions), that the lady was young, blonde and beautiful. Her taste in dress, her social position, her slender neck and tiny feet, all these and other details were deduced as cleverly from the cloak itself as were Sherlock Holmes's conclusions about Henry Baker from a scrutiny of his hat, or his description of Dr. Watson's brother from an examination of his watch.

When detective fiction came to be written, quite impressive deductions were based upon the same kind of reasoning. When Monsieur Lecoq deciphered footprints on snow-covered ground, and thus learned of a flight, a pursuit and a struggle, he was using 'Serendipity'. Sherlock Holmes, studying the marks left on a moorland path by cloven hoofs, noticed that their sequence showed a trot, a canter and a gallop. They could therefore have

[1] Samuel Johnson, *The Rambler*, November 12th, 1751. *Collected Edition of the Works of Samuel Johnson*, Cowie, 1825, Vol. 2, p. 236.

been made only by horses shod with specially constructed shoes counterfeiting the tracks of cattle. The Three Princes would have reached the same conclusion.

Between the Persian Princes and a modern detective-hero is, however, a wide gap which could not be bridged until many social changes had come about, and the reading public had become interested in the work of the police, particularly in their methods of interpreting tracks and material clues, a development which did not manifest itself until the nineteenth century was well advanced.

*   *   *

Before leaving the eighteenth century we must notice the immense popularity of the 'Tale of Terror,' both in this country and in France, where it was called *'le roman noir.'* The vogue began in England with Horace Walpole's *The Castle of Otranto* (1764) and continued well into the nineteenth century. Novels of this type transport their readers to mysterious ruined castles haunted by the spectres of ancient warriors or murdered nuns. Such themes have little in common with detective fiction, for they appeal, not to the reader's logical faculty, but to his fear of the unknown, his dread of the supernatural. Yet the most widely known of all writers of 'Tales of Terror,' Mrs. Ann Radcliffe, introduced into her romances two features which link them unmistakably with the detective novels of the nineteenth and twentieth centuries.

In *The Romance of the Forest* (1791), *The Mysteries of Udolpho* (1794) and *The Italian* (1797), as in the typical Gothic romance, Mrs. Radcliffe relates the ordeals of beautiful, ill-used heroines who wander through gloomy ruins honey-combed with secret passages, and come upon indications suggesting that terrible crimes have been committed. But Mrs. Radcliffe, unlike other writers of such tales, was careful to give, at the end, a reasonably rational explanation of the enigmas created in her ingenious plots. She was particularly skilful in devising apparently supernatural happenings that, when investigated intelligently, proved to be due to human agency, or to some natural, if far-fetched, coincidence. Her manner of presenting such solutions was not quite in the spirit of detective fiction, for her explanations are often too-long delayed, and sometimes so banal that the reader feels unfairly tricked. Nevertheless, her great and increasing popularity indicates that any disappointment her readers suffered on this score did not quench their thirst for her next mystery novel. They enjoyed being thrilled and puzzled, and the convention of 'fair play' between author and reader had not yet come into existence.

It is quite possible that Mrs. Radcliffe was influenced by Schiller's *Der Geisterseher*, published in 1789 and issued in English translation in 1795. In this novel, Schiller's Prince refuses to accept certain 'marvels' as supernatural until every possible rational explanation has been fully examined, a policy which at last reveals that they have been contrived by a clever juggler. A further point is that these investigations are discussed between two people, one who is clever and can immediately grasp all the logical implications, while the other needs to have everything fully explained. Whether Mrs. Radcliffe borrowed this technique from Schiller and amplified it to suit her purpose, or whether she devised it for herself, she certainly used it to good effect in her novels, particularly in *The Italian*, and presented her explanations in the form of a conversation between two characters in the story, one of whom knows more, or has noticed more, than the other, who, as much in the dark as the reader, is consumed with curiosity and persistently asks questions until all is made plain. This useful device was frequently employed when detective fiction came to be written, and we are at once reminded of those illuminating dialogues between Dupin and his anonymous friend; Sherlock Holmes and Dr. Watson; Hanaud and Mr. Ricardo; Hercule Poirot and Captain Hastings; and countless similar partners in detection. Thus, though Mrs. Radcliffe never wrote a detective story, or created a character analogous to a detective-hero, definite steps were taken in her novels towards formulating the distinctive pattern of detective fiction as we know it today.

Other details of this pattern can be traced in an English novel of a very different type, written in the closing years of the eighteenth century by William Godwin (1756—1836). He was educated for the Nonconformist ministry, but later devoted his energies to social studies far in advance of his time, and came to believe that social injustice could be ended by the exercise of reason. When his great philosophical treatise on this subject failed to reach and convert the reading public he embodied his precepts in a novel which he called *Caleb Williams: or Things as They Are* (1794).

The political purpose of this work was overlooked by its readers in their pleasure at the fascinating story and the originality of the plot, and the novel became extremely popular. In it, Godwin introduced several features which were not present in the Tale of Terror, or, indeed, in any earlier literature, and it will be useful to give a brief outline of the plot of *Caleb Williams* to show what these features were.

Caleb Williams, who relates the story, reviews his life from the day when, as a studious youth, he entered the service of a rich young land-owner, Falkland. A quarrel had recently taken place between Falkland and his neighbour, Tyrrel. When Tyrrel is found murdered, Falkland is suspected and accused, but acquitted, two local men being later condemned and executed for the crime, as there is some circumstantial evidence against them.

Caleb, noticing Falkland's gloomy moods, begins to suspect his master, and partly out of pity for the men who have been executed, but mainly to satisfy his own passionate curiosity, he determines to discover the truth. As Falkland's secretary, he has access to his master's personal papers and can keep close watch on him. He contrives a method of psychological detection by subtle questions that inflict acute mental distress on Falkland, who comes to realise that Caleb suspects him of Tyrrel's murder. When he finds Caleb searching a chest in a secret closet, in desperation he confesses to the crime, but is determined that no one but Caleb shall know of this.

To discredit Caleb, in case he should be tempted to talk of the crime, Falkland has him imprisoned on a charge of theft, but he escapes and joins a gang of thieves whose leader befriends him. Another member of the gang, Gines, is dismissed for his cruelty to Caleb, and, in jealous fury, devotes his life to hounding down his supplanter, acting first on his own account, later as a police spy and Falkland's agent. (Only his intense desire for revenge could induce him to desert 'the manly calling of a thief' and sink to the level of a police spy—a remarkable indication of the relative status of a thief and a detective at that period). Caleb is given no respite until he and his former master are brought face to face again, so that Godwin may propound his theories regarding social injustice, after which Falkland openly confesses his crime and dies of shame, while Caleb is overcome with remorse for his action in ferreting out Falkland's guilt.

In this very involved story are several details that became familiar in detective fiction. Godwin gives considerable emphasis to the 'great joy' Caleb feels when satisfying his intense curiosity, and the ingenious questions he thinks out in the hope of making Falkland betray some guilty knowledge. He is, literally, an 'amateur' in detection, inspired solely by his determination to reason out the truth. The professional police-spy, Gines, is an inflexible, implacable blood-hound of a man such as we shall see again, more sharply defined and even more ominous, as Javert in Victor Hugo's *Les Misérables*. Falkland, a kind man of good repute, seems the most unlikely person to have committed such a crime; there is no humour in the novel, and no love interest. But in addition to these features, which long persisted in detective fiction, there is another of much greater importance—the method of construction Godwin invented when planning this book.

Taking a course which more than one famous writer of detective stories has adopted since, William Godwin set down in detail the way he wrote his 'best seller.'[1] First, he carefully studied all the books he could find, including the *Newgate Calendar*, to give him authentic information about criminals and their prac-

[1] In his preface to *Fleetwood* (1832), pp. 11-12.

tices. Then, having gained the right 'atmosphere,' he deliberately planned and wrote the final volume first, working backward to the beginning. He was almost certainly the first novelist to think out and follow exactly a plan of construction which is essential to the detective story, a plan which Poe advocated in his essay on *The Philosophy of Composition*,[1] and which has not only been followed but openly acknowledged by writers of detective fiction ever since. Conan Doyle made his view quite clear: —

> 'People have often asked me whether I knew the end of a Holmes story before I started it. Of course I did. One could not possibly steer a course if one did not know one's destination.'[2]

This method of construction, so vitally important in a detective story, may sometimes not apply to other types of fiction. Writers have on many occasions declared that even when the construction of a plot has been determined in advance, the characters in the story would not always conform to that plan, but would, as it were, take their lives into their own hands and prove to be quite unpredictable. François Mauriac, discussing this point at some length, has affirmed that he is in no way disturbed when his characters give such proofs of their own vitality, for he regards it as an additional strength.[3]

Here is a fundamental distinction between other types of fiction and the detective novel. In the latter, the primary importance lies in the complicated, ingenious mechanism of the plot, which must function exactly as planned. A character may 'come to life' only within the limitations of its purpose in the story, for every incident, every action, every phrase must play its pre-arranged part, either setting out the problem, complicating it with 'red herrings' or contributing to the solution. As a consequence, character-drawing is subordinate to the plot in almost all detective fiction. The prime essential in this type of novel is the 'puzzle-device,' the labyrinthine trail which the author plans

---

[1] *The Works of Edgar Allan Poe*, London, Chatto & Windus, 1872, p. 600.
[2] Sir Arthur Conan Doyle, *Memories and Adventures*, London, Hodder & Stoughton, 1924, p. 107.
[3] François Mauriac, *Le Romancier et ses Personnages*, Paris, Corrêa, 1933, pp. 126-128.

first and then camouflages for later discovery by the right person in the right way at the right time. Any attempt by a character to deviate from the prescribed lines would defeat the author's purpose and upset the whole construction of the story. Herein lies what is at once the strength and the weakness of detective fiction—that the handling of the plot takes precedence over all else, and that the conclusion must be planned first. Credit must be given to William Godwin for first creating this technique, and for recording his reasons for doing so.

In *Caleb Williams*, then, Godwin produced a novel which came closer to a detective story than any earlier fiction had done. He invented a new technique of plot construction, he based part of his story upon a searching and successful enquiry into a murder mystery, and he created two central characters foreshadowing the amateur detective and the official police agent.

We cannot, however, entirely accept *Caleb Williams* as a detective novel, because these similarities are counterbalanced by essential differences. Godwin's purpose was to teach, not merely to entertain, and he presented Caleb not as a detective-hero but as the victim of Falkland's persecution. The secret murder, and Caleb's discovery of Falkland's guilt, were devised merely to provide a convincing reason for that victimisation. Godwin did not visualize the detective pursuing the criminal, establishing his guilt or bringing him to justice. On the contrary, he made the criminal pursue the detective and 'keep him in a state of the most fearful alarm,' as a punishment for his 'over-mastering curiosity.' But such curiosity is the very mainspring of a detective's skill. Deny him the exercise of this function and he cannot exist. Penalize him for trying to find out more than others wish him to know, and you have, not a detective story, but a tale with the same central idea as *Pandora's Box*, or *Blue-beard*—'If you pry into hidden mysteries you will regret it'—a complete antithesis to the conception of detective fiction.

Caleb Williams was certainly a new type of novel which at once aroused considerable interest, provoking wide discussion and becoming very popular. In 1796 it was dramatized by George Colman the younger, and played at the Haymarket Theatre under a new title, *The Iron Chest*. The adventures of the two near-detectives, Caleb and Gines, were thus brought to the stage, a medium which concerned itself far less with Godwin's philosophical theories than with the dramatic plot, and therefore lent increased importance to their respective roles. *The Iron Chest* can, in some measure, be regarded as the first of a long series of melodramas with detective interest which were popular in the English theatre throughout the nineteenth century.

In America, since the laws of copyright did not at that time preclude such a course, the plot of *Caleb Williams* was openly borrowed and adapted in several novels by Charles Brockden Brown (1771—1810), a young visionary who absorbed Godwin's philosophies with enthusiasm. He was born in Philadelphia of a Quaker family, and at the age of twenty-three forsook a legal career to devote himself to writing, at first on social studies. Later he produced some remarkable novels, four of them having some affinity with detective fiction. *Wieland: or The Transformation* (1798) relates how a devout man, a loving husband and father, was so wrought upon by a mysterious voice urging him to kill his wife and children, his "idols," that, believing the voice came from God he at last obeyed. It is primarily a study of intense mental conflict, but Wieland's long-continued efforts to discover a natural explanation for the 'ghostly voice' are quite sound attempts at detection. In *Ormond: or The Secret Witness* (1799) the excitement of the plot lies in a theme of flight and pursuit similar to that in the third volume of *Caleb Williams*, with the important difference that the story is transferred to the American forests and the streets of Philadelphia, bringing something fresh to the wanderings of his characters. *Arthur Mervyn* (1799) gives a vivid picture of a town demoralised by the effects of a pestilence.

Mervyn is an intelligent, well-meaning lad, (very reminiscent of Godwin's Caleb), who becomes involved with a group of wicked people and tries to find out and put right the wrongs they have committed. He is, however, so artless that his efforts serve no purpose and place him in personal danger from the guilty Welbeck, just as Caleb was from Falkland. *Edgar Huntley:*

or The Sleepwalker (1799) also echoes *Caleb Williams,* particularly in the methods Huntley adopts to discover the truth about a mysterious murder committed by Clithero.

> Speaking of Charles Brockden Brown, Ernest Baker has said: —
> 'Since he contributed something to the development of fiction in English, he necessarily comes into the history of the English novel.'[1]

There seems particularly good reason to include him when considering the history of the detective novel, for he was the first to combine the features we have noticed in the works of Mrs. Radcliffe and of William Godwin—intriguing mysteries, investigations undertaken from motives of curiosity about a crime, exciting themes of flight and pursuit, a rational explanation of the mystery as the story ends—adding to them fresh, congenial details of his own devising. He sometimes made the solution of his mysteries depend on currently popular 'scientific' or 'pseudo-scientific' causes, if ventriloquism and somnambulism can be included under that heading. He also, for the first time in fiction, introduced descriptions of the North American forests and the Red Indian tribes who lived and fought therein, their ruthless fixity of purpose, their woodcraft, their amazing skill in following a trail. In this respect, Brown was the forerunner of his much more famous fellow-countryman, James Fenimore Cooper, who, some twenty years later, gave a similar background to his novels whose effect has long been mirrored in detective fiction. The figure of the redskin hunter, silent, inscrutable, keenly observant, adept at following the slightest clue, became almost symbolic of a certain type of popular detective-hero, and Conan Doyle more than once likened Sherlock Holmes to a Red Indian.

Thus, before the nineteenth century opened, there were already present in popular literature several features that later combined with others to form detective fiction. Readers enjoyed tales of crime and criminals, and had some perception of the purposes inductive reasoning could serve. Defoe had provided models of

---

[1] Baker, *Op. cit.,* Vol. V, p. 211.

crisp, realistic prose, and a self-reliant hero who captured the imagination of the general public. Mrs. Radcliffe had written mystery novels in which her readers could expect the riddles to be finally explained, often in conversations between a clever, observant character and his less quick-witted friend. William Godwin not only created an amateur crime-investigator, but invented a new technique, and, by concentrating on his plot before his characters, worked out a method of construction that was especially appropriate to detective fiction. Brockden Brown co-ordinated most of these factors, added a touch of 'science,' and introduced the figure of a highly-skilled interpreter of material clues.

It is significant that the novels of all these writers were extremely popular, and pleased contemporary taste. During the final decade of the eighteenth century and the opening years of the nineteenth there was a remarkable expansion of the reading public and a great increase in the demand for popular fiction, a demand that brought into being a number of successful circulating libraries. To satisfy this market, novels were produced in increasing numbers, and it was not long before some of them began to develop more definitely in the direction of the detective novel.

CHAPTER
II

THE CHARACTERISTIC PATTERN BEGINS TO FORM

William Godwin gathered round him in his later years a group of young idealists who reverenced his beliefs and his literary achievements. Among them was Edward Lytton Bulwer, later Lord Lytton, (1803—1873), who showed the influence of Godwin's teachings in a series of seven novels published between 1827 and 1833.

All these works are about crimes of one sort or another, and most of them set out to prove that a criminal can be reformed, but *Pelham* (1828) and *Eugene Aram* (1832) take a different line, and introduce a carefully worked-out detective theme that provides the climax of the story, with the criminal duly handed over to justice. Here is a definite step towards the development of detective fiction, and a glance at the plots of both novels will reveal points of interest in this connection.

Pelham: or The Adventures of a Gentleman was an instant success, particularly in fashionable London, where gossip busily tried to identify characters in the story with well-known society figures. The hero, young Lord Pelham, meets with all sorts of exciting adventures, and half-way through the book he becomes involved in a murder mystery. While riding home from the Races with an acquaintance, Sir John Tyrrell, his horse falls lame and he lags behind. Shortly afterwards he finds Sir John lying beside the road, killed and robbed. He immediately rouses the neighbourhood and leads a search for the murderer, but without success, and the mystery remains unsolved for months. Then Sir Reginald Glanville, brother of the girl Pelham hopes to marry, is arrested by Bow Street Runners on suspicion of the crime, and Pelham intercedes with the magistrate on his behalf, using for the first time the very language of detective fiction in his comment: "I think I am possessed of some clue." A brief delay is granted, but unless Pelham can, "by the day after tomorrow, ascertain any facts to elucidate this mysterious crime and point the inquiries of justice to another quarter," the magistrate will commit Glanville for trial. Accordingly, Pelham sets out to solve the mystery, not only to save his friend from being wrongly convicted, but to avoid the scandal that a trial would bring to Glanville's family.

Pelham starts his investigation energetically and systematically, enlisting the aid of a professional pick-pocket whom he once befriended. Together, and skilfully disguised, they follow a complicated trail through the underworld of London and eventually discover that the real murderer was the notorious Thornton,[1] leader of a criminal fraternity, who, ever since the crime, has been holding captive his former chief assistant, a rogue named Dawson.

They succeed in penetrating the well-organised defences of the gang's stronghold and reaching Dawson's prison, where they learn that he actually witnessed the murder and could prove Thornton's guilt, if only he could re-visit the scene of the crime, for he knows where the incriminating evidence is buried, including the weapon which can be identified as Thornton's property. After an exciting hand-to-hand fight, Pelham manages to set Dawson free, and on the next day takes to the magistrate all the proofs needed to ensure Thornton's arrest and Glanville's release.

Many passages in *Pelham* are clearly influenced by the Tale of Terror and the Newgate Novel, but in that part of the plot outlined above there are several important innovations which link the story unmistakably with detective fiction. Pelham, who acts as a detective, (though he could not be so described, since the term had not yet been invented),[2] is the leading figure throughout. He is quickly at the scene of the crime, is the first to find the body, and directs the initial search for the murderer.

[1] Lytton based the character and career of Thornton upon details of an actual murderer, Thurtell, brought to trial a few years earlier.

[2] The *Oxford Dictionary* traces the word ' detective ' no earlier than 1843-1844, when Sir James Graham, then Home Secretary, selected a few of the most intelligent officers of the London police to form a special group, given the title of ' The Detective Police '.

He suspects the real criminal at once, but is misled by false evidence. Then strong personal reasons cause him to take up the investigation again, and by a combination of resourcefulness, pugilistic skill and inductive reasoning he brings it to a successful conclusion.

Like many a later detective, Pelham has the advantage of some personal acquaintance with a friendly criminal from whom he obtains information and practical help. We must notice, too, Lytton's clever management of sustained suspense; the sense of urgency imposed by the narrow time-limit within which the murderer must be discovered; the marked absence of the official police, in this case the Bow Street runners, who appear only to make an arrest, and who first take into custody an innocent suspect, being unable to find the actual criminal until the private investigator has identified him and proved his guilt; and the fact that for the first time in English fiction, the detective is the hero of the novel, quite over-shadowing both the murderer and his victim. In view of Lord Lytton's sympathetic attitude towards the criminals in his other novels it is interesting to notice that in *Pelham,* his nearest approach to a detective novel, he adopts a different technique. Here, as in the typical detective novel of the twentieth century, the murderer is ruthlessly hunted out, his guilt proved and his person delivered into the hands of the law, after which no more is heard of him.

Eugene Aram was based upon an actual murder mystery that aroused great interest at the time of its discovery and long afterwards. Eugene Aram, who lived in Yorkshire from his birth in 1704 until 1745, was much respected there, and later in Norfolk, as a scholarly man of great learning and upright life. In 1759 he was accused of having murdered a certain Daniel Clark fourteen years earlier. Ever since the crime, Aram had lived a blameless, studious life in poverty, blackmailed by his former associate, Houseman, who was present when Clark was attacked. At his trial the scholar defended himself with considerable skill, making a shrewd, well-argued attack upon the circumstantial evidence brought against him, but to no avail, for he was convicted and executed.

William Godwin was particularly interested in this case, and planned a novel to show Aram as the victim of an over-harsh penal code, but found himself prevented from writing it by ill-health and advancing age. Lytton, following Godwin's plan, credited Aram with such nobility of character and intellect, inventing so many extenuating circumstances to explain away his crime, that Thackeray sarcastically summed up the novel as showing "how Eugene Aram, though a thief, a liar and a murderer, yet, being an intellectual, was among the noblest of mankind." In addition to these ideas derived from Godwin, Lytton introduced some of his own, and made the novel largely a story of detection, once again showing an amateur investigator gathering the evidence that was to prove Aram's guilt. Young Walter Lester, son of the murdered man, determines to solve the mystery of his father's disappearance many years earlier. Learning at last of his father's double life as 'Daniel Clark,' he devotes his time to searching out and questioning anyone who has any knowledge of 'Clark,' and may be able to give him some vital scrap of information. He is misled by false clues, but patiently and persistently adds one fact to another until eventually he has clear proof that the murderer was not Houseman, who has been suspected by many, but Eugene Aram, who seems the most unlikely person to commit any crime, especially one of violence. It is Lester who leads the search, obtains Houseman's statement, takes steps to confirm it and brings the officers of the law to arrest Aram. He attends the trial and gives evidence, interviews Aram in prison and finally receives his confession. Though Lytton's avowed purpose in writing this 'tragic romance' was to represent Aram in a sympathetic light, the most convincing theme in the book is the gradual unfolding of Aram's past by Lester, and this section at least of *Eugene Aram* is essentially a story of detection.

*   *   *

Meanwhile, in America, James Fenimore Cooper had begun to

write a series of novels which became world-famous, and which had an immediate, far-reaching effect upon the development of detective fiction. *The Pioneers* (1823) was followed in 1826 by *The Last of the Mohicans*, the best known of all his books. In the same year, during a visit to France, he published *The Prairie*, and after a long interval the series was completed by *The Pathfinder* (1840) and *The Deerslayer* (1841).

These novels relate the adventures of a small group of white people journeying in peril through territory occupied by hostile Red Indian tribes. Members of other tribes act as friendly guides to the travellers, and much of the story's interest lies in the skill these redskins display in following a trail, their quick perception of any sign of danger, the information they can obtain from a broken twig, a torn leaf or a faint footprint. Cooper gave his characters attractive names that captured popular fancy— Leatherstocking, Hawkeye, Big Serpent, Le Renard Subtil—and made them reason in ways at least half-way towards modern detective methods: —

> 'Some of the leaves which were exposed to the sun had drooped a little, and this slight departure from the usual natural laws had caught the quick eyes of the Indian; for so practised and acute do the senses of the savage become, more especially when he is on the warpath, that trifles apparently of the most insignificant sort often prove to be clues[1] to lead him to his object.'[2]

The guides often explain, as they go along, precisely what has led them to their conclusions, and this is an important detail. Hawkeye, when tracking the singer, David, points out to the lad with him: —

> 'Now he begins to be footsore and leg-weary, as is plain from his trail. There, you see, he has slipped. Here he totters and staggers wide of the path.'[3]

---

[1] It is interesting to note the word ' clue ' used here with exactly the same meaning as in detective stories. It had already been similarly employed by Bulwer Lytton in novels which Cooper may well have read. e.g. ' I think I am possessed of some clue ' (*Pelham*, Ch. 78). ' I will not let slip one thread of this dark clue ' (*Eugene Aram*, Book IV, Ch. 10).
[2] *The Pathfinder*, Ch. V.
[3] *The Last of the Mohicans*, Ch. 18.

A little later Hawkeye continues: —

'One moccasin like another? You may as well say that one foot is like another, though we all know that some are long and others short, some broad and others narrow, some with high and some with low insteps, some in-toed and some out. One moccasin is no more like another than one book is like another . . . Here is the patch we saw so often in the other chase . . . He is a drunkard, too. Your drinking Indian always learns to walk with a wider toe than the natural savage, it being the gift of a drunkard to straddle, whether of white or red skin.'[1]

Such expositions of tell-tale footprints were to become very familiar indeed in detective fiction, particularly at the turn of the century. Sherlock Holmes, (to mention only one of many that could be named as examples), learned a great deal from footmarks in *A Study in Scarlet, The Sign of Four, The Boscombe Valley Mystery, Silver Blaze, The Resident Patient, The Priory School* and several other stories.

The Last of the Mohicans won immediate popularity in America and England, and even greater success in France, where it was at once available in French translation. Cooper's novels appealed very strongly to French tastes in fiction at that time, portraying as they did a land unspoiled by civilisation, where men dwelt in communion with Nature, free of all restraint—a way of life in tune with the Romantic spirit that was making itself felt in French literature. The further characteristics of Cooper's Indians, their woodcraft, their powers of making expertly reasoned deductions from tiny clues, exercised the charm of novelty and called the reader's logical faculties into play. But this feature of Cooper's novels might never have assumed any special significance in the development of detective fiction, had it not been for one of those potent coincidences that sometimes occur in literature, as in life.

In 1828, while *The Last of the Mohicans* was still being eagerly read in France, the first real-life professional detective, Eugène François Vidocq (1775—1857), published in Paris the first volume of his *Mémoires,* recounting his sensational exploits

[1] *Ibid.,* Ch. 18.

in hunting down dangerous criminals almost singlehanded. Public imagination was captured by the amazing career of this ex-convict who became a detective and founded the *Sûreté*, and though the French people, then and later, had no love for their police, their interest in Vidocq awoke in them an interest in the processes of detection. As that interest grew, more than one writer of popular fiction made use of the obvious parallel between an Indian hunter stalking the foes of his tribe or the wild game in the forest, and a *policier* tracking down the criminal he means to capture. Balzac stressed this point in some detail in *Une Ténébreuse Affaire,* when describing the activities of those sinister agents of the French political police, Corentin and Peyrade.[1] Eugène Sue, in the opening phrases of *Les Mystères de Paris,* referred specifically to Cooper and stated his own intention to depict Parisian criminals in much the same light as hostile Indians on the war-path. It was a simple, quite natural step to change the background of such stories from the woods and plains of the New World to the crowded streets of the French capital, equally full of the same danger and uncertainty, and the normal habitat of the criminals whose exploits form the basis of the plot.

Vidocq, whose vigorous personality and adventurous career created a vivid impression in France and England of what a detective should be, was born at Arras in 1775. After a mis-spent youth and a checkered army career he found himself in prison at the age of twenty-one, and contrived to escape. During the next ten years he was frequently arrested or re-captured, but always succeeded in escaping again, thus becoming as familiar with convicts and prison life as with the methods and organisation of the police. While at liberty he audaciously approached M. Henry, Head of the Criminal department of the Paris police, and offered his services as a secret agent. They were accepted, and Vidocq soon showed a brilliant capacity for his new rôle.

At that time, 1810, Paris was divided into districts, each with its own *Officier de Paix* whose authority was limited to his own section. There was no central control, and provided a criminal

[1] Honoré de Balzac, *Une Ténébreuse Affaire,* Edition Calmann Levy, 1892, p. 111.

kept on the move he could feel fairly safe from any police action. Vidocq changed this, and organised his own band of agents, with authority to pursue escaped prisoners in any district, keep a watchful eye on suspicious characters, particularly ex-convicts, and investigate any baffling crimes committed in Paris or its suburbs. In 1811 he was appointed *Chef de la Sûreté*, a position which he held until 1827, and again from 1831 till 1843.

It is not surprising that Vidocq met with bitter opposition from the regular police, who resented his presence in their districts. They were particularly indignant that an ex-galley-slave, an escaped convict who had not even been officially pardoned, should enjoy the status of a high-ranking *agent*, empowered to conduct enquiries and make arrests on his own responsibility, answerable only to the Chief of Police in person. Above all, they were jealous of his phenomenal success.

His *Mémoires* gave detailed accounts of how he conducted the various investigations entrusted to him, almost all of them concerned with robberies or frauds carried out by organised gangs, and described his shrewd methods. His complete familiarity with the vernacular of criminals, their signs and counter-signs, their manner of life, even their thought processes, enabled him to enter their haunts without arousing suspicion, often in the guise of a newly-escaped convict, and win the confidence of the very men he was hunting. His memory for facts and faces was prodigious, and on learning the details of a robbery he could generally make an astute guess as to the identity of the thieves. He was a master of disguise, and could maintain his assumed personality for days and sometimes weeks at a stretch, living side by side with his suspects until the moment when he could make his arrests, recover as much as possible of the stolen property, and place clear evidence before the Chief of Police. These innumerable little stories of practical detective work, many of them almost certainly fictional and added by successive 'editors' of Vidocq's own records, follow much the same pattern; stating the 'case'; explaining the reasons for every action, every deduction; relating the steps in the pursuit of the criminals; and recording their arrest.

The organisation he established and conducted so efficiently soon became famous throughout France and beyond. If his *agents*, men and women, were usually ex-convicts, so were those employed by the police themselves, and Vidocq, at least, controlled his assistants effectively. He had a flair for publicity, and built for himself a remarkable reputation for professional acumen, discretion and personal elegance, maintaining his own resplendent offices, far more imposing than the Headquarters of the police. At the age of fifty he finally left the *Sûreté* and founded the earliest known private detective agency. Its original function was to provide business and professional men, for an annual fee, with confidential information as to their clients' financial stability, but its scope was soon extended to include private consultations with Vidocq on personal problems. His success in this enterprise, coupled with his earlier triumphs in a more official capacity, made him an almost legendary figure in Paris, the first detective-hero France, and the world, had ever known.

At this period of his life Vidocq was a figure of some social importance, fêted at dinners attended by illustrious guests. The English prison-reformer, Sir Francis Burdett, made a point of entertaining him whenever he visited Paris. Honoré de Balzac, who received him in his own home, regarded him with much admiration and curiosity, and out of his knowledge of Vidocq created his famous Vautrin who appeared and re-appeared throughout *La Comédie Humaine*.

While Vidocq was at the head of the *Sûreté* the term 'detective' was still unknown and the first *roman policier* had not yet been written. Before he raised it to the status of a profession the ignoble occupation of a thief-taker was looked upon with scorn, not only by the public but by felons themselves. In England, in 1725, Jonathan Wild was reviled more bitterly for his activities in this field than for his many crimes, and this was still the general attitude a hundred years later, in Vidocq's day. In France, public hatred had for generations rested impartially upon the police and any who assisted them. Only a man of striking personality and extraordinary ability could have overcome this deep-rooted antipathy and succeeded in winning a measure of esteem.

The fact that Vidocq was openly and fiercely attacked by the official police of the time may well have increased his popularity in his own country. He was almost as well-known in England as in France, for George Borrow translated his *Mémoires* as soon as they appeared, and incidents from them were at once brought to the stage by Jerrold, in *Vidocq, The French Police Spy*, played at the Surrey Theatre in 1829. Lord Lytton, in *Night and Morning* (1845) introduced an episode about a gang of coiners and the detective who was on their trail, a Monsieur Favart, who was clearly copied from Vidocq and described as "a man of the most vigilant acuteness, the most indefatigable research, who awed rogues with his very eye, and had never yet failed in any enterprise he undertook." Lytton obviously felt that Vidocq had been overpopularised, for he parodied him throughout this passage and made Favart meet his death in the coiners' den, where, in spite of his 'impenetrable disguise,' he was recognised and murdered.

In that same year, 1845, Vidocq spent some time in London and opened an exhibition in a Regent Street shop. Surrounded by gruesome relics, he discussed some of his famous cases and appeared in several disguises to entertain the constant stream of visitors.[1]

Vidocq's tremendous personality, his remarkable success in the profession he originated, gave the general public in his own country and abroad a very clear conception of the 'ideal detective,' and it was from him that many later detectives of fiction, Sherlock Holmes, for example, inherited such characteristics as great physical strength, patience and endurance; skill in disguise and an insight into criminal mentality; their reputation for inevitable success and their moments of dramatic personal triumph. "I am Vidocq!" the phrase which, over and over again, dumbfounded a captured criminal in the *Mémoires*, re-echoed down the years to become "I am Hawkshaw, the detective!" in *The Ticket of Leave Man*, Tom Taylor's popular melodrama,

[1] Cf. The *Times*, June 9th, 1845, reporting the opening of Vidocq's Exhibition.

and, in Conan Doyle's *The Valley of Fear*, "Yes! Birdy Edwards is here. I am Birdy Edwards!"

Another legacy from Vidocq is the general assumption, sometimes expressed in detective fiction, that the regular police are inept, inefficient and resentful of the gifted amateur, without whose aid they would seldom bring an investigation to a successful conclusion. Poe's Dupin endorsed this idea by the ease with which he out-classed the Prefect G——, in *The Purloined Letter*, and his thinly veiled scorn for the same official expressed in the final paragraphs of *The Murders in the Rue Morgue*. Half a century later, Sherlock Holmes held precisely the same view, grudgingly conceding that Lestrade and Gregson, "the best of the Scotland Yarders," showed energy and persistence but no real acumen or intelligence, and this, oddly enough, at a period when, in England at least, public appreciation for the sound work of the police was steadily growing. It is surprising how long this idea persisted, and even when detective fiction came to accept the convention of a friendly 'working partnership' between an amateur detective and the official police, the amateur was still the leading figure. What success could be expected from Lomas without Reggie Fortune, Pike without Colonel Gethryn, or Mr. Parker without Lord Peter Wimsey?

Later detectives inevitably acquired skills which Vidocq, living when he did, could not possess. The microscope and the test-tube were not yet considered as aids to detection, and he was in no sense a scientific detective. He relied almost exclusively upon his knowledge of criminals, his quick grasp of a situation, his intelligence and resourcefulness—in brief, on certain fundamental aptitudes displayed in varying degrees by every successful detective.

In considering the influence Vidocq exerted upon popular literature, it must not be overlooked that before becoming a detective he had spent long years as a convicted felon and a leader among his fellow-prisoners. It was this side of Vidocq that inspired Balzac to create his cunning, utterly ruthless Vautrin, and was the source of that keen interest in the affairs of criminals so often expressed by Balzac and by many other novelists for more than a quarter of a century. In his writings[1] Vidocq revealed the terrible conditions then existing in French prisons, his own dreadful experiences in the chain-gangs, the galleys and the appalling dungeons at Brest and Toulon. Public interest, perhaps also the public conscience, was sharply aroused, and novels presenting the sufferings of convicts or ex-convicts became very popular in France from the 1830's onward, still exerting a powerful appeal some thirty years later, when Hugo wrote *Les Misérables* (1862).

It seems a strange paradox that Vidocq, who wrote primarily of his detective exploits and was renowned for his success in that sphere, should have awakened such widespread sympathy for the criminals he hunted. The explanation may well lie in the fact that popular opinion in France at that time could readily feel compassion for the victims of a harsh penal code, but was by no means prepared to applaud the activities of a detective. Very strong prejudices still persisted against 'informers,' and though Vidocq was famous as an extremely successful thief-taker and a brave, brilliantly clever man, he had been a thief himself. There seemed, perhaps, some hint of treachery to former associates in using his knowledge of their habits to send criminals, his old comrades among them, to the prisons in which he himself had suffered so terribly.

Thus, in his own country at least, the influence of Vidocq, the detective, was less quickly felt in popular fiction than the influence of Vidocq, the convict. Yet one effect of this preoccupation with criminals was to open up a path for the later development of detective fiction. It is a simple, natural progression from compassion for a convict to special sympathy for a man unjustly accused. Thence it is a short step to the perception that he needs someone to champion his cause and set about proving his innocence, preferably by finding out where guilt actually lies— that is to say, he needs the help of a detective. Balzac makes this point very clear in *Une Ténébreuse Affaire*, when the lawyer, Bordin, comments that the French legal system offers no protec-

[1] *Les Voleurs* (1836). *Les Vrais Mystères de Paris* (1844). *Quelques Mots* (1844). *Les Chauffeurs du Nord* (1845).

tion to an innocent man, charged with crime. The prosecution can draw upon all the resources of the state to obtain evidence in support of its case. Who will do the same for the accused?[1]

Thus Vidocq's two apparently conflicting influences both led, in their separate ways, to an increased interest in detection, in France and in the English-speaking world. When his *Mémoires* were read by Edgar Allan Poe, in America, they inspired him to create his masterly detective, Dupin. English fiction, it is true, had already produced amateur detectives in Caleb Williams, Lord Pelham and Walter Lester, each of whom for personal reasons investigated the circumstances of a mysterious murder. Vidocq, however, was of a very different calibre. He was a professional detective—the first of his kind—who devoted himself with zest and intelligence to this work as his sole occupation, bringing to a successful conclusion an almost endless series of apparently insoluble problems. He inspired the conception of an all-knowing detective from whom nothing can remain hidden, and because he was a Frenchman he was largely responsible for creating the impression, which we shall find expressed by many later writers from Edgar Allan Poe to Robert Louis Stevenson, that there was something peculiarly French about detective fiction. In considering the development of this type of popular fiction in the Western world, it would be difficult to over-estimate the degree to which it was influenced by the career and personality of Eugène François Vidocq.

[1] p. 204 in the edition consulted, Calmann-Lévy, 1892.

CHAPTER
III

THE RISE OF THE *ROMAN-FEUILLETON*. DETECTIVE THEMES IN THE NOVELS OF HONORE DE BALZAC, EUGENE SUE AND ALEXANDRE DUMAS

In France, during the second quarter of the nineteenth century, there was a rapid increase in that section of the reading public which, lacking the cultural background of earlier generations, demanded little beyond the sensational and the topical. Such readers satisfied their taste with periodicals or *journaux*. Every political party produced its own *journal,* and so did each religious group, relying upon loyal adherents to buy the publication regularly, preferably by annual subscription, and thus to provide funds for its continued existence.

Such periodicals were expensive. Moreover, each limited itself to expressing the views of its own party or sect, ignoring or abusing those who held other opinions, with the result that the public was not adequately informed. Largely through the business acumen of Emile de Girardin, a new type of *journal,* called a *feuilleton,* was devised to appeal to all classes of readers, irrespective of their beliefs or political opinions, and in July, 1836, Girardin issued the first number of *La Presse,* at a price exactly half that of the old-established *journaux.* To balance its finances it accepted advertisements; and to attract regular purchasers it included, every day, an instalment of a new and exciting novel. Within a few months *La Presse* had a rival, *Le Siècle,* planned on similar lines, and they both became so popular that older periodicals were forced to follow suit if they were to survive.

Thus modern, competitive journalism began to develop in France. To obtain a satisfactory revenue from advertisers a *journal* needed to maintain a wide circulation, not only among its own yearly subscribers but also by sales to casual purchasers, who would buy one *journal* in preference to another according to whether it pleased their fancy and held their interest.

The popular device to ensure that readers would buy every copy as it appeared was a serial story, or *Roman Feuilleton*. This was written in such a way that each day's instalment aroused keen curiosity as to how the characters could be extricated from the predicament in which they were left at the moment when the serial was interrupted. A subscriber who failed to buy the next issue would lose the thread of the story, and might never be able to satisfy his curiosity. Annual subscribers, who represented a valuable source of income, could be encouraged to continue their support by the commencement of a new, and if possible even more exciting, serial shortly before subscriptions were due for renewal. Indeed, a successful *roman feuilleton* might run for a year, and in some cases even two.

The French public greatly enjoyed these serials, and the success or otherwise of a *journal* came to depend increasingly upon the powerful appeal of a daily instalment of suspense, adventure and excitement. Consequently, writers of really popular serials could command a large salary. Eugène Sue, for instance, whose *Les Mystères de Paris* had doubled or trebled the circulation of *Le Journal des Débats*, was offered by another periodical a fee of 100,000 francs a year for his next serial, *Le Juif Errant*, before one word of it was written.

Until the vogue for the *roman-feuilleton* declined in the middle years of the nineteenth century, a tremendous flood of serial stories poured forth in response to the public's desire for such fiction. These novels, usually sensational and often worthless as literature, were not detective stories. Indeed, many of them were written from day to day as required, without a predetermined plot, and thus could not be constructed as a detective novel. But certain features of the *roman-feuilleton*—a sense of drama and suspense, a preference for subjects involving sensational crimes, a special interest in individual criminals and in the ways they were brought to justice—were retained when detective fiction came to be written in France, more particularly those types of detective fiction intended for the uncritical masses. Of the *romans feuilletons* that were re-issued in volume form, by far the most successful were those having some affinity with the *romans policiers* of the generation which followed. The development of the *roman feuilleton* in the direction of detective fiction was particularly influenced by the novels of Honoré de Balzac, Eugène Sue and Alexandre Dumas.

Of these three prolific writers, incomparably the greatest was Honoré de Balzac (1799—1850), and it was he who had the most far-reaching effect upon detective fiction. He co-ordinated elements of detective interest which we have already noticed in the novels of Mrs. Radcliffe and of Fenimore Cooper, enriching them with details inspired by Vidocq and adding to them completely new features of his own creation.

In his early years Balzac felt a lively admiration for the English writers of *romans noirs,* and introduced similar themes of horror and mystery in some of his *oeuvres de jeunesse,* for example *Le Vicaire des Ardennes* (1822) and its sequel, *Annette et le Criminel* (1824), later given the title of *Argow le Pirate.* Argow commits many crimes, including murder, but there is little need for detection since he confesses early in the story, and the only doubt is whether he will escape punishment. At his trial he is made to walk in sand so that his footprint can be used in evidence, a detail that may have been suggested by episodes in Cooper's *The Pioneers,* published in the previous year.

In 1827, Balzac, an enthusiastic admirer of Cooper, wrote *Le Dernier Chouan,* a title generally considered to be closely based upon *The Last of the Mohicans,* which appeared a year earlier. Balzac's novel was not published until 1829, the title being changed to *Les Chouans.* Some parts of the plot are very reminiscent of passages in Cooper's novel, and both stories relate the adventures and perils that threaten two young women travelling with an armed escort through wild country and lonely forests at a time of revolt. The *Chouans* themselves take names very like those of Cooper's braves—Galope-chopine, Pille-Miche, Marche-à-terre—and carry out their expeditions in much the same way as the Mohicans managed their raids. Cooper's influence is even more apparent in *Une Ténébreuse Affaire* (1841), when Michu binds the hoofs and nostrils of horses to prevent their making a sound or leaving tracks, places his ear to the ground to detect any pursuing footfall, and follows the trail of horsemen along forest paths.

Far greater was the influence of Vidocq, the ex-convict, upon Balzac, inspiring him to create Vautrin, whose adventures extend through *Le Père Goriot* (1834-35), *Les Splendeurs et Misères des Courtisanes* (1843—47), and *La Dernière Incarnation de Vautrin* (1847). All Vidocq's energy and ruthlessness are reproduced in Vautrin, his great prestige in the criminal underworld, his almost incredible skill in disguise, above all, his remarkable intelligence and subtlety. Throughout his *Comédie Humaine* Balzac introduced outstandingly clever criminal or reprobate heroes and presented them as characters to be admired, not because they were criminals, but because they were clever. Balzac's own appreciation for the special qualities which mark great men, even when these qualities are displayed by criminals, is particularly evident in his Preface to *L'Histoire des Treize* (1833—1835) and in the phrases he uses to describe the members of that terrifying secret society, *Les Dévorants*.

When creating the various *agents de police* who appear so frequently in his novels, Balzac again drew largely upon his knowledge of Vidocq, this time in his detective capacity. M. Gondureau, the officer who succeeds in capturing Vautrin in *Le Père Goriot*, employs Vidocq's characteristic methods of patient reconnaissance and is given Vidocq's title of *Chef de Sûreté*, even his official address in the *Petite Rue Sainte-Anne*. Peyrade, the very active *agent* who appears in *Une Ténébreuse Affaire* and in *Les Splendeurs et Misères des Courtisanes* has a great deal of Vidocq about him in his self-confidence, his physical strength, his deceptive joviality and his eye for a pretty woman. But it must be noticed that though Balzac many times gave a hero's role to the criminal, he never made a hero of a detective. He recognised that such *agents de police* might possess remarkable powers of intelligence, but scorned the uses to which those powers were applied by the political police of his day, and frequently spoke of the hostility these men aroused in the general public, their need to become impervious to insults, and the many other humiliating disadvantages under which they worked. Balzac did, however, take a great interest in the way their work was planned and carried out. His friend, Léon Gozlan, has described the zest with which he delved into their methods of obtaining evidence and building up a case, priding himself on his own skill in making subtle deductions from apparent trifles; Balzac's delight when Vidocq assured him that he, too, possessed a marked flair for 'smelling out a criminal'; even an occasion when Vidocq and Balzac set out to solve a crime-mystery together.[1]

Balzac's aptitude for sustained inductive reasoning, and his perception that such a theme could make entertaining reading, is clearly shown in a brief article published in *La Silhouette* on January 9th, 1830, with the rather significant title of *Etude de Moeurs par les Gants*. It is an exercise in 'pure' detection, not in any way concerned with crime, and relates in amusing detail a conversation in the salon of a countess who surprises her friends by deducing, from simple indications, various secrets they had thought to be well-concealed. In particular she discusses how the stains on a pair of light-coloured gloves can reveal exactly what their wearer had done during an evening's festivities; whether he had danced, and with which partners; his choice of food and his table-manners; the furniture he touched, possibly even the way he went home. Everywhere in his novels Balzac shows the same appreciation of how informative slight indications can be, introducing that thought even when it has no special bearing on his story. When, in *L'Histoire des Treize*, M. de Maulincour shelters from a storm in a doorway and idly watches the porter's wife sweeping out the rubbish, Balzac comments, in passing, that the life and habits of everyone in the house could be revealed by those odds and ends. Countless similar examples could readily be quoted.

In some of his novels such lines of reasoning do not remain as mere asides, but are given a definite importance in the plot. Balzac was the first really great novelist to devote serious atten-

[1] Cf. Gozlan, *Balzac Chez Lui*, Paris, Lévy Frères, 1862, p. 160, p. 210, and pp. 225-302.

tion to the working out of detective themes in fiction, and two of his works in particular, *Maître Cornélius* (1831)[1] and *Une Ténébreuse Affaire* (1841), will repay examination from this point of view.

Balzac's introduction to *Maître Cornélius* describes it as 'an ancient jewel, re-shaped to the present fashion,' and he gives it a detective interest. Moreover, in this case he shows considerable respect for the investigator, who, unlike those in his other novels, has no connection with the police. This short historical romance of Tours in 1459 relates how King Louis XI took upon himself the task of solving the mystery of a puzzling robbery, 'flattering himself that, as a king, he possessed enough perspicacity to uncover the secrets of thieves.'

Cornélius Hoogworst, a rich, miserly moneylender, has often complained of being robbed, and each time his unfortunate apprentice of the moment has been convicted and hanged for the theft. A young nobleman, Georges d'Estoutville, ventures to enter the miser's service, incognito, in order to be near his lady-love, whose home is adjacent to the house of Cornélius. When another robbery occurs the police arrest Georges, who refuses to explain his absence from his room at the time of the crime. Actually he had climbed over the roof-tops to visit Mme de Saint-Vallier, a natural daughter of King Louis, and when her lover is arrested the lady tells her father the whole story and begs his help. The king decides to investigate the matter, and satisfies himself, by examining the scene of the crime, that the young man could not possibly have entered the locked room by the chimney, as alleged, without leaving traces of soot upon the floor. Louis therefore covers the floor of the strong-room with flour and pays a surprise visit to the house at dawn. The flour shows fresh footprints, and when Louis follows the trail he discovers that they were made by Cornélius himself. The old miser, a somnambulist, had removed and hidden his own gold, unawares.

[1] It is interesting that *Etude de Moeurs par les Gants* and *Maître Cornélius* were written at a time when Balzac was much affected by Cooper's influence. Cf. Balzac's letter to Victor Ratier, the editor of *La Silhouette*, written from La Grenadière, in Touraine, dated July 21st, 1830.

Here we find a surprising number of features that are familiar in detective fiction. The crime is committed in a sealed room, some ten years before Poe made use of the same device in his *Murders in the Rue Morgue*.[1] The police are completely at fault, and a serious miscarriage of justice is prevented only through the intelligence of a distinguished amateur investigator who undertakes the enquiry for his own interest and pleasure. He makes logical deductions from personal observation at the actual scene of the robbery, systematically eliminates every impossibility, obtains the footprints of the thief, and at last brings the tale to an unexpected ending by proving the guilt of the most unlikely person. All these details are so much in the spirit of modern detective fiction that Balzac's term *'la mode d'aujourd-hui'* might well refer to the present day, instead of to more than a century ago.

The second of Balzac's novels in which a detective investigation formed a major part of the plot, *Une Ténébreuse Affaire*, appeared as a serial in *Le Commerce* during January and February, 1841, the title of the first section, *Les Chagrins de la Police*, striking at once the characteristic note. As Balzac made plain in his Preface when it was published in volume form, it is largely a reconstruction of certain events which took place in France, early in the century, and his purpose was primarily to expose the methods employed by the police of that time. He shows them challenged by one or two keenly intelligent minds, and the story is consequently full of detective interest.

Michu, a morose gamekeeper, has for years been despised by his neighbours, even by his wife, as a traitor to his former master, guillotined during the Revolution. In reality, and in spite of appearances, Michu has faithfully obeyed the orders of his late *patron*, guarding the secret of his buried wealth until his two sons could safely return from exile and take their rightful position in society. Misled by premature news of an official pardon, the young men come back to France at a moment when the political police are conducting active investigations in the

---

[1] Balzac was not the originator of this device, which had more than once occurred in earlier literature, and may stem from the story of *Bel*, in the Apocrypha.

neighbourhood of their old home, suspecting, rightly, that the *Comtesse de Cinq Cygne,* cousin of the exiles, has been secretly in communication with these 'enemies of the state,' who will be executed if found on French soil. Unaware of their danger, the brothers are actually approaching their cousin's house at a time when the police are searching the premises.

In this emergency Michu reveals his loyalty to his old master, braving great danger to convey a warning to the returning exiles, arranging an escape through the forest under the very noses of the police, restoring their fortune, providing them with a secret hiding-place, performing prodigies of strength and cunning until at last, by a stroke of misfortune, the police obtain sufficient evidence to arrest him and those he has done his utmost to serve. The third and final section is devoted to the drama of their trial, with the court swayed now in favour of the accused, now against them.

By ending his novel with a judicial trial, Balzac took a course which was followed by several later writers of detective fiction, particularly those who, like Balzac, had a special interest in, and knowledge of, the law. His father was a man of considerable legal attainments, who for nineteen years held the important position of a *Secretaire du conseil du roi,* and Balzac himself studied law before becoming a novelist. He was thus familiar with criminal legislation and judicial procedure, and in this trial scene he presented with convincing accuracy the tense drama of cross-examination and the subtle interplay of personality between opposing counsel. He went further, and gave in full the evidence, much of it deduction from material clues, upon which the police based their case, weaving a net of proof from the tracks made by horse-shoes which the blacksmith could identify; the peculiar green wax used by Mme Michu to seal her wine bottles; the pattern left by the bricks of an oven on the bottom crust of a loaf, and the use that Michu made of a bag of cement.

Balzac's novel is, of course, more than a story of detection. It is a *roman de moeurs,* in which the portrayal of character is more important than the construction of the plot, exciting though that may be. In this respect *Une Ténébreuse Affaire* differs from the typical detective novel, in which, as we have already seen, the first consideration is the plot, the delineation of character being usually a secondary matter. Nevertheless, this work contains so much of detective interest that it cannot be disregarded in any serious study of this type of fiction.

In considering Balzac's characters in general, it is interesting to note that those whom he presents as worthy of admiration are almost invariably observant, perspicacious and not readily deceived. Whenever he portrays people who are weak, those who are victimized or cheated by others, it is their lack of perception that he tends to emphasize, often with some considerable scorn. Though Balzac never created a detective-hero, (indeed, such a figure did not appear in French fiction until more than ten years after his death), he did much to familiarize his readers with the idea, on which detective fiction largely depends, that a man is to be specially admired when he possesses unusually intelligent powers of observation, when he is quick to perceive the significance of small details that others would entirely overlook.

An innovation of considerable importance in Balzac's work, one which has been extensively followed in detective stories and only rarely in other types of fiction, was his habit of introducing characters into more than one novel. Fenimore Cooper's "Leatherstocking" had already appeared in three novels, and was to figure in two more, but Balzac conceived the idea on an immensely greater scale, and made some 460 of his characters appear and re-appear in the long series of novels that form *La Comédie Humaine*. In one book alone, *Splendeurs et Misères des Courtisanes*, he introduced more than 150 persons already known to readers of his earlier works. He first made this a definite part of his system in 1833, when writing *Le Père Goriot*, and subsequently rewrote some of his earlier stories to bring them into line with this new development, which was to become a constantly more important feature of his technique. Edgar Allan Poe adopted this device in his three stories of Dupin, with the important difference that he made it apply only to three characters, the detective himself, the narrator, and, to a lesser degree, the Prefect of Police. In this modified form the technique first introduced by Balzac became almost conventional. Conan Doyle employed it in his sixty-odd tales of Sherlock Holmes, and almost every popular detective in twentieth century fiction is the hero of a long sequence of investigations, supported by one or two associates long familiar to readers.

One other feature that Balzac was the first to introduce into fiction is the technical language he employs on appropriate occasions, and his readiness to give, in the course of a novel, a little dissertation on some scientific or pseudo-scientific subject, as, for example, at the end of *Maître Cornélius*, when the old man's physician discourses learnedly upon the nature and treatment of somnambulism. In the opening paragraphs of *Une Ténébreuse Affaire*, Balzac affirms that "the laws of physiognomy are exact, [. . .] and the science of Lavater and Gall proves beyond question that [. . .] there are signs in a man's face that reveal not only his character but his destiny." Here, Balzac is taking certain liberties with the theories of these contemporary scientists, for their treatises do not state, or even imply, that a man's future is to be seen in his face, as Balzac suggests. They went no further than expressing their belief, based on long research, that the talents and disposition of a human being could be accurately inferred from the external appearance of the skull. It was Balzac's own, often-expressed, conviction that a man's future could be inferred from his present condition and circumstances, and the theories of Lavater and Gall doubtless seemed in accord with this idea, but Balzac was inaccurate in attributing to those scientists any 'proof' that a man's 'fate,' (not merely his talents and disposition), could be deduced from his face. Many a later writer of detective fiction, following the same course as Balzac, has rounded off a story with a little lecture on some 'scientific' matter, or entertained his readers by drawing sensational, but sometimes inaccurate, inferences from the 'new discoveries' of his day.

Balzac frequently refers appreciatively to another contemporary scientist, Cuvier (1769—1832), the French naturalist whose analytical deductions from the fossilised bones of prehistoric animals created so much interest from 1812 onwards. One particularly illuminating comment occurs in *Louis Lambert* (1832), when Balzac says of his hero that "he knew how to deduce, from a fragment of thought, enough to build up a complete reconstruction, as Cuvier did in a different order of things. All science depends on deduction, [. . .] whereby one moves from cause to effect, and back from effect to cause." When Dupin, (and, later, Sherlock Holmes), astonished his friend with an impressive display of thought-reading, he was manifesting precisely the same skill that Balzac attributed to Louis Lambert, and building up a complete reconstruction from 'a fragment of thought.'

*   *   *

It is a sharp descent from Balzac to Eugène Sue (1804—1857), yet this novelist, with his dandyism and his socialistic ideals, was notable in his day. Sainte-Beuve considered him Balzac's equal 'in invention, fertility and technique,' and his superior in the ability to create an accurate impression of the social conditions of the time. Like Balzac, he went to work on an enormous scale and constructed his complicated plots with great ingenuity. He was not concerned with devising detective problems, but his novels, portraying as they did the criminal world of Paris, had some influence on later detective fiction, especially in France.

His first important serial, *Les Mystères de Paris*, appeared in the *Journal des Débats* between June 1842 and October 1843, and when concluded was at once published as a novel. It relates in ten long volumes the adventures of Rodolphe, Prince of Gérolstein, who is living incognito in the slums of Paris as a self-imposed penance, devoting himself to helping the poor and unfortunate. He is quickly in conflict with a gang of thieves and murderers, proving himself as cunning and courageous as Vidocq in dealing with criminals, and equally knowledgeable concerning their habits and vernacular. After an almost interminable series of desperate encounters he captures the leader of the gang, the redoubtable 'maître d'école.'

59

Les Mystères de Paris is not a detective novel, but it contains passages in which Rodolphe acts as a detective, undertaking complicated investigations to discover the parentage and past history of Fleur-de-Marie and of François Germain, or ferreting out, then circumventing, the best-laid plans of his criminal opponents, finally causing their destruction. Many of the mysteries in the novel eventually prove to be due to natural causes, just as in the works of Mrs. Radcliffe, whom Sue greatly admired. Like her, he loved to terrify his readers with stories of nightmarès, horrible suggestions of the supernatural or descriptions of dreadful tortures. But to this background Sue added an extensive knowledge of prison-life, a familiarity with the psychology of criminals and a close acquaintance with their slang, which he was the first to employ in *feuilletons*. In addition, Sue introduced a new idea which does not seem to have appeared in fiction before, a conclusion he may have reached from his own observation, or possibly from following a line of thought suggested by the works of Lavater and Gall. Throughout his novels he expressed his conviction that certain types of criminals characteristically commit only certain types of crime.

English detective fiction owes a special debt to Eugène Sue, for Matthew Phipps Shiel, writing his *Prince Zaleski* in 1895, seems to have borrowed many of his hero's remarkable personal idiosyncrasies from two of Sue's characters, both, like Zaleski, of royal blood—Prince Rodolphe, in *Les Mystères de Paris,* and the Prince of Hansfield, who appeared in *Paula Monti* (1842). Like Rodolphe, Zaleski, troubled by memories of an old, unhappy love affair, has renounced the luxury and ceremony of a palace to become a voluntary exile in a strange land, tended only by one devoted negro servant who is a skilled physician. When Rodolphe (or Zaleski) penetrates the secret meeting of a murderous society and barely escapes with his life, his faithful David (or Ham) nurses him back to health single-handed. The parallel is even more striking between Shiel's hero and the Prince of Hansfield, who might be Prince Zaleski himself, except that he does not occupy occasional moments of leisure in solving crime-mysteries brought to him by a friend, being, indeed, sufficiently concerned with a similar problem of his own. Both men have withdrawn from the world to live in one room of a great mansion, where all daylight is shut out and the passing of time disregarded. Both find solace in playing for hours upon a magnificent organ; both choose a long black tunic as their normal garb, and both have furnished their retreat in the same way, with rich but dust-laden velvets, strange weapons, terrifying pictures and gruesome relics. Though Shiel has related how, 'lying idle one day, gazing at the sky,' he 'conceived the idea of writing *Prince Zaleski*,' one cannot help feeling that he must have had Sue's novels very much in mind.

There is little other detective interest in Sue's numerous serials, which are chiefly concerned with making sensational expositions of social injustice and suggestions for improving the conditions of the working classes, penalised at that time by harsh laws. He was a prolific and talented writer, rather than a great novelist, but he was, beyond question, extremely popular in his lifetime; he was one of the first writers in the nineteenth century, devoid of a title, who was accepted in aristocratic society. Indeed, it was largely because of this social success that Balzac, already established as a novelist but not as a popular celebrity, entered the ranks of the *feuilletonistes* in anticipation of enjoying similar favours.[1]

Eugène Sue was widely read in England as well as in France, several editions of his novels being published here in translation and also in the original text. Harrison Ainsworth published *The Revelations of London* (1844—1845) in open imitation of *Les Mystères de Paris*, and another series of stories in similar vein, *The Mysteries of London,* appeared in the *London Journal* between 1845 and 1855, the editor, Reynolds, describing them as 'from the French of Eugène Sue.'

The popular and prolific writer of a very different type of serial fiction, Alexandre Dumas (1802—1870), gave his most famous novels a setting in complete contrast to that chosen by

[1] The friendship between Balzac and Sue dates from approximately 1831, and its warmth is apparent from comments made by Balzac on the subject in his letters to Madame Hanska, though he made certain reservations in some of his remarks. Cf. Jacques Boulanger, *Les Dandys*, Ollendorff, 1907, pp. 307-309.

Sue, and, indeed, by most serial writers of the period. Instead of the squalid underworld of contemporary Paris, Dumas took his readers into the royal courts of seventeenth century France, which formed a magnificent background for the adventures of D'Artagnan, Porthos Aramis and Athos. Here were heroes to be admired for their quick perception as well as their physical strength and bravery. The reader could trust them to unravel all the intrigues and uncertainties of the plot, feeling from the start a comfortable assurance that, whatever their difficulties, they would triumph in the end, as, indeed, they invariably did in *Les Trois Mousquetaires* (1844), *Vingt Ans Après* (1845) and *Le Vicomte de Bragelonne* (1848—1850).

That Dumas was interested in analytical deduction from apparently trivial indications is everywhere apparent in his novels. In *The Count of Monte Cristo* (1845—1846) he even foreshadowed those 'psychological' or 'intuitional' methods that were to become so popular in detective fiction during the early twentieth century. There is a remarkable similarity between the thought-processes of the Abbé Faria and those of that later churchman, Chesterton's Father Brown, particularly during the discussions between Edmond Dantès and his aged fellow-prisoner in the Chateau d'If, when the abbé proved, by analysing the puzzled young sailor's own recollections, that his imprisonment had been contrived by certain treacherous friends for reasons that could be clearly established. Dantès himself showed sustained powers of detection when, as the Count of Monte Cristo, he ruthlessly set out to uncover the hidden secrets of the men who had betrayed him and to bring retribution upon them, while his investigations into the murders attempted or committed by that secret poisoner, the second Mme de Villefort, would of themselves constitute an excellent detective story.

It was in 1846 that Poe's first detective story, *The Murders in the Rue Morgue,* became widely known in France, and may well have impressed Dumas, for his next novel, *Le Vicomte de Bragelonne,* published in ten volumes between 1848 and 1850, introduced a brilliant display of detective reasoning by D'Artagnan, who was sent by King Louis to discover all he could about the details of a secret duel that had just been fought in a forest glade. After examining the terrain D'Artagnan reported what he had observed and the conclusions he had reached. Two horsemen had made tracks in the grass or the soft earth, and one of the horses was black. (Hairs from its tail had caught in the brambles). The contestants had fired at least two shots—D'Artagnan picked up the wadding of their pistols—and one of them was extremely agitated, for he had spilled half the charge when re-loading. D'Artagnan revealed the whole sequence of events from clues he had discovered and interpreted—the angle from which a bullet was fired, since it severed a hat-plume and the branch of a tree; the place where the wounded man had been left for dead; the bloodstains showing the position and severity of his wounds; the two newcomers on foot, who between them had led him away to find shelter and medical aid. It could be Sherlock Holmes speaking, and Louis, like an early Dr. Watson, marvels at the investigator's subtle deductions; asks the questions the reader wants to have answered, such as 'How could you know the unmounted cavalier was wounded in his right hand and then in the chest by the same ball?'; finally exclaiming in amazement "From your wonderful reconstruction I can picture the whole scene!"

It is an interesting point of technique that the reader has already been given an account of this combat in an earlier chapter. Thus it seems Dumas's purpose was to focus the reader's attention upon D'Artagnan's acumen in interpreting the evidence and arriving at what the reader knew to be the truth, leading him to applaud, as Louis himself did, the detective skill shown by the musketeer.

Earlier in the same novel Dumas introduced a detail, new at that time, which has often been used since in detective fiction. Mme Vanel discovers the secret plans of Colbert through his having written a memorandum with a hard pencil on the top sheet of a pad of paper, thus leaving a readable impression on the second sheet. Many a modern detective has obtained information in just the same way, and Sherlock Holmes expressed considerable disappointment when, in *The Case of the Missing*

Three-quarter, such a source failed to provide the data he expected: —

> 'It is a pity he did not write in pencil. [. . .] As you have no doubt frequently observed, Watson, the impression usually goes through.'

But it is in *Les Mohicans de Paris* (1854—1855) that Dumas made his nearest approach to a detective novel. The title itself is suggestive, and the special skills of Cooper's redskin trackers, their habits of minute observation and shrewd deduction, are adapted to detective purposes by the various characters who investigate the crimes of Gérard Tardieu. The elegant Jean Robert, poet and amateur detective, interprets signs and traces in just the manner of an Indian guide, while Salvator, that aristocratic gentleman of leisure who enjoys probing into mysteries, can piece together fragmentary clues to such good effect that he is often credited with more than human powers. Incidentally, Salvator sometimes has the help of an extremely intelligent dog, clever enough, for example, to discover for his master the secret grave of Tardieu's murdered nephew. This 'Brésil,' or 'Roland,' may well be a fictional ancestor of those sagacious hounds employed by certain later detectives, from Rocambole, and once or twice Holmes himself, down to Nick Carter and Sexton Blake!

In this novel, for the first time in French fiction, Dumas presented a police officer in a 'sympathetic' light, giving him an important place, even if not precisely that of 'hero.' Monsieur Jackal, with his occasional silent laugh in the manner of Leatherstocking, learns a great deal from scrutinizing footprints on a garden path, or the marks made in soft earth by a ladder. He even carries out an impromptu experiment to discover what weight would cause the ladder to make a similar depression! His habit of 'thinking aloud' tends to rob his conclusions of any dramatic effect, but he is an efficient detective and arrives at solutions to problems quite cleverly at times, as, for instance, when he proves that Mina must have been abducted from the *pension* of Mme Desmarets with the aid of the only other woman

Vidocq

G. K. Chesterton

Mary Roberts Rinehart

Sir Arthur Conan Doyle

A. E. W. Mason

Dorothy Sayers

in the house who had a room to herself. He will always be remembered as the originator of that oft-quoted dictum, *Cherchez la femme!*

M. Jackal habitually wore green-tinted spectacles, not in order to see better, but so that others could not perceive where his glances were directed, exactly as Poe's Dupin had done in *The Purloined Letter*, published twelve years earlier. One particularly interesting feature in *Les Mohicans de Paris* is the relationship between M. Jackal and Salvator, the keenly intelligent amateur whom he would have liked to enrol as his chief assistant. While firmly declining any official status, Salvator was quite willing to work in close collaboration with M. Jackal, sharing his discoveries and theories. This association between an amateur and an official detective may possibly have been suggested to Dumas by the somewhat guarded friendship between Dupin and Monsieur G—— in *The Purloined Letter*, but whereas Dupin merely handed the missing document to the baffled Prefect of Police, telling him nothing whatever of how it had been retrieved, Salvator freely discusses with M. Jackal the problems they are both endeavouring to solve, and something approaching a working partnership thus comes into existence. Such an alliance was to become an almost conventional feature, so much so that it would be difficult to name any successful amateur detective in twentieth century fiction who lacks a personal contact with the official police force.

In M. Jackal's day, however, a police agent, clever though he might be, was still regarded with disfavour by the French public, and though Salvator was prepared to discuss his ideas with M. Jackal, he considered him quite impossible as a social acquaintance, in spite of his quiet manner and scrupulously neat appearance, and was most reluctant to sit beside him in a carriage. Indeed, M. Jackal accepted without offence this estimate of his personal status, for though he enjoyed his work he had no illusions as to the stigma attached to his profession in France at that time.

This strong prejudice against the police and any who assisted them, which was portrayed even more clearly by Balzac than by Dumas, prevented the creation of a detective-hero in French fiction at that period, and though the writers considered in this chapter all introduced themes of detection, each adding his individual innovations, none of them made this the chief subject of a novel, or gave the leading rôle to a detective. In detective fiction, as we know it today, the author makes it his primary purpose to devise an entertaining, baffling problem which will be unravelled by the detective, who thus becomes the central figure, the focal point of the reader's admiration. For the earliest emergence of this technique, the first complete examples of the modern detective story, we must look to America, where, during the lifetime of Honoré de Balzac, Eugène Sue and Alexandre Dumas, the various threads we have traced hitherto were all woven together to form a distinctive pattern, and a new type of story with a magic of its own was created by Edgar Allan Poe.

CHAPTER
IV

THE SHORT DETECTIVE STORY
EDGAR ALLAN POE

In contrast to the slow development of the detective novel, the emergence of the short story as a literary form was quickly followed by the appearance of the short detective story. Vidocq's *Mémoires* could conceivably be regarded as a series of such tales, for each 'case' is complete in itself, but they are little more than factual reports, written with dramatic or humorous touches but quite lacking in literary quality. Few short stories, other than fables or cautionary tales for children, appeared in literature before the early nineteenth century, but at that time English writers began to experiment with the production of fiction in this form for the new magazines just commencing publication, *Blackwood's* for example, which issued its first number in 1817.

Edgar Allan Poe (1809—1849), born in Boston, published his first work, *Tamerlane, and Other Poems* in 1827, and a second volume of poetry in 1831. These brought him some esteem but little financial reward, and he realised that, to live by his pen, he must concentrate on writing fiction. Accordingly he carefully studied the short stories already popular in *Blackwood's* with special reference to their construction and subject matter, the advantages and limitations of presentation in this form, and thus perfected the techniques he used so effectively in those detective stories and tales of the macabre for which he is chiefly remembered today. Conan Doyle considered him 'the supreme original short story writer,' and has stressed the debt that all later writers of detective fiction owe to 'those admirable stories of M. Dupin, so wonderful in their dramatic force, their reticence, their quick dramatic point.'[1]

In these three stories the Chevalier C. Auguste Dupin became the first detective-hero of fiction. He is the most important figure

[1] Sir Arthur Conan Doyle, *Through the Magic Door*, London, Smith, Elder, 1907, p. 114.

in each tale, and the whole plot is designed to display his powers of observation and deduction. Dupin is a scholarly recluse who in moments of leisure discusses with his friend, the narrator, ways in which analytical reasoning can be applied to practical problems, and certain mysterious crimes committed in Paris serve as examples for elucidation. Why Poe, writing in Baltimore, decided to give his detective stories a French setting is a point of particular interest. It seems certain that Poe never selected a background for any work without careful thought, and chose for each of his tales a setting to accord closely with its subject and atmosphere. For that sentimental fragment of fantasy, *The Oval Portrait*, he chose a castle in the Apennines very similar to those in the gothic romances of Mrs. Radcliffe, whom he mentioned in the text. The tortures he described in *The Pit and The Pendulum* had a Spanish setting, and *The Cask of Amontillado*, telling of gay carnival and sinister revenge, had Southern Italy for its background. For a tale of fearful peril at sea, Poe chose the northern coast of Norway, and for his three great detective stories he considered Paris the natural setting. It seems clear that in Poe's opinion there was some close affinity between France and the application of inductive reasoning to the detection of crime, a thought-provoking detail, particularly since no detective fiction, as such, had yet been written in France. The explanation may well be that the ideas which inspired him to plan this new type of story were associated in his mind with France because they had reached him from French sources.

Poe had certainly read Vidocq's *Mémoires,* for the methods of searching a house he described in *The Purloined Letter* are those that Vidocq often used, and in *The Murders in the Rue Morgue* he comments: —

'Vidocq was a good guesser and a persevering man. But, without educated thought, he erred continually.'

A detective who possessed the advantage of a sound education would obviously be much more successful, so Poe created just such a character in Dupin.

Una Pope-Hennessy suggests that Poe borrowed some of the

details he used in *The Masque of the Red Death* from 'the seven coloured palaces of the Princes of Serendip, whose adventures Poe may have come across as a boy,'[1] and this could well be true, though Poe does not mention the three princes and their camel anywhere in his writings. He does, however, refer to Zadig in his humorous tale *Hopfrog*, and would know of Zadig's clever deductions from observation in *Le Chien et Le Cheval*. Indeed, he uses similar arguments in *The Murders in the Rue Morgue* to prove to his friend that the only creature capable of making the marks he had found was an ourang-outang, and Poe's indebtedness to Voltaire's story was noticed by French readers as soon as this tale appeared in French translation.[2] To identify the peculiar characteristics of the ourang-outang, Dupin quotes a passage in the work of the French naturalist, Cuvier, famous for his skill in deducing the details of a whole skeleton from a fragment of fossilised bone, a skill which had also impressed Balzac. In making Dupin talk so learnedly and so often about "The Calculus of Probabilities" Poe may again have been influenced by a French source, for the French mathematician, le marquis de Laplace, wrote his *Théorie des probabilités* in 1812, and an English translation of his *Mécanique céleste,* containing this particular treatise, was published in Boston between 1829 and 1839, a period when Poe was closely connected with that city.

Whatever may have been Poe's reasons for setting his tales of Dupin against a French background, he went to some length to build up that background in convincing detail. His hero, a Frenchman of noble family, has a good address in Paris, and during his walks through well-known streets of the French capital he discusses local topics such as the performances in the various theatres; the reviews in the *Musée*; the gossip about the professional ambition and personal handicaps of an actor whose latest show was a failure. Dupin is a regular reader of the *Gazette des Tribunaux,* inserts an advertisement in the personal column of *Le Monde,* and is prone to round off his little lectures

---

[1] Una Pope-Hennessy, *Edgar Allan Poe, A Critical Biography*, Macmillan, 1934, p. 140.
[2] Cf. The *Quotidienne*, June 11th, 1846.

on detection with a quotation from Rousseau's *La Nouvelle Héloïse* or Crébillon's *Atrée.*

In complete contrast with Vidocq, Dupin is a man of culture, familiar with the classics and equally at home when discussing chemistry, anthropology or 'algebraic analysis' with his anonymous friend, the narrator of the stories, who is humbly over-awed by the brilliance of Dupin's massive intellect, and serves him, by turns, as a foil, a confidant or a willing assistant, in the same way as Dr. Watson was to serve Sherlock Holmes, half a century later. Dupin made his début in *The Murders in the Rue Morgue* (1841) and was presented to the reader simply as a young man of illustrious family, living in poverty and seclusion, a student whose only luxury was his books, whose learning was immense. Poe gave no information about his physical appearance: the reader was not to be interested in his looks, but in his thought-processes, his brilliant analytical mind. He first displays his powers of perception and deduction by correctly reading his companion's thoughts—an impressive parade of detective virtuosity that serves as an effective curtain-raiser to the main story. Dupin and his friend, reading the *Gazette des Tribunaux*, learn of the brutal murder of Mme L'Espanaye and her daughter in a locked room at the top of a house, the windows being 'firmly closed.' When the police arrest a man who once rendered Dupin a service, the savant decides to investigate the mystery, studies the newspaper reports, and examines the bodies at the scene of the crime, after which he keeps his friend in suspense till the next day. He then casually mentions that he is expecting a sailor to call in answer to an advertisement, and while waiting he gives his long-suffering companion a lecture on the salient details of the case, making for the first time in fiction that statement so often quoted since, "the more extraordinary a problem appears, the easier it will be to solve." He first challenges the statement that there was no possible exit from the victims' apartment, and explains every link in the chain of reasoning that led him to conclude, before he touched it, that "there *must* be something wrong about the nail" in one of the windows.

While at the scene of the crime, Dupin 'disentangled this

little tuft of hair from the rigidly clutched fingers of Mme L'Espanaye,' an action apparently unobserved by the *gendarme* who accompanied him.[1] The nature of this hair, coupled with Dupin's discovery that the impression left by the fingers which strangled the woman does not correspond with the grip of a human hand, convinces him that the victims were killed by an ape. Dupin places a volume of Cuvier in his friend's hands, directing his attention to 'a minute anatomical and generally descriptive account of the large fulvous Ourang-Outang of the East Indian Islands,' and thus, for the first time in detective fiction, not only gives a scientific interpretation of the evidence, but substantiates it by reference to a text-book which the detective is able to take from his own bookshelves. Dupin's reconstruction of the crime is fully confirmed by the long-awaited sailor, who is then allowed to depart unhindered, still hoping to recover his dangerous pet. Dupin placed his information before the Prefect of Police, who instantly released his earlier suspect, but 'could not altogether conceal his chagrin at the turn which affairs had taken, and was fain to indulge a sarcasm or two, about the propriety of every person minding his own business.'

The Prefect's jealousy of Dupin's detective acumen, and Dupin's poor opinion of police intelligence, almost certainly reflect the rivalry between Vidocq and the French police. Poe's purpose in stressing this situation in his tales of Dupin may well have been to make their French setting still more convincing, and this effect would have been heightened for Americans conversant with current affairs in France by a recent lawsuit that attracted a great deal of public interest. In 1837, the Official Police brought an action against Vidocq in the French courts, challenging his methods and disclosing how much their own position was prejudiced by his success. The verdict was given in Vidocq's favour, and his prestige was thereby enhanced. He

[1] Such an action would not have been considered ' fair play ' in later English detective fiction for the convention became generally accepted that a detective, other than a police official, must not remove evidence. Cf. the action taken by Sherlock Holmes after the mysterious death of Mortimer Tregennis, in *The Devil's Foot*. He is scrupulously careful to take for his own experiments only half of the ashes of a drug burned on the smoke-guard of a lamp, leaving the other half available for the police, ' had they the wit to find it '.

was less fortunate in 1843, when a second police prosecution brought him a term of imprisonment. Poe wrote these stories in 1841 and 1842, when Vidocq's reputation stood high and that of the police was at a low ebb. But the fact that this state of affairs was related to France, not to England or America, was largely overlooked by those later writers of detective fiction, from Conan Doyle onwards, who followed Poe's lead and made their amateur detectives outshine the police of their day as a matter of course.

Another feature that has been widely borrowed from Poe is his device of building separate stories around the detective, his admiring chronicler and one particular police official. In creating this pattern Poe was possibly influenced by Vidocq's series of investigations, but more probably he adapted Balzac's technique of introducing the same characters in several different novels. Such a striking innovation, developed as a special feature by the greatest contemporary figure in French literature can hardly have escaped the attention of such a keen student of France as Edgar Allan Poe. But if he followed Balzac's example he modified it to suit his own purpose, making it apply to three characters only.

After his first success, Dupin continues his lectures on the mathematics of detection in *The Mystery of Marie Roget* (1842). By giving this quite different story the sub-title *A Sequel to The Murders in the Rue Morgue,* Poe makes it plain that the essential theme, the link between them, is 'the mental character of my friend, the Chevalier C. Auguste Dupin.' The centre of interest is Dupin's brilliant analytical reasoning, and other men or women who appear in the tales serve merely to create the problems he is to solve. For the first time in fiction, the detective-hero and the detective theme monopolize the reader's attention.

The Murders in the Rue Morgue may have been based on an account in a contemporary English newspaper of the damage caused by a trained chimpanzee that escaped from captivity.[1]

---

[1] Cf. Pope-Hennessy, Op. cit., p. 203. Eugène Sue used a similar theme in his *Coupe-en-deux,* an instalment of *Les Mystères de Paris* published at about the same time. Sue does not, however, present it as a detective story, in the way Poe does.

Whether this was so or not, Poe presented the story simply as fiction. It was otherwise with *The Mystery of Marie Roget,* in which Dupin gave a practical demonstration of his detective powers by putting forward an explanation of a mystery that had aroused the excited interest of the American public for several months before this tale appeared. Though its background is still, nominally, Paris, it is a detailed reconstruction of an actual murder committed in New York in August, 1841, a case that was still unsolved when Poe's story was published in November, 1842.[1]

Because of this it is a different type of story, an impersonal exercise in analytical deduction. There is no action, and since the mystery of Mary Roger's death was still occupying the New York police when the story appeared, the conclusion could not be entirely explicit, Dupin merely indicating the lines which, in his opinion, the enquiry could most usefully follow. The French background is far less convincing than in *The Murders in the Rue Morgue,* despite the French names of all the characters and the newspapers to which Dupin refers, for the features of the actual scene of the crime, an essential part of the evidence, destroy the illusion. Everyone knew that ferryboats plied across the Hudson, and on the further bank at that time were the 'deserted glades' and 'dense thickets' where the little boys of the neighbourhood 'gathered the bark of the sassafras,' but to transfer such features to the Seine in Paris placed a considerable strain on the reader's credulity.

There is a subtle difference, too, in the relationship between Dupin and the Prefect G——, for 'after the powers of the police had been taxed to their utmost for several weeks' it is the Prefect himself who asks for Dupin's help, offering him a 'liberal proposition' that Dupin 'accepts at once.'[2] The chevalier has not,

---

[1] In *Graham's Lady's and Gentleman's Magazine.* When, a few years later, this story was issued with others in volume form, notes were added to explain the circumstances under which it was written, and to point out that Dupin's deductions proved correct in every detail.

[2] The Editors of *Graham's* added a careful footnote to place on record that ' when the result desired was brought to pass the Prefect fulfilled punctually, though with reluctance, the terms of his compact with the *chevalier* '.

however, modified his own opinion of 'the myrmidons of police,' and shows how little he values their best efforts by sleeping quietly, though 'in an attitude of respectful attention,' while the Prefect relates all the evidence his department has collected. Once he embarks on his task, Dupin's methods of detection remain much the same as in *The Murders in the Rue Morgue,* and, as before, Poe shows him scrutinizing newspaper reports, arguing at length about the 'Calculus of Probabilities,' and discoursing on scientific subjects, this time on the nature of fungi; the rate at which grass grows; 'chemical infusions that will preserve the animal frame for ever from corruption'; and whether the firing of a cannon over water would cause a drowned body to rise to the surface.

The third story, *The Purloined Letter,* is lighter and more conversational in tone, and opens on a scene very similar to that which Conan Doyle often used as an introduction to his tales of Sherlock Holmes. The narrator and the detective are sitting by the fire in their study one autumn evening, enjoying their comfort all the more because of the gusty weather outside, smoking their pipes after talking about recent successful investigations, when their old acquaintance, Monsieur G——, Prefect of the Paris police, unexpectedly arrives to ask Dupin's opinion about a troublesome problem which is "very simple, but excessively odd."

An unscrupulous and powerful politician, *Le ministre D*——, has by a trick gained possession of a compromising letter, and is blackmailing the owner, a charming member of the royal household, who had the good sense to take her problem in confidence to the police. They have made the most minute and painstaking search of the minister's house and grounds, even of his person, but have failed to discover where the letter is hidden, though it must be readily accessible. An enormous reward is offered for its recovery. Can Dupin suggest what the police should do next? The detective is singularly unhelpful at the time, but a month or so later, when the Prefect, more depressed than ever by his continued failure to find the precious document, calls on him again, Dupin enquires casually whether he would really, as promised, "pay fifty thousand francs to anyone who could obtain that letter?" "Certainly!" "In that case, fill me up a cheque for the amount mentioned, and I will hand you the letter!"

After the Prefect, speechless with amazement, has departed, clutching the paper in a perfect agony of joy, Dupin explains to his friend how he managed to locate and gain possession of it, when the police had so repeatedly failed. The letter had not been concealed, but left in full view in an old letter rack, turned inside out and torn almost in half, as though of no importance. The obvious is generally overlooked, a truism that Poe was the first to use as the basis of a detective story. It has often been employed since. G. K. Chesterton, with his love of paradox, found it particularly to his liking and introduced it several times in his tales of Father Brown.

In *The Purloined Letter*, Dupin is no longer an abstract logician. His character is drawn 'in the round,' and he has come to life as a person, holding normal, even humorous, conversations with the Prefect, and chatting amiably to his friend the narrator about methods of detection, especially about the boy who won all the marbles in the school by estimating the astuteness of his opponents, and accurately deducing their thoughts from their expressions. The poor recluse of *The Murders in the Rue Morgue* has re-entered the social life of Paris on such an exalted level that the powerful Minister D—— receives him personally as a close acquaintance, and Dupin is now rich enough to be able to leave behind him, 'accidentally,' a gold snuff-box to serve as an excuse for a second visit. He is certainly in business as a consultant-detective, and accepts the Prefect's cheque without even a word of thanks. His subsequent career might have been particularly interesting, but, alas, *The Purloined Letter* is the last of the Dupin stories.

In addition to these three famous tales, Poe wrote two others that contain some detective interest of a different type, *The Gold Bug* and *Thou Art the Man*. Though *The Gold Bug* was not published until 1843, when it won a hundred-dollar prize in a competition arranged by *The Dollar Magazine*, part of it may have been written years earlier, during the period 1827—1829 when Poe was serving in the army at Fort Moultrie, on that same Sullivan's Island, off the coast of South Carolina, which he made the setting for this tale of buried treasure, the hoard of the notorious pirate, Captain Kidd. Once more, Poe's hero is a Frenchman, this time a Monsieur Legrand, who, like Dupin, comes of an ancient, illustrious family, reduced to poverty. By chance, Legrand discovers that a scrap of parchment, picked up on the seashore, bears a memorandum written in cipher with invisible ink. After intense concentration he decodes the cryptogram, plans and carries out his investigations, finally recovering the treasure with the help of an old family servant and the friend who relates the story. Not until the end, when the reader, like the narrator, is 'dying with impatience for a solution of this most extraordinary riddle,' does Legrand explain exactly how he deciphered Captain Kidd's memorandum, and how the clues he found in it led him to the buried treasure.

Some passages in this story—the descriptions of scenery and the humorous interludes with Legrand's negro servant, Jupiter —were probably composed during Poe's sojourn at Fort Moultrie, while the greater part was written some years later and reflects Poe's absorbing interest in Cryptography. If not exactly a detective story, *The Gold Bug* is certainly a story of detection, based on observation and logical deduction, and it has one or two details that later became familiar in detective fiction, such as the enigmatic title, (for the beetle itself is of merely incidental importance), and Legrand's habit of expecting the utmost co-operation from his hard-worked assistants, telling them nothing until it suits him to satisfy their curiosity.

Poe's last story of crime and detection, *Thou Art The Man*,[1] is less well-known, but merits some notice in spite of its unpleasantly macabre conclusion. It is presented in an oddly humorous vein, quite unlike the atmosphere of the Dupin stories, and this time it is the narrator who acts as a detective, though this is not revealed until the final paragraphs. The setting is a small American country town, where the wealthiest citizen has mysteriously disappeared while riding in the woods. The missing

[1] Published in Philadelphia, *Godey's Lady's Book*, November, 1844.

man's closest friend, 'Old Charley,' leads the search and finds enough evidence to bring about the arrest of a young nephew of the victim, who is accordingly sentenced to death. Before the sentence is carried out, the anonymous narrator quietly investigates the clues that secured the lad's conviction, and discovers that they have been deceptively arranged by 'Old Charley' whereupon he arranges a terrifying hoax and so obtains a public confession from the murderer.

Here there are no learned discussions, no mention of the 'mathematics of detection' or of any scientific matter, and no specific reference to the police. It is a simple, straightforward detective story, and contains several features that were new in Poe's work—the murder trial in a magistrate's court; a trail of false clues, such as the 'bloodstained' clothing, the home-made bullet that had been fired by the accused man's gun, the victim's pocket-book hidden in his nephew's room; and, in contrast to the unemotional endings of the Dupin tales, a dramatic *dénouement* revealing the guilt of the most unlikely person.

Thus, in this small group of five short tales, Poe gave a pattern for several different types of detective story. *The Murders in the Rue Morgue* is the typical tale of sensational crime, with gruesome details of frightful injuries inflicted on the victims; *The Mystery of Marie Roget* is an intellectual *tour de force* in which the detective, without leaving his armchair, solves the problem purely by inductive reasoning. In *The Purloined Letter* lies the germ of the 'Secret Agent' story, with crime in diplomatic circles, a missing document, blackmail, a beautiful lady in distress, and intense police activity handicapped by the need to avoid at all costs any politically dangerous scandal. *The Gold Bug* is the forerunner of tales in which a cryptogram holds the secret of buried treasure, and *Thou Art The Man* tells of crime in a peaceful little town, with all the neighbours watching every move, a strong case against the murdered man's heir, and the actual criminal a highly respected citizen, unmasked at the last moment by the detective skill of a quiet local lad.

Poe's *Tales of Mystery and Imagination* were quickly popular in America, and Howard Haycraft has remarked that Abraham

Lincoln himself was 'the first of the countless eminent men who have turned to the detective story for stimulation and solace,' and that he enjoyed Poe's account of Dupin's investigations so much that 'in the words of a contemporary writer, " he suffers no year to pass without a perusal of this author.' "[1] This is hardly surprising when one recalls that Lincoln displayed considerable detective skill himself, during his career as a barrister.

For instance, he secured the acquittal of his client, William "Duff" Armstrong, charged with murder at Beardstown in May, 1858, by proving in court, with the help of an almanac, that the chief witness for the prosecution was lying when he claimed to have seen the crime committed by moonlight, on a certain date at a certain time. It is more remarkable that, during the election campaign for the Presidency of the United States in 1860, Lincoln's 'admiration for the absolute and logical method of Poe's tales' was particularly mentioned in an address to the electorate by one of his supporters, as a detail likely to win the approval of the voters, which argues a widespread appreciation for detective fiction as an intellectual diversion in America, beyond anything felt in England at that period.

A selection of Poe's stories, including *The Gold Bug* and the three tales of Dupin, was published in London in 1846,[2] during the author's lifetime, and another collection which included the same group of detective stories appeared in 1852.[3] Neither of these issues seems to have made much impression on contemporary English readers, whose tastes were more amply satisfied by the three-volume novels popular at the time, and another twenty years elapsed before a further edition of this American writer's work was published in England.[4] In France, however, there was a ready market for such material in the popular *journaux*, and in 1846 two rival newspapers independently

---

[1] Howard Haycraft, *Murder for Pleasure*, London, Davies, 1942.

[2] By Wiley and Putnam.

[3] *Tales of Mystery, Imagination and Humour*, by E. A. Poe. (Vol. 1 of a series called *The Parlour Bookcase*.) Published in London and Belfast by Simms and Mc'Intyre, 1852.

[4] *The Works of Edgar Allan Poe*, London, Chatto & Windus, 1872.

published translations of *The Murders in the Rue Morgue*.[1] Charges of plagiarism were hotly contested in a law-suit that entertained the literary world of Paris and made Poe's name familiar, translations of other examples of his work following in quick succession. But it was his tales of Dupin that especially appealed to French-readers. and the vogue for the *roman feuilleton* had prepared a fruitful soil for this new growth. In *The Murders in the Rue Morgue*, which by the beginning of 1847 had been adapted and translated at least four times in the French Press, the public found a crime-story as sensational as any in *Les Mystères de Paris*, but presented from a completely different viewpoint. It was no longer enough for the reader to feel horror at the crime and sympathy for the victim, or possibly for the criminal. He was expected to think, and to think analytically; to take pleasure in following in detail the logical arguments whereby an explanation is found for the whole mysterious chain of circumstances. This new type of story told of crimes, but not of criminals; and it presented a detective as the hero.

French fiction had already produced romantic heroes, Eugène Sue's Prince Rodolphe for example, who occasionally embarked on detective enquiries to further some special purpose of their own. *Agents de police*, such as Balzac's Corentin and Peyrade, had ruthlessly carried out various criminal investigations with complete success but they were not presented as deserving any admiration from the reader. In complete contrast with both these types, Dupin was a 'sympathetic' character whose logical deductions were very much in tune with French habits of thought. A point that doubtless had its effect on French readers

[1] In June, 1846, the Quotidienne began publishing a serial version with the title *Un Meurtre sans exemple dans les fastes de justice* and the adaptor, who signed himself G.B., allowed himself considerable latitude in changing the names of the characters (Dupin, for instance, became M. Bernier), and in emphasising the sensational details. In October of the same year another version, this time with the title *Une Sanglante Enigme*, began to appear in *Le Commerce*. This adaptation was signed ' Old Nick ', the pseudonym of a celebrated French journalist, E. D. Forgues, who, as it happened, had just been engaged in a controversy with *La Presse*, and had accused that journal of plagiarism in one of its recent *feuilletons*. *La Presse* retorted that ' Old Nick ' was himself guilty of such practices and had copied *Une Sanglante Enigme* from the columns of the *Quotidienne*. When the case came to court, Forgues proved conclusively that both *feuilletons* were based on Poe's story.

was that Dupin was a Frenchman, a Parisian of good family. He had a poor opinion of the regular police, whose methods he distrusted as did most Frenchmen of the period, though for a different reason, and nowhere in the stories did he bring about an arrest. If his detective activities reminded French readers of Vidocq, he was nevertheless a man of a very different intellectual calibre, familiar with the work of such national celebrities as Lavater, Laplace and Cuvier, and able to argue convincingly that the detection of crime was also a science.

Baudelaire's translation of Poe was read by the young Emile Gaboriau, who was so filled with admiration for the Dupin stories that he determined to write, on similar lines, a new series of his own, to be called *Récits Etranges*. This project never materialised in that form, but when, in the 1860's, Gaboriau created the first great detective hero in French fiction, M. Lecoq, he made him in some respects a re-incarnation of *le chevalier* Dupin.

Poe's influence in England was long delayed, but it made itself felt for the first time at a most opportune moment. The edition published in 1872 contained his detective stories and also his essays on literary composition and on Charles Dickens. The sudden death of this great novelist in 1870 brought not only grief and shock to his immense circle of readers. It left them with a tantalising enigma, his half-finished serial story of crime and detection, *The Mystery of Edwin Drood*. Poe's essay on Charles Dickens, made available to English readers two years after the novelist's death, revealed that from a study of the first two instalments of *Barnaby Rudge,* Poe had accurately deduced almost the whole plot of the novel, and had published his reconstruction in the *Philadelphia Saturday Evening Post* on May 1st, 1841, shortly after *Barnaby Rudge* had begun to appear in serial form in England. A keen interest in Poe's methods of reasoning must have been felt by those who still longed to satisfy their curiosity as to how Dickens meant to develop and conclude *The Mystery of Edwin Drood*.

Poe's essay on Charles Dickens is largely an analytical examination of the construction of *Barnaby Rudge*, considered as a crime-story, and in the course of it he sets out very precisely the technique to be followed when writing such a story, a technique that has been followed ever since by writers of detective fiction, and by no-one more closely than Conan Doyle, one of Poe's most enthusiastic admirers. Here, for the first time, is a blue-print of how a detective novel must be planned: —

'The *thesis* of the novel may be regarded as based upon curiosity. Every point is so arranged as to perplex the reader, and whet his desire for elucidation. [. . .] The impression here skilfully conveyed is that the ghost seen is that of Reuben Haredale, and the mind of the not too-acute reader is at once averted from the true state of the case. [. . .] There can be no question that, by such means as these, many points which [. . .] would have been comparatively insipid if given in full detail in a natural sequence, are endued with the interest of mystery.
The design of mystery, however, being once determined upon by an author, it becomes imperative, first, that no undue or inartistical means be employed to conceal the secret of the plot; and secondly, that the secret be well kept. [. . .] A failure to preserve it until the proper moment of *dénouement* throws all into confusion. If the mystery leak out, against the author's will, his purposes are immediately at odds and ends, for he proceeds upon the supposition that certain impressions *do* exist, which do *not* exist, in the mind of his readers.'

Poe goes on to point out several pitfalls that are difficult to avoid when writing a novel about a mysterious murder, and gives instances of how Dickens was once or twice forced to change his plot on encountering such difficulties.

One characteristic effect produced by detective fiction is the delight readers take in discovering any inconsistencies or inaccuracies in the plot. Even a writer as careful as Conan Doyle occasionally received letters in this strain from readers, and certain discrepancies in a Sherlock Holmes story were once challenged by a newspaper.[1] It is interesting to note that Poe, 'the father of detective fiction,' enjoyed doing precisely the same thing when he in turn became a reader. Before ending his

[1] Cf. Sir Arthur Conan Doyle, *Memories and Adventure*, London, Hodder & Stoughton, 1924, p. 108.

essay on Dickens he could not resist pointing out that: 'The interval elapsing between the murder and Rudge's return is variously stated as twenty-two and twenty-four years,' and 'It may be asked why the inmates of The Warren failed to hear the alarm-bell which was heard by Solomon Daisy.'

What Poe did in this way for Dickens, others have done for Poe. Régis Messac comments[1] that sash windows were unknown in Paris at the date of *The Murders in the Rue Morgue;* that ferry-boats do not ply across the Seine, and sassafras does not grow on the banks of that river. Fosca adds[2] that a Prefect of Police at the time of Louis Philippe could not have signed a cheque; and that if a wide strip of material, torn from the hem to the waistband of Marie Roget's skirt, was long enough to pass three times around her body and form a loop in the way described, then her total height must have been about four metres—over twelve feet! Somerset Maugham, possibly in less serious vein, maintains that the description of the method of entry, in *The Murders in the Rue Morgue,* is based upon a fallacy. It is inconceivable that any Frenchwomen of the period and class indicated would have been preparing to go to bed at three o'clock in the morning in a room with an open window![3]

*   *   *

The 1872 edition of Poe's works was quickly followed by a still more comprehensive collection, published in 1875[4] and re-issued five times before 1883. His poetry and his tales of horror were commended by contemporary literary critics, but as successive *Selections* from his works came to be published to satisfy popular demand, it was increasingly apparent that his fame with the

[1] Regis Messac, *op. cit.,* pp. 348-354.
[2] François Fosca, *Histoire et technique du roman policier,* Nouvelle revuè critique, 1937, pp. 191-192.
[3] W. Somerset Maugham, ' The Decline and Fall of the Detective Story ', *The Vagrant Mood,* Heinemann, 1952, p. 115.
[4] *The Works of Edgar Allan Poe,* Ed. John H. Ingam, Edinburgh, Black, 1875, 4 Vols.

general reader rested mainly upon his stories of Dupin. By the early years of the present century Poe had won a secure hold upon the reading public, and the warm appreciation of some of the foremost writers of the period. Under the auspices of the Authors' Club, a dinner in honour of the centenary of Poe's birth was given in London on March 1st, 1909. Sir Arthur Conan Doyle presided, and speaking of 'this great man's work' he said:

'It is not, I think, upon his strange and haunting poems that Poe's fame will rest. They are musical to a degree, original, masterful, and yet so aloof from life, so devoid of message, that one feels their limitation. But his tales were one of the great landmarks and starting points in the literature of the last century for French as well as for English writers. For those tales have been so pregnant with suggestion, so stimulating to the minds of others, that it may be said of many of them that each is a root from which a whole literature has developed. . . . His original and inventive brain was always . . . opening up pioneer tracks for other men to explore. Where was the detective story until Poe breathed the breath of life into it?'[1]

While it is certainly true that stories with detective interest existed before Poe created M. Dupin, they occurred as episodes in novels of a general type. Poe took this theme of deduction from observation, made it the central interest, and presented it with a new technique, deliberately stimulating the reader's curiosity to a high pitch of intensity and refusing to satisfy it until the end. He added the figure of a detective hero to conduct the reader through this exciting experience, a figure new to fiction. Thus a new *genre* came into being with its own distinctive shape, substance and individuality, and it is to Edgar Allan Poe that we owe the detective story as we know it today.

[1] The *Times*, March 2nd, 1909.

CHAPTER
V

FROM CONVICT - HERO TO
DETECTIVE - HERO IN ENGLAND

While Poe was creating this new type of story in America, fiction in England, as in France, was still strongly marked by that fondness for criminal heroes which had persisted for fifty years. The prevailing trend was strong enough to cause Thackeray to write *Catherine* (1838), based on the life of a notorious criminal, Catherine Hayes, though such a subject may well have been far from congenial to him, judging from his Introduction to *Pendennis* (1850), in which he explained why this time he had written a different type of story. But readers as well as writers were by then growing tired of novels about criminals, and though such works continued to appear their popularity was waning, and novels with some detective interest were beginning to take their place.

Thomas De Quincey (1785—1859) was one of the first English writers to turn from this pre-occupation with convicts, and to give instead some objective consideration to crime itself. One immediately thinks of his *Murder Considered as One of the Fine Arts*, but of the three essays which form this work, (the first written in 1827 and the second in 1839), only the final one, which appeared in 1854, contains any reference to detective investigations. Though he deals with two murder mysteries that had recently disturbed the public, he does little more than record the facts as they were known to have occurred, and was certainly far from perceiving that detection might become a subject for study, or that it, too, could be 'considered as one of the fine arts.'

De Quincey's nearest approach to a detective story is his *The Avenger*,[1] which tells of a series of mysterious murders in a little

---

[1] It is probable that *The Avenger* was noticed by Edgar Allan Poe, for it appeared in *Blackwood's* in August, 1838, at the time when Poe was studying this Edinburgh magazine with particular care, in preparation for his own humorous skit on 'How to write a Blackwood Article', which was published in the *American Museum* in December, 1838.

German town, crimes that baffle the police. De Quincey gives a wonderfully realistic account of two young girls who catch sight of the murderer hiding in a cupboard, try to act as though they have not seen him, and manage to escape with their lives. This passage is in the spirit of detective fiction, and so is the fact that the reader's curiosity is evoked and stimulated to a high pitch, to be satisfied only at the end of the story, but there is no detective in *The Avenger*, no question of clues or analytical reasoning, and the mystery is at last explained by the murderer himself.

England produced no such remarkable convict-turned-detective as the celebrated Vidocq, but one or two English convicts wrote accounts of their own criminal careers. The author of *The London Spy, or The Frauds of London* (1809) described himself as 'The Celebrated George Barrington, Superintendent of the Convicts at Botany Bay.' This was the same George Barrington mentioned by Major Arthur Griffiths in his *Chronicles of New-gate*,[1] whose real name was Waldron, by turns a strolling player, a false clergyman and a 'gentleman of fortune.' He was sentenced to transportation for life, and on the voyage to New South Wales warned the captain of an intended mutiny. As a reward he was given some slight official standing, and assumed for himself the high-sounding title of 'Chief Constable' at Parramatta, an almost meaningless term that did, however, lend a semblance of truth to his claim on the title page of his reminiscences.

A somewhat similar volume, *The London Guide and Strangers' Safe-Guard* (1818) was written by William Perry, who described himself as "A Convict and a Gentleman who has made the police of the Metropolis an object of enquiry for two and twenty years." These professional thieves, who undoubtedly had first-hand knowledge of the conditions then prevailing, made it plain that such criminals had little to fear from the forces of law and order. The only mobile London police were the Bow Street Runners, known as 'peace-officers,' who could be sent by the Justices to pursue anyone suspected of a serious crime. The novelist Henry Fielding, who was a Justice of the Peace, founded the organisa-

[1] London, Chapman & Hall, 1884.

tion in 1748, making his own private house in Bow Street the headquarters to which his men reported. This force of 'special constables' did useful work under Fielding, and represented a definite step forward in the war against criminals. They usually hunted in couples, acting on their own initiative and without direct supervision, often at a distance from London. Many of them were honest and trustworthy, and one of Fielding's best men, Saunders Welch, seems to have been a worthy fore-runner of Vidocq, particularly in his great strength and courage, and his dramatic captures of elusive gang-leaders. With the passing of time, however, the Bow Street Runners fell into disrepute. It was not in their personal interest to prevent crime, and it was by no means unheard-of for them to accept bribes from the men they were sent to arrest, or to share with them the rewards offered for the return of stolen goods. The great fortunes left by some of them could hardly have been acquired honestly, and by the beginning of the nineteenth century, conditions were such that drastic reform was a matter of extreme urgency. In 1829 Sir Robert Peel laid the foundation of a better system, and organised the Metropolitan Police upon a principle that was extended to the provinces during the following ten years. In spite of all that the public had suffered from the wholesale depredations of thieves, the initial reaction to the new police system was at best non-committal, and often frankly hostile. People feared that the remedy might be worse than the disease, and greatly distrusted any plan of control which might become arbitrary or tyrannical, as had happened at certain periods in France. But this opposition softened to toleration, and gradually changed to appreciation as the new police force conducted itself discreetly and efficiently, bringing about great improvements in the prevention and detection of crime, the suppression of vagrancy and the maintenance of good order.

The Bow Street Runners disappeared, as an organisation, with the formation of the new police force, though some of the best-known of them opened in business as private enquiry agents. Charles Dickens mentioned his personal recollections of them in a letter to his friend Walter Thornbury, a frequent contributor to Dickens's magazine *All The Year Round,* from whose office this letter was written on April 18th, 1862.

'My Dear Thornbury,

The Bow Street Runners ceased out of the land soon after the introduction of the new police. I remember them very well as standing about the door of the office in Bow Street. They had no other uniform than a blue dress-coat, brass buttons, (I am not even now sure that that was necessary), and a bright red cloth waistcoat. The waistcoat was indispensable, and the slang name for them was 'redbreasts' in consequence.

They kept company with thieves and the like, much more than the detective police do. I don't know what their pay was, but I have no doubt their principal complements were got under the rose. It was a very slack institution, and its headquarters were The Brown Bear, in Bow Street, a public house of more than doubtful reputation, opposite the police office. [. . .]

Field, who advertises the Secret Enquiry Office, was a Bow Street Runner, and can tell you all about it. Goddard, who also advertises an enquiry office, was another of the fraternity. They are the only two I know of as yet existing in a 'questionable shape.'

Faithfully yours always,

Charles Dickens.'

The detective police, to whom Dickens referred, did not come into existence until some fifteen years after the Metropolitan police force began to function, by which time it had become apparent that criminal investigation and the detection of crime should be made the special concern of a separate section of the force. In 1843—44, Sir James Graham, then Home Secretary, decided as a tentative measure to appoint a few keen, intelligent officers to undertake these duties, dressed as ordinary people. These first "plain clothes detectives" numbered only three inspectors and nine sergeants, with half-a-dozen constables as auxiliaries. From such small beginnings grew the now world-famous Criminal Investigation Department at Scotland Yard. During the hundred years and more that have passed since that time, several officers of this branch have, on retirement, written an account of their personal experiences. One of the very first to do so was William Russell, who, under the pseudonym of "Waters," produced his *Recollections of a Detective Police-Officer* (1856).[1]

He gives an informative picture of police work in England at that time, and of his own duties, first as a constable, later as a detective. Apart from one case of attempted and one of actual murder, he deals with confidence tricksters, thieves, or clever forgers, and to arrest his suspects he travels up and down the whole length of the country, sometimes by stage-coach, sometimes on the trains of the period, where the passengers almost freeze to death in open trucks.

Waters' first case is dated 1836, some years before the detective force came into being, while he was an officer in the Metropolitan police. He is placed in sole charge of a delicate and difficult enquiry, carrying out his duties so efficiently that while rescuing a young man from a gambling den he also rounds up a gang of forgers whose counterfeit banknotes have been the despair of the authorities for years. Waters is congratulated by his Superintendent, and so takes "the first step up the ladder to my present exalted position in public service."

Promoted to the status of a detective, Waters conducts various investigations on his own initiative with two assistants, one of whom possesses such useful talents as a skill in ventriloquism, and the ability to feign a drunken stupor so convincingly that criminals unsuspectingly discuss their plans in his presence. In view of the low status accorded to the police in France at this time, and in England to the Bow Street Runners of a decade or two earlier, it is interesting to note that Mr. Waters meets with friendly co-operation and esteem from the general public, from managers of important hotels and the landlords of country taverns. He is a dependable, self-respecting family man who loves his work and is proud of his position.

Recollections of a Detective Police-officer was so successful that it started a vogue for such reminiscences. Alexandre Dumas was so impressed by Waters' book that he had it translated and

[1] Published by J. & C. Brown of London.

published in Paris with his warm recommendation in the Introduction, to give French readers information about English
police organisation. Careful footnotes were added to explain
details of English judicial procedure and to point out that
English policemen enjoyed a status and a measure of popularity
quite unknown to their counterparts in Paris. Only a few years
later, France was to have her first fictional detective-hero, like
Waters a police officer, in the person of Monsieur Lecoq.

Meanwhile, some of the popular melodramas written in
England began to introduce detective interest in their plots,
possibly as an interesting change from the exploits of Dick
Turpin and Jack Sheppard, or Gothic romances such as *The
Mysteries of Udolpho,* which had almost monopolised the stage
during the first quarter of the nineteenth century. *Presumptive
Evidence: or Murder Will Out,* written by John Baldwin Buck-
stone, was produced at the Adelphi in 1828. A thieving rascal
'borrows' the uniform of a young naval rating on shore leave,
and wears it as a disguise while committing a burglary. He is
surprised by the householder, kills him, and escapes, leaving
beside the body the sailor's Trafalgar Medal. As a consequence
the sailor is arrested, tried and convicted, but is saved from
execution at the last moment when the murderer confesses. The
play is sheer melodrama, but, as the title suggests, some importance is attached to the question of proof, and the audience is
left in no doubt that evidence, especially circumstantial evidence,
needs to be scrutinised with great care.

Jerrold used Vidocq's *Mémoires* as a basis for his *Vidocq, The
French Police Spy,* played at the Surrey theatre in 1829, with the
hero appearing in a caped coat and square hat, elegant knee
boots and a lace stock, carrying a riding crop. In less spectacular
garb, the 'plain clothes detective' was a familiar figure on the
English stage, though usually in a minor role, long before he
appeared in English fiction. Detective reasoning played a part
in that immensely popular melodrama *Maria Marten: or The
Red Barn,* based upon an actual crime, and showing the dramatic
way in which William Corder was proved guilty of murdering
his sweetheart at Polstead, in 1828. The girl was believed to have

gone to new employment, and no anxiety was felt for her until her stepmother, troubled by a recurring dream, caused a search to be made in the Red Barn, where her body was discovered. At the inquest, medical evidence established that her wounds corresponded exactly with certain weapons found in Corder's possession. The case attracted tremendous interest at the time, and the story quickly became a stock melodrama in the repertoire of barnstormers all over the country, with Corder, dressed in black and twirling his long, black moustache, as the public's favourite villain. Every company produced its own version, for the play was not written, but the invariable high-lights were the step-mother's dreams and the dramatic climax that developed as Maria's wounds were compared with the weapons that made them.

Dramatic detective sequences also played a part in *The Factory Assassin: or The Dumb Boy of Manchester*, written by Barnabas Rayner (or possibly adapted by him from a French source), and produced at Astley's Theatre in 1837. The dumb boy is defended by a barrister, Mr. Palmerston, who notices that the murder in Manchester has points of resemblance with another mysterious crime just committed in Dieppe. The French police had found in the victim's hand a locket, snatched from the murderer's neck as he bent to strike. Mr. Palmerston travels to Dieppe and somehow gains possession of the locket, which he produces at the trial of his hapless client, and proves that the portrait it contains will identify the murderer. This learned counsel certainly acted as a private detective with much success, though the plot is more concerned with the apparently hopeless plight of the dumb boy, and the dramatic court scene which clears him, than with the logic of the steps that achieve this result.

The first popular melodrama to give a really important rôle to a detective was Tom Taylor's *The Ticket of Leave Man*, produced at the Olympic in May, 1863. Bob Brierly, a respectable, ingenuous young workman, is tricked by a gang of forgers, convicted on circumstantial evidence, and after serving a prison sentence finds it almost impossible to obtain steady, honest employment. Meanwhile Hawkshaw, 'the smartest detective in the

Force,' on the track of the forgers, appears on the stage in various disguises until finally, helped unwittingly by Bob Brierly, he obtains all the evidence needed, whereupon he tears off his disguise and triumphantly declaims: "I am Hawkshaw, the Detective," a dramatic moment that forms the climax of the plot.

The play gave almost equal importance to these two counterbalancing personalities, the 'criminal' and the detective. In the original production the leading rôle was undoubtedly that of Bob Brierly, the ticket-of-leave man. The difficulties that beset him in his almost hopeless struggle to re-establish himself were, in fact, a shrewd and well-timed piece of social criticism, for in the same year that this drama was first played, the whole ticket-of-leave system was debated in Parliament and certain anomalies removed. Bob Brierly was thus a significant figure at that time, arousing sympathy for the misfortunes of others as well as for his own. He was, however, the last notable convict-hero of popular melodrama, for the taste of the public was changing. Improvements in the law and in prison conditions had some bearing on this change, for when a convict's punishment is not harsh or inhumane he no longer disturbs the public conscience. A further reason was the increasing interest in the detective police and their methods of setting about their work. In later revivals of *The Ticket of Leave Man*, (and there were several in the nineteenth century, some even in the twentieth), the ex-convict lost his original position as the chief figure, and the rôle for the 'leading man' was Hawkshaw the Detective.

This eclipse of the convict-hero by the detective-hero, this new trend that captured the imagination of the general reader and gave his interest a new direction, received a good deal of its initial impetus from certain novels of Charles Dickens and Wilkie Collins. Thousands of English readers first became interested in detectives, amateur or professional, through seeing them at work in *Bleak House*, *The Woman in White*, *The Moonstone*, or *The Mystery of Edwin Drood*, and these two novelists, the most widely-read fiction writers of their day, both in their different ways exerted a remarkable influence upon the development of the detective novel in English.

91

CHAPTER
VI

DETECTIVE THEMES IN THE WORKS
OF CHARLES DICKENS AND WILKIE COLLINS

Towards the middle of the nineteenth century in England, the popularity of the three or even four volume novel, beautifully produced to appeal to the leisured or the well-to-do and costing several guineas, was increasingly challenged by popular, inexpensive magazines designed to entertain the growing multitude of middle-class readers. Many successful periodicals were published at regular weekly, monthly, or even quarterly intervals, and Charles Dickens himself owned at different times three widely-read magazines, *Master Humphrey's Clock, Household Words,* and *All The Year Round.* The serial stories which were a recognised feature of such publications were usually reprinted as complete novels immediately after the final instalment had appeared, and quickly sold in thousands at a shilling or two per volume, thus reaching a very wide circle of readers.

These magazines were published less frequently than the *journaux* which in France produced the *romans-feuilletons,* and each instalment of the serial was considerably longer. There was consequently less need for a rapid succession of melodramatic crises with which to break off the instalments, and more opportunity to develop the story naturally and create fiction worthy of being preserved in volume form. The success or otherwise of a serial, and indirectly of the magazine in which it appeared, depended largely upon how strongly the subject and method of treatment appealed to the reading public. Charles Dickens and Wilkie Collins were both extremely sensitive to the changing trends in popular taste, and it is remarkable how often their novels deal with criminals who are eventually punished, or mysterious crimes that are at last explained.

In *Oliver Twist,* which appeared as a serial in *Bentley's Miscellany* during 1837, Dickens introduced a whole community of thieves, among them a brutal murderer, and retribution over-takes them all in the end, though Dickens, who was not as yet particularly interested in the work of the recently established metropolitan police, gave no special place to the ways and means that brought about this result. Yet even in this early novel Dickens introduced a definite, if brief, detective interest with Mr. Brownlow's investigation to discover Oliver's history. Keeping his own counsel until his enquiries are complete, Mr. Brownlow finally confronts the malignant Monks, producing his clues, leading in his witnesses, marshalling his proofs, explaining every mysterious circumstance, acting as a competent detective four years or so before Poe's Dupin made his first appearance.

Still earlier, in his first literary work, *Sketches by Boz* (1833—1834), Dickens displayed an interest in inductive reasoning, and in 'Meditations in Monmouth Street' he 'amused himself' by examining second-hand clothing and deducing from its cut and quality, its stains and marks of wear, the former owner's physical appearance, occupation, habits and personality, though he arrived at his conclusions in fanciful vein, rather than strictly rationally.

By the time Dickens founded, in 1850, a twopenny weekly magazine called *Household Words*, he had become very interested in the work of the detective police force, particularly in the way they applied methods of observation and deduction to the detection of crime.[1] He was on friendly terms with several officers at Scotland Yard, and between 1850 and 1856 he wrote for *Household Words* a whole series of articles about the Metropolitan Police. 'On Duty with Inspector Field' describes a night patrol in the slums of London; 'The Detective Police' reports how certain officers succeeded in capturing a gang of warehouse thieves, a clever forger, and a notorious horse-stealer known as "Tally-ho Thompson." 'Three Detective Anecdotes' is an account of 'Sergeant Witchem's'[2] success in identifying and arresting a

---

[1] Cf. *The Letters of Charles Dickens*, London, Macmillan, 1893, in particular p. 244, giving Dickens's letter to W. H. Wills, April 3rd, 1851.

[2] ' Sergeant Witchem ' was a thinly veiled alias for that well-known Scotland Yard Detective, Inspector Whicher, who was the model used by Wilkie Collins for his Sergeant Cuff, in *The Moonstone*.

murderer, a rogue who robbed hospitals, and another thief whom he cleverly tricked into handing over to him a very valuable stolen diamond. Such articles continued to be popular for a remarkably long time, and in 1867 Dickens warmly approved his friend Mr. Thornbury's suggestion of writing for *All The Year Round* a comparison between the practices of the old Bow Street Runners and the work of modern detectives. At the same time, Dickens, well aware that the public had grown much more interested in the police than in the tales of convict-heroes, turned down Thornbury's further suggestion of articles about Vaux and Barrington, two rogues who had been celebrated a few decades earlier.[1]

The first novel in which Dickens made a major part of the plot depend on a mysterious crime was *Barnaby Rudge*, which appeared as a serial in *Master Humphrey's Clock* in 1841. This at once attracted the special interest of Edgar Allan Poe, who, as we have already noticed, studied the opening instalment or two with such perspicacity that, in an article published in the *Philadelphia Saturday Evening Post* on May 1st, 1841, he forecast so accurately the lines that the plot would follow, even foreseeing certain unexpected difficulties the author would later encounter, that Dickens is said to have exclaimed in amazement: "The man must be the devil himself!" In his second article on the subject, ('Charles Dickens', *Graham's Magazine*, February, 1842), Poe criticised the ending of *Barnaby Rudge* as 'a change of plan,' going on to give his own opinion of how the crime mystery (ignoring almost everything else in the plot) should have been developed. Poe considered that the chief interest lay in the discovery of the truth about Haredale's murder, and the author should have progressed without deviation towards this *dénouement*, the pre-determined climax of the novel. This was Poe's method of plot construction, as it had been William Godwin's in *Caleb Williams*, a thought that Dickens clearly had in mind when he wrote to Poe, following the American's

---

[1] Cf. Dickens's letters to Mr. Thornbury, *Op. cit.*, pp. 635 and 622. James Hardy Vaux, in his *Memoirs* (1819) described many sneak-thief tricks that were employed by the Artful Dodger and Noah Claypole in *Oliver Twist*.

'examination of the mechanism of *Barnaby Rudge*.'[1] But this was not the method generally followed by Charles Dickens, whose plots were prone to digress from his main theme, or even to present several human dramas, only lightly linked, in the same novel. Though the plot of *Barnaby Rudge* turned upon a mysterious murder, Dickens did not make of it a detective problem, as Poe would have done.

In *Bleak House*, however, which appeared as a serial in *Household Words* between 1852 and 1853, Dickens did construct an important part of the plot in the form of a detective story, beginning with an intriguing problem and leading on to a murder mystery. After an innocent suspect has been arrested on circumstantial evidence, the murderer is at last identified and captured by 'Inspector Bucket of the Detective,' in whom Dickens created the first police detective-hero in English fiction. He is a notable figure who creates an impression of purposeful efficiency, an atmosphere of mystery and authority, in sharp contrast with his commonplace appearance. The reader first meets him as a shadowy figure standing in the background as a witness is interviewed in a lawyer's office.

'He stands there with his attentive face, a composed and quiet listener. He is a stoutly built, steady-looking sharp-eyed man in black, of about the middle age. Except that he looks at Mr. Snagsby as if he were going to take his portrait, there is nothing remarkable about him at first sight but his ghostly manner of appearing.'

The reader catches a glimpse of him from time to time as he busily follows his lines of enquiry, but learns nothing more until his investigations are complete. When that time comes, Inspector Bucket calmly takes command of the situation, even in the presence of Sir Leicester Dedlock. He is superbly confident that the baronet (like the reader) is all agog to hear every step that led to his success, every item of incriminating evidence. It is interesting to note that a good deal of this evidence reaches

---

[1] Poe quoted Dickens's letter in the opening paragraphs of his essay on 'The Philosophy of Composition', reprinted in *The Works of Edgar Allan Poe*, London, Chatto & Windus, 1872, p. 660.

Inspector Bucket through the close co-operation of his wife, who, in the most natural manner in the world, helps her husband whenever she can, even receiving as a lodger his suspect, Mlle Hortense. When the French maid writes anonymous letters, Mrs. Bucket not only sees them written and posted, but 'secures the fellow half-sheets and the corresponding ink.' The Inspector finds 'the wadding of the pistol with which the late Mr. Tulkinghorn was shot,' and his wife discovers in her lodger's room the remainder of the sheet of paper from which that wadding was torn. Mrs. Bucket shadows Mlle Hortense and sees her throw the murder-weapon in a lake. The Inspector and his men recover it. Such an efficient partnership in detection by a husband and wife was a complete innovation in detective fiction at that time, and, indeed, has seldom been used since.

Another new feature is that in *Bleak House* Charles Dickens, for the first time in English fiction, devoted an explanatory chapter to the culmination of the detective theme, with Inspector Bucket triumphantly holding the centre of the stage. The actual murderer is among his listeners as he recounts the details of his investigation, his reasons for each decision, and the conclusions that lead him to arrest Mlle Hortense, who, until then, is quite unsuspected by those around her. In thus creating a 'clearing-up chapter' in which to present a *résumé* of the detective's successful work, Dickens produced a pattern that became more or less conventional in detective novels.

As though reluctant to leave the theme of detection, and perhaps feeling that his readers, (who had not been kept informed during Bucket's investigations into the murder of Mr. Tulkinghorn), might like to observe the Inspector in action, Dickens showed him conducting a further enquiry, this time into the disappearance of Lady Dedlock, and portrayed with lively appreciation his powers of logical deduction, his patience and endurance, his skill in directing the men under his command. Inspector Bucket is not only a successful detective, but also a man of tact and humanity, respected by all who meet him. Occasionally he assumes a disguise, with complete success,

Agatha Christie

Michael Innes

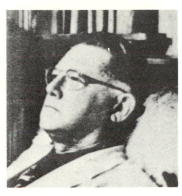

Erle Stanley Gardner

Georges Simenon

John Dickson Carr

Margaret Millar

but normally his own dignified personality is sufficient for his purpose, and with calm assurance he takes control whenever he appears. "I am Inspector Bucket of the Detective, I am,"[1] he says, and is as proud of his profession, as well as of his own status in it, as 'Waters,' whose *Recollections of a Detective Police-officer* appeared three years later. *Bleak House*, Dickens's first experiment with a plot of this type, was at once tremendously popular. As he himself remarked in a letter to a friend: —

'It has retained its immense circulation from the first, beating dear old Copperfield by a round ten thousand or more. I have never had so many readers.'[2]

Dickens's next story of detection, *Hunted Down*, was written for an American magazine, the *New York Ledger*, where it appeared as a serial during 1859. This time, Dickens took a further step, and made the detective theme dominant. For this reason the tale should not be overlooked, though it is, in itself, slight and unsatisfying. In brief, it tells how Mr. Sampson, Manager of a Life Assurance Office, came to suspect that a client, Mr. Slinkton, has killed one of his two nieces and is slowly poisoning the other. The girl is taken to safety, and her uncle's guilt is proved, by the efforts of Mr. Sampson and a young colleague, Mr. Meltham, who was the sweetheart of the first niece, and since her death has devoted all his time and energy to shadowing her murderer. Both Sampson and Meltham act as private detectives, separately and jointly, but the reader does not know this until the end, nor are their methods entirely convincing. Dickens was not so much at home with such characters as with the regular police, nor had he mastered the special technique of the 'pure' detective story.

Some months after its appearance in the U.S.A., the story was serialised in *All The Year Round*, and Dickens's English readers must have recognised it as a fictional adaptation, (as far as the

---

[1] In this phrase, which occurs several times without variation, Inspector Bucket uses the word ' detective ' as an abbreviation for ' the detective police force ', i.e. the organisation. He never employs it to describe himself or any other individual.
[2] *The Letters of Charles Dickens*, p. 293.

crimes were concerned), of incidents in the career of a well-known London journalist, Thomas Griffiths Wainewright, who, finding himself in financial difficulties in 1830, insured the life of his sister-in-law for £18,000. The lady died in the same year of strychnine poisoning, and enquiries set in motion by the Insurance companies discovered that Wainewright, before killing his sister-in-law, had used the same poison to murder his uncle, his mother-in-law and a close family friend. The case attracted considerable attention, and Wainewright's guilt was established at his trial. While he was in Newgate he was seen and talked to by Dickens, who was visiting the prison with his friend, Macready, the actor. Wainewright escaped execution and was transported to Australia where he died in 1852, some seven years before Dickens wrote this story.

That Dickens was becoming increasingly interested in murder mysteries is very plain from his letters. In 1867 he was heatedly discussing with W. H. Wills the case of Eliza Fenning, (convicted of murder by poison and executed in 1815), challenging the evidence, objecting to 'the unfairness of the judge,' affirming his belief in her innocence and suggesting alternative explanations for the facts established by the prosecution. While in America in January, 1868, he made a point of visiting the laboratory at Harvard, where, in 1850, Professor Webster killed his colleague, Doctor Parkman, and disposed of his body in the furnace. After examining 'all the gruesome paraphernalia' Dickens wrote home, full of excited interest, to tell Wilkie Collins the 'terrific story.'

The novel Dickens was writing when he died was a tale of mysterious murder, constructed as a detective story. *The Mystery of Edwin Drood* was to consist of twelve monthly instalments, and the first number appeared in *All The Year Round* at the beginning of April, 1870. Two more instalments were published before the author's sudden death on June 9th of that year, and a further three that were already written brought the story exactly half-way to its conclusion. Nothing, it seems, can be more tantalizing than an unfinished detective story! Novels of a different type, when left incomplete by their authors, are seldom provided with a conclusion by another hand. But the unfinished *Mystery of Edwin Drood* offered an almost irresistible challenge to the reader's ingenuity, and a remarkable number of attempts have been made to deduce from the first half of the book the plan Dickens had in mind for the second. At least four 'adaptations' appeared before the end of 1870, while a dramatic version, devised by a Mr. Walter Stephens 'by permission of the executors and publishers of Mr. Dickens' was played at the Surrey theatre on November 4th, 1871, as a 'Preface' to *The Ticket of Leave Man*. Wilkie Collins, who had sometimes collaborated with Dickens in the course of their long friendship, was asked to catch up the broken threads, but refused. A score of attempts were made in the nineteenth century to provide the novel with a logical ending, and still more have appeared during the twentieth. Almost all of them are serious analytical studies in detection, basing their conclusions on a minute scrutiny of every possible clue to be found in the completed number or in the proposed illustrations for the whole novel, which Dickens discussed in advance with the artist, Luke Fildes.

Was Edwin Drood really murdered? If so, how and by whom, and where was his body hidden? Did Dickens intend to develop the plot on somewhat the same lines as in *Hunted Down*, making the killer Drood's uncle, the opium-smoking cathedral chorister, John Jasper? Could his guilt be proved? Above all, who was Dick Datchery, that enigmatic, obviously disguised figure who quietly settled in Cloisterham after Edwin Drood's disappearance and devoted himself to making such persistent enquiries into Jasper's every action? Datchery has been identified, in turn, with almost every male character in the novel for whom the rôle would not be manifestly impossible, while several authorities have put forward good reasons for believing that Datchery, with his large white wig and his always hidden hands, was a woman, Helena Landless. The unfinished *Mystery of Edwin Drood* may well have stimulated a more lively, long-lasting interest in the application of inductive reasoning to a detective problem than did any of Dickens's completed novels, not excepting *Bleak House*!

Charles Dickens made very definite contributions to the development of English detective fiction, particularly to those special characteristics which distinguish it from French and American fiction of this kind. In spite of his close association with France, Dickens's stories of detection owe little or nothing to French influences. The police officers who appear in so many of his novels—*Great Expectations, Our Mutual Friend* and *Bleak House* in particular—are all typical of the contemporary London policeman and have no affinity whatever with the political police of Balzac's novels or with those ex-convicts turned *agents de police,* so familiar in French popular fiction. Dickens was the first novelist to portray the English police, their special place in the community they served, their organisations and the methods employed by the new 'detective force,' symbolised by Inspector Bucket.

America seems to have had no more effect than France upon this aspect of Dickens's work. Dickens corresponded with Poe, actually met him in America, agreed to introduce some of Poe's stories to London publishers, and had almost certainly read his few short tales of detection, yet he was in no way influenced by Poe's example. There is, indeed, a striking contrast between Dickens's management of detective themes and the detective story as created by Poe. With the possible exception of *The Mystery of Edwin Drood,* Dickens never wrote a tale solely, or even chiefly, for the purpose of propounding and in due course solving a baffling problem of detection, nor did he ever make a detective, not even Inspector Bucket, so important as to monopolize the reader's attention to the virtual exclusion of other characters, as Poe did in his stories of Dupin.

With Dickens, all characters have their individual completeness, an identity of their own. His criminals and their victims are not, as in Poe, mere depersonalised ciphers existing only to create a puzzle for the detective to solve. John Jasper, and to an even greater extent Bradley Headstone, is presented as a convincing psychological study, a human being with normal as well as evil impulses, known to the reader in his ordinary environment before the crime was committed or even contemplated.

His motives, the steps of his moral downfall, are as important in Dickens's novels as his criminal act and its consequences. With Mlle Hortense, Dickens adopts a rather different technique, and the reader knows her simply as a jealous, vindictive servant whose acquaintance with Mr. Tulkinghorn is of the slightest. When he is shot, several other persons, Lady Dedlock, for instance, are far more likely suspects. But after the arrest is made we learn why, as well as how, the murder was committed, and the psychological causes that led Mlle Hortense to plan the deed are given their true importance.

Edwin Drood and Mr. Tulkinghorn are not merely 'victims,' as are Mme L'Espanaye and her daughter, or Marie Roget, of whom the reader hears only after they are dead. Drood's personality, his way of life, his family background are familiar to the reader before he disappears. Mr. Tulkinghorn is especially interesting in this connection because we know enough about him to be aware that several people had a possible motive for killing him and the opportunity to do so. He is a special kind of victim, one whose murder does not in the least surprise the reader, for he is a man of such rigid professional rectitude, such inflexibility of purpose, and has such disregard for the tragedies his proposed actions could cause, that only an act of violence could prevent him from carrying out his expressed intentions.

Dickens showed particular skill in depicting the character of Mr. Tulkinghorn and the emotions he inspires in all who have dealings with him. He has no vices, except, perhaps, his implacable persistence, and even that could be attributed to zeal for his employer's interests, yet he arouses active dislike because of his total lack of human kindness. In making the victim a man of this calibre, without one saving grace, Dickens fore-shadows in *Bleak House* those numerous twentieth-century detective novels in which the problem is not: "Why was this person killed?" or even: "How was the crime committed?" but "Which one, of all the people who had good reason to hate him, did, in fact, murder him?"

One further relevant feature of Dickens's writing is his power of evoking a dreadful apprehension, a certainty that something terrible is about to happen. In *Barnaby Rudge*, for instance, when the little bell-ringer reaches the inn door after his uncanny experience at the church, he is so convincingly drawn, so helpless and speechless with terror, that the reader, like his friends in the bar-parlour, is 'palsied with fright' even before knowing what has alarmed him. *Edwin Drood* is full of passages that conjure up fearful possibilities, mysteries that stimulate the reader's curiosity to an almost unbearable tension. This particular quality, this atmosphere which is certainly present in many detective stories, may have been uppermost in Osbert Sitwell's mind when he called Dickens "the father of the modern thriller."[1] The term 'thriller' is not, however, quite synonymous with 'detective novel,' and as far as the latter type of fiction is concerned it would be more accurate to describe Charles Dickens as the originator of a new kind of novel, whose primary purpose was the normal one of depicting human relationships, but which, in addition, made an important part of the plot depend on the work of police detectives, sympathetically presented. Except for this important point of sympathetic presentation, such a description would apply to many of the novels of Balzac, who showed as much interest as Dickens in the processes of detection, but Dickens, in contrast to Balzac, expressed a friendly admiration for the police themselves, and thus took the development of detective fiction an important step forward.

The only contemporary English writer whose influence on the detective novel equalled or even surpassed that of Charles Dickens was Wilkie Collins (1824—1889), his close friend for some fifteen years. Both men were, in the phrase of the period, "sensation novelists," satirizing social evils, attacking legal anomalies and championing the cause of those who seemed to them the victims of injustice. Both were interested in tales of mysterious crimes and in the work of the police, but there is a remarkable contrast between their respective methods of handling detective themes. Dickens developed a technique of his

---

[1] Cf. *The Dickensian*, 1931, p. 252, quoting from ' a recent lecture by Osbert Sitwell on " Modern Fiction ".'

own unaffected by foreign influences. Wilkie Collins, however, in his novels of crime detection—the only ones by which he is remembered today—owed a great deal to Poe and even more to certain French sources.

These two writers were spending the spring of 1856 in France together, when, as Collins related to a personal friend, an incident occurred to stimulate his interest: —

> 'I was in Paris, wandering about the streets with Charles Dickens, amusing ourselves by looking into the shops. We came to an old book-stall, half shop and half store, and I found some dilapidated volumes and records of French crime —a sort of French Newgate Calendar. I said to Dickens, "Here is a prize!" So it turned out to be. In them I found some of my best plots.'[1]

These volumes were Maurice Méjan's *Recueil des Causes Célèbres* (1807—1814), and they remained in Collins's library until his death.[2]

They served him first as the source for a series of articles in *Household Words* in 1858 on notable French criminal trials in the eighteenth century, to which he gave the significant title 'Cases Worth Looking At.' Most of them are simple tales of strange or terrible crimes, but the second in the series, *The Poisoned Meal*, is essentially a detective story. After setting out the evidence, Collins proceeds to examine it in close detail, devoting some thirty pages to analytical deductions from the established facts, and giving logical reasons for his conclusions concerning the innocence of the accused and the identity of the real criminal.

Collins had already contributed to *Household Words* between 1852 and 1856 a number of short stories which owed a good deal to French sources, particularly to Vidocq and to Balzac, and also to Poe. Five of them were later issued in volume form (linked by a thread of narrative and increased by a sixth not previously published) with the title *After Dark*. The first story, *A Terribly*

---

[1] Wybert Reeve, ' Recollections of Wilkie Collins ', *Chambers Journal*, Vol. IX, p. 458.
[2] Cf. Kenneth Robinson, *Wilkie Collins: A Biography*, Bodley Head, 1951, p. 98.

THE DEVELOPMENT OF THE DETECTIVE NOVEL

Strange Bed, tells of a murderous attack upon a young English-man at a disreputable gambling house in Paris. Vidocq once had a somewhat similar experience in a country inn, *l'auberge du Veau,* and the police who come to the aid of Collins's Englishman set to work with all the energy and efficiency that Vidocq so often described in his *Mémoires.* The attempted murder is related with mounting terror and suspense by the intended victim (an interesting technique which Collins em-ployed again in some of his later works) and the passage in which the young man comes to realise with horror that the top of the great bed is slowly descending upon him, is a close parallel of a similar dramatic situation in Poe's *The Pit and the Pendulum.*

The second of Collins's tales, *The Stolen Letter,* presents a detective problem of a completely different type, related as an amusing battle of wits. A rich young man, whose happiness is threatened by a blackmailer on the eve of his wedding, seeks the help of his lawyer, the narrator of the tale, who undertakes to recover the compromising letter. The blackmailer is a thoroughly convincing scoundrel, cunning enough to circumvent the traps devised by the lawyer, who has to exert all his detective skill, and in addition to discover the meaning of a cryptic memorandum, before he gains possession of the letter. Several details of this tale, including its title, are clearly reminiscent of Poe's *The Purloined Letter,* for both stories tell of a blackmailer who threatens a lady's good name, a stolen document which must be recovered, and the success of an amateur detective who receives a substantial reward in cash. In each case the detective substitutes for the letter a note devised to postpone the black-mailer's discovery of his loss, and phrased to cause him acute annoyance. In Collins's story, however, the letter is cunningly concealed, not left in full view, and additional urgency is given to the search by a narrow time-limit within which the document must be found.

The third tale in this series, *Sister Rose,* is a story of the French Revolution, the fourth, *Gabriel's Marriage,* a romance of a Breton fishing community, and the fifth, *The Yellow Mask,* is a tale of imaginative horror very much in the manner of Poe. In the sixth, *The Lady of Glenwith Grange,* Collins once more introduced a detective interest as an important part of the plot. It tells, with delicate sympathy and restraint, the tragic story of a woman whose young sister is married to 'a rich nobleman of France, Baron Franval,' later discovered to be an impostor and an ex-convict. A courteous, very efficient *agent de police* arrives at the Grange during the baron's absence and tells the elder sister of his suspicions, the steps already taken by the French authorities, and his own plan for settling the matter beyond all doubt. The passage in which the self-styled 'baron' is proved to be the ex-convict, Monbrun, bears a detailed resemblance to the scene in Balzac's *Le Père Goriot,* when Vautrin is identified with Jacques Collin, the escaped convict. Both men are examined while unconscious, and are found to bear on their shoulder the prison brand T.F. (for Travaux Forcés); they have committed similar crimes and received the same sentences; both have been leaders of convict organisations, both escaped from prison and successfully eluded all the efforts of the police to recapture them; both are confident of being able to escape again whenever they choose.

To finish our consideration of Collins's short stories before passing to his long novels, we must glance at two tales with some detective interest that were included in a collection called *Little Novels* (all reprinted from various periodicals) published in 1887, only two years before Collins's death. *Mr. Lepel and the Housekeeper* contains an account of how a wealthy bachelor, Mr. Lepel, falls into a decline which baffles his doctors. He rejects as a ridiculous prejudice his friend's suspicion that his housekeeper is slowly poisoning him, though the reader is given good reasons for thinking this may well be true. Once more, the story is related by the intended victim, though Mr. Lepel, unlike the hero of *A Terribly Strange Bed,* is quite unaware of his own danger. Collins cleverly conveys by subtle hints that the over-attentive Mrs. Mozeen, so trusted by her employer, is secretive and treacherous. She knows of his will in her favour; she has access to poison and administers with great care the medicine that, instead of alleviating, aggravates his symptoms. It is an innovation in technique that Collins clearly expects the reader to deduce the implications of the clues placed without comment before him. A fortunate accident saves Mr. Lepel's life at the last moment and his quiet housekeeper hastily leaves his service,[1] still retaining her employer's confidence, though the comments of his doctor leave the reader in no doubt of her guilty intentions.

The second of the *Little Novels, Mr. Policeman and the Cook,* is a murder mystery with some detective interest, again marred by an unsatisfactory ending. A former police constable confesses, on his death-bed, that although he knew a certain woman was a murderess, he avoided carrying out his duty and allowed her to go free. As a young, ambitious officer he had devoted his leisure to trying to solve a case that had baffled his superiors. From a little detective work, aided by a great deal of coincidence, he discovered that the crime was committed by the young girl who brought news of it to the station-house. She was a cook with whom he had been 'keeping company,' and on learning of her guilt he cast her off, suppressed the evidence and resigned from the force, keeping silent on the matter until he lay dying.

Dickens never presented a Police Officer in an unsympathetic light, and his warm regard for the Force is evident throughout his work. But Collins, notwithstanding his notable Sergeant Cuff, shows no such general admiration for the police, and in this story, at least, he conveys a contrary impression, for the constable, loyal neither to his profession nor to the girl he has promised to marry, with his smugness and conceit, his underhand methods, his grumbles about 'the responsible and ill-paid duties of his vocation,' completely fails to win the reader's respect, far less his admiration.

Collins's interest in the processes of detection is manifest in

[1] The inconclusive ending to this part of the story is at variance with the normally accepted pattern of detective fiction, for a secret poisoner, even when unsuccessful, is the one type of criminal who is never allowed to go unpunished. More often than not he dies from a dose of his own poison, and Dickens's Mr. Slinkton, in *Hunted Down,* follows a course far more in keeping with the conventional ending of such a story than does Collins's Mrs. Mozeen, who simply packs her bags and departs.

these short works, but the form in which they were cast gave inadequate scope for his most outstanding quality as a writer, his skill in creating long, extremely involved plots. This power is displayed in all Collins's novels, but nowhere to greater advantage than in his best-known works, *The Woman in White* (1860), and *The Moonstone* (1868), both of them detective problems.

An important part of the plot of *The Woman in White* was derived from the old volumes of French crimes that had already served Collins well. One of the cases Méjan related was that of a certain Marquise de Douhalt, who, in December, 1787, set out for Paris to take legal action against her brother who had wrongfully seized her inheritance, leaving her and her aged mother in great poverty. She broke her journey to rest for a few days with relatives who, unknown to her, were in league with her brother. They drugged the unfortunate lady and had her shut up in the Salpétrière as a lunatic under another name, cut off from all contact with the outside world. She was presumed dead, and all rights to her property had already passed to her brother before Mme de Douhalt managed to communicate with an old friend who finally obtained her release. She could produce nothing to support her claim to her own identity except the white dress she was wearing when admitted to the asylum, which was returned to her when she left. The French courts considered this insufficient proof, and the poor lady died in 1817 without ever regaining her identity in the eyes of the law.

In his novel Collins complicated the story still further. A woman of similar appearance had been substituted for the heiress, Laura Fairlie, and had died and been buried in her name. When Laura escapes, she thus finds almost insurmountable obstacles in the way of establishing her legal identity. That she does at last succeed in doing so is due to the very involved detective work carried out by Walter Hartwright, the young drawing master, and by Marian Halcombe, the real heroine of the book, a woman of great sincerity, intelligence and charm.

Though the most notable feature of *The Woman in White* is the ingenious dove-tailing of its plot, the main characters, few in number and sharply differentiated from each other, are completely convincing, and two of them memorable. Marian Halcombe, with her plain face, her kindness and integrity, her brilliant mind, is the most resourceful opponent of that quite unforgettable villain, Count Fosco, suave, plausible, devoted to his canaries and the tame white mice that run freely over his ample person while he sits peacefully planning his diabolical schemes. Collins adopted an unusual technique when making the reader acquainted with Fosco, (a technique, incidentally, which Poe used when introducing Dupin). He does not describe him at all, but makes us gain our impressions of him from the opinions recorded by other characters, impressions which are at first conflicting, but rapidly become increasingly ominous. Fosco looms terrifyingly larger as the climax approaches, but his victim is rescued at the last moment and he meets a terrible death at the hands of an Italian secret society.[1]

The Woman in White began as a serial in *All The Year Round* on November 26th, 1859, and created a sensation from its opening chapter, exceeding even the popularity of *Bleak House* some six years earlier. Immediately after its conclusion in serial form it was re-issued as a volume with phenomenal success, not only in England, where the entire first impression was sold on the day of publication, but also in America, where one New York publisher alone sold 126,000 copies.

In *The Moonstone* (1868) Collins returned to a detective theme with even more sensational success, and crowds of enthusiastic readers waited in the streets to buy the next instalment the moment a new number of *All The Year Round* came from the press. The mystery formed the chief topic of conversation at many a fashionable dinner table; large bets were laid as to where the moonstone would be found; while the very street porters and errand boys stopped to devour the latest issue in odd

---

[1] The conception of a secret society, powerful enough to exert itself in mysterious ways and for sinister purposes, had already appeared in French fiction in Balzac's *Histoire des Treize*, but was still new and sensational in England at the time when Collins was writing *The Woman in White*. It is possible that he borrowed this idea from Balzac, whom he greatly admired, and of whose life and work he wrote a special study. (Cf. Collins, *My Miscellanies*, London, Sampson, Low, 1863, 2 vols: Vol. i, pp. 205-249.)

moments snatched from their work.[1] Although the tantalising secret thus became known to readers everywhere as soon as the concluding instalment appeared, the public rushed to buy the novel in volume form as soon as it was re-issued, not only in London but also in America, where four separate editions were published simultaneously.

The Moonstone contains some of Collins's most powerful descriptive writing and his finest characterisation, but is even more remarkable for its extremely intricate plot, which gives ample scope for the working out of several lines of enquiry, curiosity and suspense mounting as the circle of suspects narrows. As in *The Woman in White*, the tale is unfolded in a series of reports, with various characters relating what they have each seen, heard or discovered, and though these amateurs all contribute something to the progress of the enquiry, in *The Moonstone* Collins also introduces a police detective, Sergeant Cuff.

Collins based this officer upon that same Inspector Whicher, of Scotland Yard, for whom Dickens had used the alias of "Sergeant Witchem" when describing some of his cases in *Household Words* twelve years earlier. Since that time, this distinguished detective had been the victim of an unfortunate experience. He was in charge of investigations into the tragic murder case at Road in 1860, but his conclusions were rejected by the court that acquitted Constance Kent, and his career was seriously jeopardised in consequence. In 1865, Constance Kent's confession showed that Inspector Whicher's deductions at the time of the crime had been perfectly sound. This case was still fresh in public memory when *The Moonstone* began to appear in January, 1868, and readers would at once recognise certain items of evidence that Collins borrowed from it, details concerning a washing-list and a missing night-gown, for example. Even more clearly remembered were the individual police concerned in the Road Case, the local man, Inspector Foley, reproduced by Collins as the dull-witted Superintendent Seegrave, and the clever Scotland Yard officer, whose fictional counterpart in *The Moonstone*

1 Cf. William Tinsley, *Random Recollections of an Old Publisher*, Simpkin, Marshall 1900, Vol. I, pp. 114-115.

was assured of the interest and sympathy of contemporary readers.

The moment Sergeant Cuff arrives at Rachel Verinder's home, he assumes control with perfect composure, interviewing each guest and servant in turn, examining the house with minute care. It is worth noting his appearance, as described by the steward, Gabriel Betteredge: —

> '——a grizzled, elderly man, so miserably lean that he looked as if he had not got an ounce of flesh on his bones in any part of him. He was dressed all in decent black, with a white cravat around his neck. His face was as sharp as a hatchet, and the skin of it was as yellow and dry and withered as an autumn leaf. His eyes, of a steely light grey, had a very disconcerting trick when they encountered your eyes as if they expected something more from you than you were aware of yourself. His walk was soft, his voice melancholy, his long lanky fingers were hooked like claws. He might have been a parson, or an undertaker, or anything else you like, except what he really was.'

This might well serve as a composite picture of many later nineteenth century detectives of fiction. In it we catch glimpses that instantly link Sergeant Cuff with his near-contemporaries, Detective-Inspector Bucket and Gaboriau's Père Tabaret, as well as with such later figures as Ebenezer Gryce; Baroness Orczy's "Old Man in the Corner," whose long thin fingers played incessantly with a piece of string; even with Sherlock Holmes himself, hatchet-faced and lean, while Betteredge's concluding sentence has served to describe innumerable detective heroes. To complete the picture of Sergeant Cuff, Collins adds one or two individual touches—a dry humour, a passion for growing roses, and the human failing of being sometimes wrong in his conclusions. He is methodical, rather than brilliant, and though he makes a good start by proving that the diamond was taken between midnight and three o'clock in the morning by someone whose clothing must bear traces of paint, thereafter he makes only slow progress, disappearing from the scene for long periods and leaving various amateur investigators to unravel much of the mystery until he re-appears towards the end to weave the threads into a decisive pattern.

In *The Moonstone,* even more than in *The Woman in White,* the complicated plot was devised as a game of skill between writer and reader. Collins's technique of making different characters relate various episodes is most valuable in this connection because it enables the author to keep secret anything he does not wish the reader to know, and also allows him to convey impressions, false in themselves, but necessary for the development of the plot. Dickens had already used this technique in *Barnaby Rudge,* with the same purpose. It was Dickens's plan to make his readers believe that the steward, Rudge, had been killed when his master was attacked, but he does not say so himself, which would have misled the reader unfairly. Instead, he makes Solomon Daisy relate how "the body of poor Mr. Rudge was found," expressing the general belief. Dickens does, nevertheless, fall into the error of referring to Mrs. Rudge as 'the widow,' though, as he reveals later, her husband is still alive. In Collins's hands the technique is employed more meticulously and more extensively, becoming a special feature, a convention of 'fair play' which he observes to perfection. Anything stated by one of his characters may possibly be inaccurate, but whatever Collins states himself, as author, can be accepted by the reader as true.

For the rest, *The Moonstone* is a kaleidoscope of changing suspicions, red herrings and doubtful alibis. For the first time in English fiction there is an ingenious juggling with details of time and place, careful reconstruction to determine how long certain actions would take, and though the secret is skilfully guarded till the end, Collins is scrupulous in giving the reader enough clues to enable him to deduce the solution for himself, if he is sufficiently perspicacious.

One detail which stands out in both these novels, and in all Collins's work, is his attitude towards domestic servants, so far in advance of his time as to seem almost revolutionary to his Victorian readers. To him, far more than to any other contemporary writer, even Charles Dickens, a servant was not a being to be patronised, regarded as humorous or of negligible importance, but a real person with a heart and mind, eyes and ears, as likely as his master to be truthful or observant. The detective story, perhaps more readily than any other type of fiction, takes the same democratic standpoint, giving impartial consideration to statements made by duke or farm-labourer, mistress or char-woman, and Wilkie Collins is the first English writer to express that view with perfect naturalness.

Sergeant Cuff, though certainly the best known, is not Collins's only detective. In *No Name* (1862) and *The Law and The Lady* (1875) he made two attempts to create a woman detective, but with no sustained success. In *My Lady's Money*, first published in the Christmas number of *The Illustrated London News* (1877), he introduced a private investigator, "Old Sharon," whose 'analytical faculties' are at the service of clients who consult him. He 'thinks better when smoking,' and on entering his room one sees, through the clouds from his pipe, a little elderly man, plump and bald, swathed in a flannel dressing gown, sitting in an armchair with a pet dog on his lap and a French novel in his hands. Old Sharon's perspicacity is, however, somewhat limited, and unless Conan Doyle borrowed his pipe and dressing gown for Sherlock Holmes some ten years later, Collins's last detective had little or no effect upon subsequent fiction.

At the time when *The Moonstone* was delighting English readers, detective fiction in France reached a new level of popu-larity in the novels of Emile Gaboriau, and it is possible to note the striking contrast between this first English detective novel and the typical contemporary *roman policier*, in atmos-phere, in the nature of the central problem, and in the technique of plot construction. In the works of Gaboriau and his imitators, the story generally opens with the discovery of a brutal murder, every wound, every blood stain, all the wild disorder at the scene of the crime being described in gruesome detail. The victim is unknown to the reader until his (or, more often, her) disreput-able past is gradually uncovered by the police, and the murderer is usually a melodramatic 'wicked baronet.' The other characters, with the exception of the detective, are little more than stock figures. The interest of the plot lies solely in the well-devised puzzle and its solution, the background being almost invariably a long drawn out tale of intrigue, passion and violence in aristocratic circles. *The Moonstone*, notwithstanding its steadily mounting drama and suspense, has a quieter tempo, an atmosphere of gracious living, and deals with theft, not murder. We know the characters as individuals living their normal lives before the robbery takes place, and when Sergeant Cuff examines the scene of the crime he finds no greater disturbance than a small smudge upon a newly painted door. But the puzzle is quite as baffling as any solved by Monsieur Lecoq, the plot even more intricate, the human drama far more credible, the contest of wits between writer and reader conducted with a precise regard for 'fair play' that is virtually unknown in the *roman policier* of the same period.

The credit for creating the English detective novel, and giving it characteristic features which still persist, belongs almost wholly to Charles Dickens and Wilkie Collins. Dickens was writing with warm appreciation about the work of the English detective-police long before Collins's first story appeared in print. In *Bleak House* he made a detective story an important part of the plot; invented a special type of victim and kept the reader in suspense as to the motive as well as the identity of the murderer; gave English fiction its first police detective-hero and introduced the device of a 'clearing-up chapter.' Had Dickens lived to complete *The Mystery of Edwin Drood*, in which, for the first time, he gave paramount importance to a detective theme, there seems good reason to believe, from a study of the existing chapters, that it would have equalled or eclipsed *The Moonstone* in power and originality. In *The Woman in White* and *The Moonstone* Wilkie Collins gave a new literary dignity to the detective novel. The plot in each of them is sensational but never incredible; the puzzle theme, intricate and well-sustained though it is, does not eclipse the human characters in interest or importance; and in these works Collins devised and presented the 'fair play convention' which has had such far-reaching effects.

Detective-Inspector Bucket and Sergeant Cuff, taken jointly, form the prototype for the characteristic English police detective in later fiction. They are sound, dependable, self-respecting men of the middle-class, taking a pride in their work and very conscious that they function not merely as individuals but as members of a great organisation. They perform their duties with all the energy and efficiency of which they are capable, but they are not infallible. Sometimes they are at a loss, sometimes they are helped by amateurs, sometimes they must rely on their own dogged persistence, but eventually they bring their cases to a successful conclusion, enjoying the limelight while they explain just how this has come about. They are happy in their home life, devoting their leisure to hobbies as other men do, so that the reader feels he knows them personally.

Amateur detectives differ widely in their personal characteristics, and have been particularly susceptible to influences from France and from America. But when an English detective novel has an English police-officer for a hero it is remarkable how often, even in the middle years of the twentieth century, that hero retains qualities linking him with Detective-Inspector Bucket and Sergeant Cuff. In this, as in the management of plot and the method of presentation, the example set by Charles Dickens and Wilkie Collins still exerts an active influence on the English detective novel.

CHAPTER
VII

THE RISE OF THE *ROMAN-POLICIER*

The national strife that disturbed France in the middle years of the nineteenth century cut sharply across the cultural interests of the people and brought to an end the first and best period of the *romans-feuilletons*. When quieter conditions again prevailed, and the public once more had time and inclination for reading, a new generation of serial writers had appeared, hack-journalists for the most part, whose purpose was simply to satisfy popular tastes in fiction, and so to earn the best living they could with their pen. Many of them were extremely prolific. Paul Féval, for example, was the author of more than a hundred books and several plays. Ponson du Terrail wrote seventy-three novels within two years! In general, the sensational serials published in the popular press of the day were little more than copies of the cloak-and-dagger romances or the melodramatic crime stories that had captured public fancy a decade or two earlier. A few writers, however, produced novels in which the detection of crime played an increasingly important part.

Paul Féval (1817—1887) included certain detective episodes in his *Les Mystères de Londres* (1844) for which, on its first appearance, he adopted the rather surprising pen-name of "Sir Francis Trolopp," perhaps to suggest that the author was British. It is a curious tale of an Irishman who tries to avenge his country's 'wrongs' by planning various crimes against Englishmen, and the hero, *le chevalier de Lagardère*, takes upon himself the task of administering whatever retribution he considers just, in much the same way as did Sue's Prince Rodolphe or Dumas' Count of Monte Cristo, using, like them, a certain amount of detective skill to establish the guilt or to uncover the secrets of those he punishes. Part of the plot is based upon the activities of those notorious Irishmen, Burke and Hare, who murdered some fifteen people in Edinburgh between 1827 and 1829 in order to sell their bodies for dissection in medical schools. A most interesting detail of the novel, from our present point of view, is that in it Féval created an English private detective named Robin Cross, very long and thin, with an obsequious manner and the businesslike habit of insisting on payment in advance for his services.

Féval's *Les Couteaux d'Or* (1856) reflects Fenimore Cooper's influence by introducing an Indian brave, Towah, who cleverly trails his enemies through the streets of Paris, helped by his sagacious hound, Mohican. In *Les Habits Noirs* (1863) Féval returns to his earlier type of hero and makes 'Trois Pattes' a sort of Monte Cristo turned beggar, who tracks down his foes from motives of revenge, and depends at least as much upon his powers of disguise as on detective acumen. The title itself refers to a gang of successful thieves whose exploits were planned after careful reconnaissance which called for a good deal of ingenious deduction from observation. One of them, called Lecoq, was a prepossessing rascal, unusually quick to notice informative trifles and clever in arranging misleading evidence to divert suspicion from himself. In the character of a commercial traveller for a firm of Paris safe-makers he collected valuable information which he either passed to his confederates or exploited for his personal advantage.

Most of Féval's novels related the adventures of similar romantic bandits, who often employed detective methods for their own purposes but were not detectives.[1] Indeed, the criminal-hero was still the most popular figure in contemporary French fiction, and his pursuers, if any, were as relatively unimportant as his victims. Sometimes, as in Féval's serials, it was the cunning and daring of a thief that engrossed the reader's attention; sometimes it was the sufferings of a convict or his struggles towards rehabilitation after his release or escape· but,

---

[1] In his later years Féval became an ardent Catholic, and then felt that his chronicles of crime might have exercised an evil influence, being too informative as to ways and means. He therefore devoted his old age to re-writing his novels from his changed point of view, but there seems no indication that these revised works were received with the acclaim given to the original versions.

whatever the angle of approach, the dominating figure was the criminal, not his detective-antagonist, who, if he appeared at all, played merely a subsidiary role. Even as late as 1862, in Victor Hugo's *Les Misérables*,[1] the primary theme is the long struggle of Jean Valjean, the ex-convict hero, to regain peace and security. Javert is important only as the pursuing Nemesis that threatens to overtake him.

The section of *Les Misérables* which most nearly resembles a detective story is the second volume of Book V. Here, Hugo develops the *motif* of flight and pursuit, using the very terms employed in a deer-hunt, Javert being the tireless, implacable hound, trailing his quarry through a maze of Paris slums and only just failing to bring him down. But the hero is still the hunted man, not the hunter. All the reader's sympathy is drawn to Valjean, and is heightened by the circumstance that in his flight for life he is burdened by the child, Cozette. The *agent de police* is merely a personification of merciless retribution, and there is no suggestion that Javert is to be admired for his skill, or even for his devotion to duty. He inspires no emotion but fear.

But though no French writer had as yet given the rôle of hero to a police officer or a private detective, that step was soon to be taken in the works of two popular fiction writers who fostered a closer interest in detection, *per se*. They were Pierre Alexis de Ponson, known as Ponson du Terrail (1829—1871), whose Rocambole became a sort of detective-adventurer, and Emile Gaboriau (1833—1873), whose Monsieur Lecoq was to dominate the field of detective fiction far beyond the borders of France until he was at last eclipsed by Sherlock Holmes.

Ponson du Terrail met his first literary success at the age of twenty-four, when he was commissioned to write a serial in a hundred instalments. As he frankly acknowledged later,[2] he began writing with no settled plan, beyond that of introducing

---

[1] Hugo's convicts and police officers really belong to a much earlier period than 1862. The sentences said to have been passed on Valjean were quite out of date in their severity, and not in accordance with French law at the time of the story.

[2] In his *La Verité sur Rocambole*, Ch. V.

into his story as many as possible of those features which had already proved popular—sensational details of the criminal under-world of Paris, a missing heiress whose vast wealth is coveted by a wicked baronet, and a noble philanthropist who sets out to punish vice and reward virtue in the slums of the capital, exactly as Sue's Prince Rodolphe had done in *Les Mystères de Paris*, twenty years earlier. Even the title of the new serial, *Les Drames de Paris*, linked it with Sue's best known work, and the similarity extended still further. One of Sue's central characters was an unsavoury old woman, who was always accompanied by a precocious little street urchin, Tortillard. Ponson du Terrail introduced a similar old tavern keeper, *La Mère Fipart*, and as her companion he created a cheeky, twelve-year old ragamuffin, nicknamed Rocambole.

This was the figure, at first of minor importance, that came eventually to play the leading rôle in a very long sequence of sensational romances. In the first of them he becomes the personal servant of the villain; in the second, *Le Club des Valets de Coeur*, he is a gay, cynical youth of twenty, the audacious leader of a gang, and now so elegant in person and behaviour that he is everywhere accepted as the viscount he claims to be. The third serial, *Turquoise la pécheresse*, continues his criminal adventures and ends with Rocambole en route for London, the scene of *Les Exploits de Rocambole* (1859). When this long series of some twenty-two tales drew to a close, Ponson du Terrail was, understandably, thoroughly tired of Rocambole, and, to terminate his career had him terribly burned with vitriol and left for dead.

But the public demanded more stories of Rocambole, and another serial, *Les Chevaliers du Clair de Lune*, appeared in 1862. In the prologue Rocambole's face bore deep and terrible scars,[1] but these became less conspicuous as the tale proceeded, until in Chapter 54 he is once more an elegant young man with

---

[1] Ponson du Terrail realised that this was a serious error. (Cf. *La Verité sur Rocambole*, Ch. 18.) French readers would not accept a disfigured hero. It is interesting that, whereas English detectives of fiction are seldom good-looking, and often quite eccentric in appearance, their French counterparts are almost invariably strikingly handsome.

no disturbing imperfections. Yet this serial was not a success with the public.

After a break of a few years Ponson du Terrail began a new series, *La Résurrection de Rocambole* (1866), with his hero completely rejuvenated, once more 'handsome as a fallen angel.' His success was immediate, and greater than ever. The five volumes of this work were followed by *Le Dernier Mot de Rocambole* (1866), also in five volumes, and *La Verité sur Rocambole* (1867) in one volume. Even then the public was not satiated with this hero, and the whole series of his adventures re-appeared as novels, successive editions testifying to his continued popularity.

But with his 'resurrection' Rocambole became a changed man, repenting of his crimes and determined in future to apply his talents to countering the activities of his former associates and other evil-doers, thus following in Vidocq's example, though for a different reason. He is an ex-convict still in touch with habitual criminals, a past-master in disguise, unsurpassed in physical strength and courage, superbly self-confident. He does not accept an official position, as Vidocq did, but sets himself up in business as a sort of private detective, to whom members of the aristocracy bring their personal problems in the strictest confidence. The subsequent Rocambole stories, almost a dozen long serials, report his adventures and investigations in that capacity. It is, perhaps, not irrelevant that Rocambole's metamorphosis from criminal to detective took place in the same year, 1866, in which Gaboriau's police detective, Monsieur Lecoq, first captured the enthusiastic interest of the French reading public.

In addition to the qualities which he inherited from Vidocq, Rocambole possessed all the skill of Cooper's Indian trackers, and also one or two habits that link him with Poe's Dupin— such tricks, for instance, as trying to divine his enemy's thoughts by copying his facial expression, or arranging a disturbance outside a house to distract attention while he gains possession of what he wants inside it, as Dupin had done in *The Purloined Letter*.

But Rocambole also had something about him that was new,

119

his gay exuberance in the rôle of detective, for instance, especially when he scored a success over the police. Vidocq had distrusted the police for their malpractices and vindictive jealousy towards him; Dupin was contemptuous of their lack of imagination; but Rocambole took special pleasure in flouting them, even in his criminal days, because for him they stood for the conventions, the established order of things against which his ego rebelled. It is this spirit that links Rocambole with later rogue-heroes turned detective, from Arsène Lupin and Raffles to 'The Saint.'

There is an air of modernity, too, in the way Rocambole and his suspects travel across Europe by train, and juggle with railway time-tables to make or break convincing alibis, in their familiarity with revolvers, 'new weapons just introduced from America.' Everything Rocambole does is on a lavish scale. Earlier detectives lived simply; he must have luxury. They had managed to disguise themselves quite satisfactorily with a few changes of clothing and a supply of wigs; he maintains an immense wardrobe with every conceivable device, so that at a moment's notice he can transform himself into the blond Polish baron, Wenceslas, the olive-skinned dark-haired Marquis de los Montes, or any other of his innumerable aliases. Once started on his detective career he quickly acquires the arts and crafts of his new profession, carrying out chemical tests with acids or re-agents and reasoning out the implications of his results. He surpasses himself during his visit to London, where, as 'l'homme gris' he strikes terror into the hearts of evil-doers, and is naturally in conflict with Scotland Yard. On one occasion he conceives the idea that the eyes of a murdered man may retain a picture of the assassin as he struck the fatal blow, and actually produces in court the evidence thus obtained, explaining it in detail to the astonished magistrate. Unfortunately, Rocambole strains the reader's credulity rather too far when the photograph he obtains from one of the dead man's eyes differs considerably from that obtained from the other, and not only shows a later view of the scene of the crime, but even includes the figure of the victim as well as the features of the murderer! Nevertheless, this sensational idea, whether practicable or not, was more than once copied by later writers. An English author, Headon Hill, made use of it in his *Clues from a Detective's Camera* (1893), and so did Jules Claretie in *L'Accusateur* (1897), both of them working out the conception much more ingeniously than Ponson du Terrail had done, and with more regard for the probabilities.

In spite of such lapses into sensationalism, Rocambole is a figure of some importance in the detective fiction of France, forming as a private consultant a popular counterpart to his contemporary, the police official, Monsieur Lecoq. But as one serial followed another, every instalment being broken off at some harrowing crisis, the exploits of Rocambole tended to become 'thrillers,' rather than detective stories. In spite of his brilliant powers, Rocambole regularly falls into the traps devised for him by his enemies, and escapes danger only by the timely intervention of his faithful assistant, Marmouset. A typical ending shows him trapped by his enemy, Timoléon, in a building where a bomb is due to explode at any moment. As the next instalment opens, Marmouset, instinctively sensing his master's peril, follows his trail with the help of a specially trained dog, arriving in time to pull out the fuse with five seconds to spare, while the hound disposes of the lurking Timoléon. Almost precisely similar situations occur over and over again in the later series of tales about Nick Carter or Sexton Blake, with Chick or Patsy dashing up with Caesar or Pedro just in time to rescue their leader from some terrible predicament that he has not been intelligent enough to avoid.

Long before the almost interminable adventures of Rocambole at last came to an end, detectives of far greater discernment had been created by Emile Gaboriau in a small group of remarkable novels. They are sensational and melodramatic, as such fiction had to be to please its public, but they differ from *romans-feuilletons* in that the reader's attention is focussed on the detection, not the commission, of crime. In them Gaboriau originated the '*roman-policier*' which was to form a major part of French popular fiction for the next quarter of a century.

In his early twenties Gaboriau was making a living in Paris

as a journalist when he attracted the notice of Paul Féval and became his secretary. He continued to produce a considerable quantity of literary work under his own name, reports of various *causes célèbres*, for example, and a biographical study of a celebrated defence lawyer, Maître Berryer, and by 1863 he had already produced seven novels that were not concerned with detection.

His first detective novel, *L'Affaire Lerouge*, began to appear during 1863 in *Le Pays*, a moribund *journal* that ceased publication before its new serial had attracted much attention. But the story had been noticed by Polydore Millaud, the proprietor of *Le Soleil* and of its still more successful contemporary, *Le Petit Journal*. In 1865 *Le Soleil* published instalments of *L'Affaire Lerouge*, which became so popular that it was issued in volume form in 1866. Gaboriau's success was assured, and his later novels of this type were considered important enough to be serialized in *Le Petit Journal* itself, *Le Crime d'Orcival* and *Le Dossier No. 113* in 1867, *Les Esclaves de Paris* in 1868, and *Monsieur Lecoq* in 1869.

In *L'Affaire Lerouge*, the opening chapters direct the limelight upon two official detectives of established reputation, M. Daburon, *le juge d'instruction*, and the celebrated Gévrol, *chef de la police de sûreté*, and it seems as though Gaboriau's original intention was to make them the central figures in his new novel of detection. But they are quickly eclipsed by two much more interesting characters, Père Tabaret and Monsieur Lecoq. Tabaret is an elderly retired pawnbroker in comfortable circumstances, whose greatest joy in life is to investigate a mystery. He is known to his friends in the police as 'Old Tir-au-clair,' and has for years devoted his time and money to helping them with any especially difficult case, unable to resist indulging in his hobby as an amateur detective, in spite of the social stigma he would have to bear if this became known. His friends and neighbours, however, attribute his irregular hours to secret vice, an impression he does his best to foster. He it is who conducts most of the investigation into the murder of the widow Lerouge, explaining his findings and deductions to the young

Lecoq with all the zest of a master who has at last found a brilliant pupil.

On his original appearance Lecoq is introduced with scant ceremony as a comparatively unimportant figure, merely Gévrol's junior assistant for the day, and Gaboriau describes him as 'an old offender now reconciled with the law,' a particularly interesting phrase because it places Lecoq, as an ex-convict turned policeman, in the same category as Vidocq, or Balzac's Gondureau, or the typical *agent de police* of any time in the previous hundred years. The term may have been used unthinkingly, simply as a conventional description—it has that air in the text —but Gaboriau seems to have regretted the phrase later, for as Lecoq became the central figure in the novels which followed, he went to some trouble to explain away this alleged stain on his hero's good name.

While investigating *Le Crime d'Orcival* the detective himself volunteers an explanation, when chatting to friends in an expansive after-dinner mood. After studying mathematics at the University he worked for some years as assistant to a famous astronomer, Baron Moser, and finding the endless calculations boring he amused himself by devising imaginary crimes, in particular a scheme for defrauding any banker of a vast sum in a way that could neither fail nor be found out. With the complete frankness of an honest mind he put his ideas before his employer, simply as a matter of academic interest, whereupon the baron dryly advised him that, with such talents, he must decide whether to become a successful criminal or a great detective. Gaboriau gives further details of his hero's blameless past in the opening chapters of *Monsieur Lecoq*, in which, notwithstanding the heights he had attained at the *Préfecture* in the intervening novels, Lecoq, is re-introduced as a very junior police officer, an honest young man of good family and sound education, proud of his powers and position as a detective. This new Lecoq had never been a criminal, and here we have an important fresh development in French fiction. His 'crimes' were merely flights of fancy, and his personal record was as free from stain as that of Sherlock Holmes, the great detective who followed Lecoq's example, and, now and then, enlivened periods of boredom by planning a hypothetical coup.

To enable Lecoq to fill his new rôle of French police-detective hero with brilliant efficiency, Gaboriau endowed him with powers derived from all his predecessors in detection. Lecoq can follow a trail as cleverly as the Princes of Serendip or Cooper's Indian braves, and he has all Vidocq's courage and intuition, his mastery of disguise, his familiarity with criminal ways. In view of Gaboriau's admiration for Edgar Allan Poe it is not surprising to find many points of similarity between Lecoq and Dupin, and they both regard a mysterious puzzle as a challenge to their powers of perception; they reason with mathematical precision and enjoy giving little lectures on 'algebraic analysis' to their associates. But whereas Dupin was an abstract logician, an arm-chair amateur detective, Lecoq threw himself with intense energy into the physical, as well as the mental, activities of practical police work, and over and above his inherited qualities he brought fresh skills of his own to the scientific detection of crime. Lecoq was the first detective to concern himself with such practical matters as determining whether or not a bed had been really slept in, and to what extent the chaos at the scene of the crime had been contrived to deceive. He was the first detective to pick up a fallen clock pointing to twenty past three, push the hands on to the half-hour, and, from the fact that it then struck eleven, calculate correctly the time when the murder was committed. No-one, before him, used plaster to preserve a record of footprints, or drew a careful sketch of the scene of the crime, to be incorporated in the text. Lecoq and Père Tabaret are the first detectives to astonish the police (and the reader) by giving a detailed description of their suspect after making a brief examination of the scene of the crime. Père Tabaret, in *L'Affaire Lerouge,* takes a quick glance around, and remarks: —

"He is a young man, below average height, elegantly dressed and wearing a top hat. He carried an umbrella, and was smoking a Havana cigar in a holder."

Lecoq, in *L'Enquête* (the first volume of *Monsieur Lecoq*) looks at the snow-covered ground outside an inn, and at once describes the man who walked across it half-an-hour ago: —

> "He is middle-aged and very tall, wearing a soft cap and a chestnut-coloured overcoat with a fleecy surface. He is very probably married."

In precisely the same way, twenty years or so later, Sherlock Holmes staggered his associates with such comments as: —

> "The murderer [. . .] was more than six feet high, was in the prime of life, had small feet for his height, wore coarse square-toed boots and smoked a Trinchinopoly cigar, [. . .] had a florid face, and the finger-nails of his right hand were remarkably long."

and Tabaret, Lecoq and Holmes are all alike in not revealing until some time later the simple indications that enabled them to make their dramatic pronouncements.

Lecoq is drawn as a man to be liked as a human being, not merely admired as a detective, and, clever though he is, he is not infallible. In *L'Enquête*, he allowed himself to be baulked of almost certain success after a long, exhausting quest, simply because he could not credit that his missing suspect was really a Duke. A chat with old Tabaret gave him fresh heart and a new line of enquiry, and at the end of the second volume he brought his case to a triumphant conclusion.

Gaboriau further enriched detective fiction by his perception of the suspense value of the 'red herring,' and often sent suspicion running on a false trail laid by circumstantial evidence. Prosper Bertomy, in *Le Dossier No. 113* and *le vicomte de Caumarin* in *L'Affaire Lerouge*, seem almost certainly guilty until, at last, new information shows them to be wrongly suspected. The case against Caumarin is so strong that he is actually on trial for murder when Père Tabaret, learning that the prisoner has no alibi for the material time, deduces that he must therefore be innocent, and begins to reconsider the evidence against him. In *Le Crime d'Orcival* Lecoq is faced with a similar need to revise his conclusions in view of conflicting indications, and in this respect Gaboriau pointed the way to that subtle and delicately balanced see-saw of detective argument which was later brought to such perfection in the novels of Freeman Wills Crofts and Father Ronald Knox.

In view of the antipathy so long felt in France towards the police, it was a remarkable achievement to win popularity for a police-hero. Indeed, Gaboriau first followed Poe's example, and in the opening instalments of *L'Affaire Lerouge* it is the amateur detective, Père Tabaret, who shines most brightly. But as the tale developed, Gaboriau invested police affairs with a glamour that caught his readers' attention, and focussed their interest upon Monsieur Lecoq. He was so typically French, and the device of a crowing cock, which he chose for his personal symbol, so aptly expressed his high-stepping self assurance, his quick eye for trifles, his bedraggled dejection when success eluded him and his exultant bravado when he was lucky! The logical force of his soundly reasoned arguments appealed to French habits of thought, and readers could also enjoy his revelations of inter-departmental rivalries within the *Préfecture;* the jealousy of a village policeman for the man sent down by the *Sûreté;* the dilemma of a *juge d'instruction,* divided between professional duty and loyalty to personal ties; the routine of prison management; and the behaviour of various types of suspect when subjected to the gruelling French system of interrogation.

In developing his novels of Monsieur Lecoq. Gaboriau found himself faced with the artistic difficulty inherent in fiction of this type. In essence, a detective story concerns itself with an analytical enquiry into a given set of circumstances, and for that reason, though the enquiry may be protracted, the tale is really episodic. The most satisfying, the most technically perfect, examples of detective fiction—the tales of Dupin and of Sherlock Holmes, for instance—are short stories. It is difficult for a longer work to concern itself with a detective theme to the virtual exclusion of that intimate study of character which is the province of the true novelist. In writing a detective novel the author generally finds himself involved in two conflicting subjects, on one hand a complicated puzzle calling for the exercise of the reasoning powers, and on the other a human drama which appeals to the emotions.

Gaboriau attempted to overcome this difficulty in *L'Affaire Lerouge* by breaking off the thread of detection at a dramatic moment (in a manner very frustrating to a modern reader) and interpolating the life-stories of the people concerned, even to the extent of taking the reader into his confidence behind the detective's back. In *Monsieur Lecoq* he went to the length of writing two separate volumes, the first setting forth the problem as Lecoq saw it, and the second relating, from the beginning, the human drama that culminated in the crime, with Lecoq completing his case in the final pages. *Le Crime D'Orcival* is much shorter, the interpolation less tedious, and Lecoq's investigations are not seriously interrupted. This book, in which Gaboriau more nearly approaches the technique of the twentieth century detective novel, is his best work by modern standards, with the possible exception of *Le Petit Vieux des Batignolles*, published posthumously in 1876, which shows a further advance towards the 'pure' detective story, and foreshadows the device of the 'trick' ending. The murderer laid a false trail with meticulous care, and was caught only because the police, in ignorance of a material fact which he assumed they would know, blundered on the truth almost by accident.

Gaboriau, who died suddenly at the early age of 38, had only seven years of full literary life, but in that brief space of time he influenced the development of detective fiction in his own country and in the English-speaking world. Almost until the end of the century, French writers continued to produce imitations of his police novels. In America, translations quickly appeared as serials in Sunday newspapers, *L'Affaire Lerouge* with the fresh title of *The Crimson Crime*, *Le Crime d'Orcival* becoming *Dark Deeds*, *Les Esclaves de Paris*, a tale of blackmail, becoming, oddly enough, *Manhattan Unmasked*, and *Le Dossier No. 113*, *The Steel Safe*, the last attracting particular attention because an actual robbery on very similar lines had just taken place in New York.

In England, Gaboriau's novels reached a very wide public.

Wilkie Collins not only read them, but retained copies on his bookshelves. For more than two decades from 1870 onwards, English literary critics were using the term, 'in the style of M. Gaboriau' as a sufficiently informative description of new fiction. Twenty years after Gaboriau's death his works were still best-sellers on the other side of the globe, where they inspired Fergus Hume to write the first of his numerous detective novels, *The Mystery of a Hansom Cab*, which was widely discussed in England in the 1890's.

The typical *roman policier* of Gaboriau and his many imitators followed an almost stereotyped pattern. The plot is constructed to focus attention on the skill of the detective, a French police official or an amateur, who appears as the chief character in one tale after another, surrounded each time by a different group of subordinate personalities. Often the criminal is of noble blood but illegitimate birth, young, handsome and ruthless, a survival of the 'romantic bandit' of earlier French fiction. The victim, usually a woman, is killed to prevent her revealing secrets, the crime is violently sensational, and the investigation uncovers a family scandal in high society, with old sins casting long shadows. The final climax may occasion a further crime, the murderer committing suicide, or being killed by someone he has wronged. This basic plot was copied fairly closely for many years by such writers as Pierre Zaccone, Alexis Bouvier, Arthur Matthey and many others, prolific and popular in their day, but now almost forgotten.

One or two authors brought new features to the *genre*, or added to it details borrowed from writers in the first half of the century. Constant Guéroult, in *L'Affaire de la rue du Temple* (1880) and its sequel, *La Bande à Fifi Vollard* (1881), took the name of '*la comtesse de Serizy*' from Balzac and a whole group of criminals from Sue. The crimes in Eugène Chavette's novels are as sensational, his detective arguments as logically reasoned, as those of Gaboriau, but his manner of presentation shows a difference. He occasionally introduces an ironic, half-joking atmosphere, as though trying to please not only readers who enjoyed a sensational *roman-policier*, but also others of more discriminating tastes, who were at least half-inclined to find this type of story amusing. His Caduchet, in *L'Heritage d'un Pique-Assiette* (1874), blunders comically at times. But the central puzzle is soundly unravelled, and one or two touches show the influence of Poe, as, for instance, when a blackmailer hides an important letter, for which the police are frantically searching, in the dining room of the detective in charge of the case, a trick adapted from the manoeuvre of *le ministre* D——, in *The Purloined Letter*.

Chavette's *La Chambre du Crime* (1875) is a 'locked room' murder mystery, and *La Recherche d'un Pourquoi* (1878) shows an Insurance Company being systematically swindled by a gang of tricksters whose secret leader is a well-known Society hostess. In *Le Roi des Limiers* (1879) the plot of which bears some resemblance to Balzac's *Une Ténébreuse Affaire*, Chavette creates a clever detective, Patapon, who employs much the same methods as Lecoq but lacks his dramatic touch. In one respect, however, Chavette improves upon Gaboriau's technique, and usually finds some rather ingenious way of introducing retrospective 'life histories' a little at a time, so that the background to the crime is given without perceptibly delaying the progress of the story.

Of those French writers who followed Gaboriau's lead, perhaps the most popular in his own country, and in England, was Fortuné du Boisgobey (1824—1891). His crime mysteries are very smoothly constructed, and, if he did not invent a detective as brilliant as Lecoq, he at least avoided the melodramatic stock figures of Gaboriau's police-novels, striking a more modern note by introducing, instead, the ordinary people of Paris—shop-keepers, artisans, sewing-girls, artists, students, all jostling each other in the crowded streets or travelling home in horse-omni-buses after a long day's work.

The central character in *Le Coup de Pouce* (1875) is a kindly old *curé*, M. Jean, an early fore-runner of Chesterton's Father Brown, who is deeply troubled by a mysterious murder committed in his parish and sets himself to discover the murderer in order to clear one of his congregation. With the aid of a young nephew of the local land-owner he at last proved that the murder was planned by a new-comer to the village, whose false alibi had been contrived by tampering with the village clock. There is a freshness in Du Boisgobey's method of inventing and handling detective problems, and his mysteries are not generally solved by the police, or by any recurring figure with special skill or past aptitude in detection. Instead, as in *Le Coup de Pouce,* characters whom we meet in their normal, day-to-day lives find themselves involved in some apparently inexplicable event, and use their own faculties of perception and deduction to discover the truth, calling on the help of their friends and neighbours if this seems expedient.

Du Boisgobey tried a variation of this pattern, in the same year as *Le Coup de Pouce,* in his *La Vieillesse de Monsieur Lecoq* (1875), an attempt to resurrect Gaboriau's police hero, but it showed him sadly changed and past his best, so forgetful of his younger days that he claimed his old master's nickname, 'Tir-au-clair,' as his own. Monsieur Lecoq returns from retirement to clear his son of an accusation of murder, which he succeeds in doing only at the last moment. Du Boisgobey lacked Gaboriau's enthusiastic interest in police affairs, and his accurate knowledge of their customary procedure, so that this novel is not entirely convincing. Writers of this type of fiction are always on the look-out for something new to grip the attention of their readers, especially some ingenious, hitherto unheard-of method of committing murder, and it is not surprising that Du Boisgobey did the same. He seems to be the first detective story writer to make an injection of curare the cause of a mysterious death, in *Le Crime de l'Omnibus* (1882). Since this poison was at that time by no means as well known (even to the author!) as it later became, he added a careful footnote to inform his readers that curare was made by savage tribes from the venom of the rattlesnake!

In *Cornaline la Dompteuse* (1887), with its background of circus life, much of the detective work is carried out by an observant young reporter, Saintonge, working on a special enquiry for his paper. Saintonge is essentially French, and so are the police officials with whom he occasionally co-operates, but Du Boisgobey may have borrowed the idea of making a newspaperman an amateur detective from an English novel, *Great Porter Square*, written three years earlier by B. L. Farjeon. Du Boisgobey's novels were published in translation, here and in America, almost as soon as the originals appeared. The first translator may well have been an American, to judge from his references to dollars, his terms for various occupations (that of a 'dry-goods clerk,' for instance) and his haphazard misuse of titled names. A new translation of *Le Coup de Pouce* appeared in England in 1884, reprints of this and others of Du Boisgobey's works being still sold in quantity during the 1890's.

Gaboriau, with his melodramatic plots, his soundly-reasoned deductions, and, above all, his entertaining hero, Monsieur Lecoq; and Du Boisgobey, with his less sensational, more realistic treatment of similar themes, were both very popular with the general public of France and England, inspiring numerous imitators whose work, if not outstanding, was for the most part ingeniously devised and well-constructed. Although French literary critics still considered such fiction as of no real importance, English reviewers were beginning to regard it more appreciatively, and to compare the French *romans-policiers* favourably with similar works written in English: —

'Our French friends [. . .] have taught us of late to be very fastidious in the matter of detective stories.'[1]

'The French are our masters in criminal romance. They bring an amount of patience to their work which is rare indeed with English novelists, and the patient thought which credibly works out all possible combinations is at least as indispensable as ingenuity and acuteness to the success of the criminal novel.'[2]

By the time these comments appeared, English writers had already given considerable attention to producing fiction of somewhat the same type, but modified to accord more harmon-

[1] *Nation and Athenaeum*, March 23rd, 1889, p. 371.
[2] Anon, ' Crime in Fiction ', *Blackwood's Edinburgh Magazine*, Vol. CXLVIII, July-Dec., 1890, p. 174.

iously with English literary traditions. The English detective novel of the 1860's, which also served new writers as an inspiring pattern, had no such clearly defined limitations as those of the *roman-policier*, and therefore the way lay open for development along broader lines. Moreover, in the hands of Charles Dickens and Wilkie Collins the *genre* had the inestimable advantage of being skilfully written by novelists who, though bitterly attacked in some quarters as 'sensationalists,' nevertheless had the interest of an educated public, and were already famous for their novels of a different type. They lent the weight of their literary reputation to the English detective novel which they created.

Those writers who first attempted to follow them in this field could not be unaware of the great popularity of the French detective story in England. Sir Hugh Walpole has commented that the French novel of this type was widely read in this country at that time.[1] He adds that it was often 'read furtively,' that 'its significance was never literary,' and that it had little or no effect upon the main trends of English literature during the 1870's and later. But it certainly had an effect upon the particular type of fiction we are considering, and in the decades between *The Moonstone* and the first appearance of Sherlock Holmes in *A Study in Scarlet,* more than one writer attempted to enliven English detective fiction with features borrowed from France, particularly from the *romans policiers* of Gaboriau and Du Boisgobey.

[1] *The Eighteen-Seventies,* C.U.P., 1929, pp. 27-28.

CHAPTER
VIII

FROM SHERIDAN LE FANU
TO MATTHEW PHIPPS SHIEL

In the period that followed the publication of *The Moonstone* and *The Mystery of Edwin Drood*, detective fiction continued to be written in England, without reaching any notable heights until the final decade of the nineteenth century. Much of it, and perhaps the best known, was the work of women writers who will be considered in our next chapter. The authors to be reviewed here were men who influenced the growth of the *genre* by introducing fresh ideas, or devising ways to interest readers of a different type. Some of them, better known for their work in other types of fiction, experimented with the detective novel in response to the increasing demand, or even as a light-hearted change from their usual choice of subject. Others chose to specialize in the *genre,* and it was during this quarter of a century that there appeared, for the first time, the 'detective-story-writer' who wrote nothing else.

Joseph Sheridan Le Fanu (1814—1873), the Irish author and journalist, was celebrated in his own country for humorous tales, ballads and lyrical poems, historical romances and stories of the supernatural. In England, his fame rests chiefly upon his ghost stories and one or two novels of crime and detection. *The House by the Churchyard* (1863), a ghoulish tale of supernatural horror, was followed by *Uncle Silas: a Tale of Bartram Haugh* (1864), equally sensational, but with the important difference that it deals with criminals, not ghosts, and introduces a certain amount of detective interest. The cunning schemes of Uncle Silas and his son to murder the heroine are at last found out and frustrated, and past crimes are eventually brought to light, but there is no central character acting as a detective, and no special emphasis is placed on deductive reasoning. *Uncle Silas* can hardly be considered a detective novel, but the introduction of analogous features is significant and indicates a new trend in Le Fanu's work, a change that reached completion in his next novel, *Checkmate,* which appeared as a serial in *Cassell's Magazine* between September, 1870, and March, 1871, being issued in volume form in 1871.

In essence, *Checkmate* is constructed purely as a detective novel, and it contains one or two features not previously used. The investigations are followed step by step to their surprising *dénouement,* and despite the years that have elapsed since the first crime the murderer's guilt is proved beyond doubt. At the outset, *Checkmate* frankly acknowledges the truism that 'murders interest people so much' and proceeds to gratify this interest, surrounding the crimes with intriguing mysteries to intensify curiosity and suspense.

In the first volume the chief character is certainly the criminal, Walter Longcluse, adept in disguise and in contriving alibis, committing one murder after another while still retaining an honoured place in society. The first man to suspect Longcluse is Paul Davies, an 'ex-detective of the police office, recently dismissed from the Force for over-zealous behaviour.' Le Fanu presents Davies as cunning and unscrupulous, clever enough to collect proofs of Longcluse's latest crime when the police fail to find a single clue. Davies blackmails Longcluse and is paid to leave the country, but before doing so he places the information he has gathered in the hands of David Arden, whose brother was murdered years earlier by a certain 'Yelland Mace' who eluded pursuit and vanished without trace.

Struck by certain similarities between Longcluse and the long-lost 'Yelland Mace,' Arden decides to investigate. In some respects he resembles his forerunner, Pelham, being a gentleman of wealth and title who undertakes a detective enquiry for strong personal reasons, an amateur, prepared to devote his own time and resources to unravelling a mystery. But Arden has a far more difficult and protracted task than Lytton's hero, and becomes more captivated by the thrill of the chase. He sets about it in a businesslike way, sending his 'confidential man' to undertake the tedious preliminary enquiries, and carefully studying his circumstantial reports, which are embodied in the text. Arden's Christopher Blount is by no means as skilled as Doctor Thorndyke's Polton, or Lord Peter Wimsey's Bunter, but he does place in his master's hand the thread that eventually leads him to the centre of the maze, and thereafter David Arden, fired with detective zeal, conducts the investigation personally. He shows no particular aptitude, makes no brilliant deductions, depending less upon inductive reasoning than on 'unaccountable suspicions,' good luck and an orderly habit of mind, but he finds out the truth and is solely responsible for the arrest of Longcluse at the end of the novel.

An innovation in *Checkmate* is that the criminal's features have been changed by a surgical operation,[1] so that Arden comes up against an apparent deadlock that almost defeats him. In 1871, when the fingerprint system of identification was still unheard-of, there were serious difficulties to overcome before it could be proved that Walter Longcluse, the city magnate, was in reality the Yelland Mace of twenty years earlier, but Le Fanu handled the matter quite convincingly. Arden at last found the obscure surgeon who performed the operation. Plaster casts of the patient's face, before and after surgery, had been preserved with careful notes of the position and effect of every incision, each alteration in cartilage or bone structure, even information that certain teeth had been removed and artificial ones arranged at a different angle, so that identification from dental records,[2] used occasionally in later fiction, finds some origin in *Checkmate*.

The plot is not solely concerned with David Arden's investigations, and introduces numerous melodramatic side-issues, but nevertheless the detective theme is certainly the main interest,

[1] This device has seldom been employed by English writers, though it was used in a short story by Beckles Willson, *The Losing of Jasper Virel* (*Strand Magazine*, July, 1909), and carried to improbable lengths. (Even the colour of Virel's eyes was said to be changed from blue to brown.) Some American detective stories in the twentieth century, and plays such as *Arsenic and Old Lace*, introduced gangsters who had their features altered by plastic surgery in the hope of avoiding identification. Cf. Erle Stanley Gardner, *The Case of the Substitute Face* (1938).

[2] Cf. Dorothy L. Sayers, *In The Teeth of The Evidence*, London, Gollancz, 1939. 'Forensic Odontology' has now been accorded a place in the scientific methods of identification employed by Interpol.

an important new development. In spite of archaic phrases and various out-moded relics from the Tale of Terror, which made it in these respects old-fashioned even when first published, the detective part of the book is surprisingly in advance of its period. Le Fanu was well abreast of contemporary experiments in photography in his references to a 'silhouette made by machinery,' and ahead of his day in his introduction of plastic surgery, almost half a century before the general public became familiar with the idea. Thus *Checkmate*, though not a great novel, is of some importance as a landmark, and must be included in that small group of English detective stories which were written in the third quarter of the nineteenth century and influenced later fiction of this kind.

Checkmate suffered seriously, as a detective story, by being planned as a three-volume novel, the required length being filled up with various digressions. Until novels of that length had fallen out of favour, writers who perceived the dramatic possibilities of a detective theme had considerable difficulty in finding material to fill this conventional structure. Major Arthur Griffiths, one of H.M. Inspectors of Prisons, who must have possessed extensive first-hand knowledge of criminals and of how they had been brought to justice, was nevertheless unequal to the task of spinning out a detective mystery to fill three volumes, though his many novels of this type were well received by contemporary readers. *Fast and Loose* (1885), a typical example of his work, deals with a bank robbery for which an innocent man has been convicted. A baronet, with a flair for detection and the leisure to indulge it, sets himself to find out the real thief, for love of the prisoner's daughter, and by the end of the first volume his investigations are so well in hand that their conclusion is obviously imminent. The second volume and most of the third are devoted to various shady characters who have little or no connection with the main plot, until the baronet's detective activities are resumed and completed in the final chapters.

In contrast to *Fast and Loose* in this respect, we may notice G. Manville's *The Dark House*, published in the same year.

The story itself has no special significance, but it broke away from the three-volume convention and presented a detective novel in one volume. Though detective novels in single volume form had been appearing in America ever since 1878, the English reading public was not quite ready for this innovation, and current reviews of *The Dark House* referred disparagingly to its lack of length, but it is interesting that the attempt was made in this country in 1885, a year or two before Conan Doyle wrote his first single-volume detective novel, *A Study in Scarlet*, in which Sherlock Holmes made his *début*.

One other English novel that appeared in 1885, *A Hard Knot*, by Charles Gibbon, deserves mention because of its well-contrived plot and the character of its excellent police detective, Hadden, a competent officer and a kindhearted man whom the reader frequently sees in his home-surroundings, in addition to following his investigations into the mysterious murder of Jean Gorbal. Hadden is clearly akin to Charles Dickens's Detective-Inspector Bucket, and Gibbon, like Dickens, was a frequent visitor at Scotland Yard, where he had personal friends among the Detective police.

Meanwhile, in America, that section of the general public which enjoyed reading 'novelettes' and cheap magazines found its tastes in detective fiction catered for by a new series of single-volume novels. These tales, which form a subdivision of that vast section of American popular fiction known as 'The Dime Novel,' stemmed to some extent from native sources. Fenimore Cooper was as popular in his own country as in Europe, and his many imitators introduced not only the redskins and white settlers familiar to Cooper's readers, but also, as time went on, the new antagonists that faced a fresh generation of Indians, 'western' heroes such as Buffalo Bill and Kit Carson, who could out-ride and out-wit their Indian foes or even surpass them at woodcraft.

Such stories were extremely popular until social changes came about in the last quarter of the nineteenth century. When settlers had turned the rolling prairies into cattle ranches, and the Red Indians, confined in reservations, were to a large extent shorn of their earlier, mainly fictional, glamour, stories of warring cowboys and Indians began to lose their appeal. Publishers of cheap fiction sought some new device, a fresh setting for tales of action and excitement. Just as the trails of the covered wagons were replaced by railroads, and the scattered stockaded settlements by rapidly growing towns, so the redskins were superseded by mail-robbers, bandits and cattle rustlers, and the cowboys by detectives, of whom the best known, in this country as well as in America, was Nick Carter.

The Adventures of Nick Carter are, for the most part, hybrid productions, the settings being purely American and the detective themes often derived from French sources. The man who invented 'Nick Carter,' John R. Coryell, was at one time under contract to write a million words a year, and did so! With such a tremendous output it is not surprising that he borrowed extensively from various suitable sources, from Ponson du Terrail and especially from Gaboriau, whose detective novels were widely read in America, where Chistern, a New York importer of foreign books, published translations almost as soon as the originals appeared in France.

Nick Carter first appeared in a serial called *The Old Detective's Pupil*, which Coryell wrote for the *New York Weekly* in 1884. The tale appealed so strongly to readers that the circulation of the *Weekly* improved remarkably, and as soon as this 'case' reached its successful climax further stories followed, Nick Carter, private investigator, becoming the hero of a series that continued for half a century, all of them nominally written by 'Nicholas Carter,' but actually the work of several authors who adhered closely to the approved pattern, the hero retaining almost unaltered the characteristics given to him by Coryell.

In the first story, Nick Carter was introduced as a young lad whose father had just been killed, and he set himself the task of discovering the murderers as a filial duty. He employed much the same methods as Père Tabaret and Monsieur Lecoq, describing his suspects in detail after a brief examination of the scene of the crime, finding a single (but very informative) hair, and identifiable shreds of material under the victim's fingernails, exactly as the Frenchmen had done in *L'Affaire Lerouge*. Lecoq was a master of disguise, employing it so habitually that only two or three of his colleagues at the *Sûreté* had ever seen his face as it really was, but Nick Carter carried the art to quite incredible lengths, and was able to masquerade convincingly as any character in the story, even as a woman. Rocambole, surpassing Lecoq in this respect, could assume a new identity at a moment's notice, but Nick Carter, and his assistants also, were clever enough to disguise themselves in the open street, without an instant's pause in the pursuit of their quarry. In some respects, Nick Carter resembles Rocambole even more closely than he does Lecoq. Both are incredibly clever linguists, for example. They have superhuman powers of mind and body, and perform similar feats of detection, yet they are both prone to find themselves trapped by the criminals they are hunting (which Lecoq never did), and have to be rescued from frightful peril by their faithful assistants.

The early Nick Carter stories, though without literary value, were nevertheless produced by men with experience and some skill in writing. Later examples, particularly those which were published in the twentieth century, sank to a much lower level. All of them, however, followed the original pattern fairly closely, opening in the middle of some sensational scene and building up from one excitement to another, with a little detective argument now and again. Their similarity was quite intentional, and was openly acknowledged on the back cover of the uniform, paper-backed volumes, where the following announcement appeared: —

'Nick Carter stands for an interesting detective story. The fact that the books in this line are so uniformly good is entirely due to the work of a specialist. The man who wrote these stories produced no other type of fiction. His mind was concentrated upon the creation of new plots and situations, in which his hero emerged triumphantly from all sorts of trouble, and landed the criminal just where he should be—behind bars. If your dealer cannot supply you with exactly the book you want, you are almost sure to find in his stock another title by the same author which you have not read.'

In other words, *The Adventures of Nick Carter* were written in conformity with a stock pattern for an uncritical public, and had two features, in particular, that never varied. 'The hero emerged triumphantly from all sorts of trouble,' danger to his person being implied, and 'the criminal must be landed just where he should be, behind bars.' There is no character study, and no trace of that romantic indulgence towards rogues which was such a strongly marked feature of English and French novels earlier in the century. Not until the twentieth century did an equivalent attitude find expression in American fiction. In the Nick Carter stories, the criminal is simply a 'bad man,' and prison is the right place for him. The pattern shows an unvarying sequence of crime, flight, pursuit and capture, with physical endurance more important than detective acumen.

*　　　　*　　　　*

Though the terms 'thriller' and 'detective novel' are sometimes used indiscriminately, it is desirable to find some line of demarcation between them. Nicholas Blake has expressed the thought-provoking opinion that 'detective fiction is read by those with a stake in the social system, the thriller by those who have none.'[1] It may, however, be advisable to look for a difference in the type of story, rather than the type of reader, and with the characteristic features of the Nick Carter stories in mind, it is possible to arrive at some conclusions on this point. Quite apart from any consideration of literary quality, the main differences between these somewhat analogous types of fiction lie partly in the subject matter, but more especially in the way that matter is presented, and in the relative importance given to the physical and the mental powers of the central figure. The 'thriller' always concerns dramatic crime; the detective story may also do so, or alternatively may deal with problems arising from other causes.

[1] In his Introduction to Howard Haycraft's *Murder for Pleasure*, London, Davies, 1942, p. xxiii.

The 'thriller' appeals chiefly to the reader's emotions; in detective fiction the primary appeal is to the reader's curiosity and to his logical faculties, though there may also be a secondary appeal to such emotions as apprehension and admiration. The hero of a 'thriller' gains his success by energetic action; the detective-hero gains his by taking thought, by bringing his intelligence to bear on the problem, sometimes not even needing to move from his chair.

Inevitably there is some over-lapping, and most detective heroes have periods when physical as well as mental effort is required. Even such figures as Reginald Fortune and Nero Wolfe, who are at pains to avoid physical exertion, find themselves forced on occasion to take action as well as thought, but it is their thought, more than their action, which solves the problem. Danger from the men they hunt may confront both types of hero, but the detective usually contrives to cope with such threats unaided, and caution saves him from anything worse than temporary inconvenience. The hero of a 'thriller,' however, frequently falls into his enemy's power, or allows himself to be trapped into highly perilous situations from which he has to be rescued by others.

While the early Nick Carter stories were reaching this country from America, English translations of Gaboriau's novels had become very popular in Australia, where Fergus Hume, a struggling young barrister with literary aspirations, learned from a Melbourne bookseller that these were his best selling lines.[1] After studying Gaboriau's works carefully, Hume produced his first attempt at a detective story, *The Mystery of a Hansom Cab* (1887). The book met with some local success, and the copyright was then sold to a group of London speculators, who formed themselves into 'The Hansom Cab Publishing Company' and re-issued the novel in this country, where it met with a phenomenal reception, some 400,000 copies being sold. Wealthy Australian settlers were much in the news at that time, which gave the story a topical interest, and Melbourne's dockland slums provided a background that was new in detective fiction, although the tale

[1] Cf. Hume's Introduction to the 1896 edition, London, Jarrold.

itself was not strikingly original, nor was the mystery by any means baffling. Its success brought Fergus Hume to England, where he produced more than a hundred detective stories which enjoyed a certain prestige, being written by the author of *The Mystery of a Hansom Cab,* but which showed no great skill in invention or plot construction, and are of little interest today.

It was in the same year, 1887, that Sherlock Holmes made his first appearance, but this great figure did not immediately capture the imagination of the reading public, and meanwhile the current popularity of detective stories inspired other authors whose work deserves mention. B. L. Farjeon (1838—1903), in *Great Porter Square* (1884), gave English fiction a new type of detective hero, a keen young newspaperman who made his own investigations into a mysterious murder in the hope of securing a 'scoop.' He is the 'special crime-reporter' of the *Evening Moon,* and most of the story is told in the form of extracts from his 'despatches' to that paper. Farjeon's *The Mystery of M. Felix* (1890) has a police officer as its hero and a well-devised plot, but perhaps his best work is *Samuel Boyd of Catchpole Square* (1899). It contains several police officials, including Inspector Robson and a persistent French *agent,* Joseph Pitou, but Farjeon again places most of the detective enquiries in the hands of a reporter, Dick Remington, who is helped by a very intelligent little girl. The character-drawing shows considerable skill, and the story is made more interesting by an unusual psychological approach. Remington finds strong reasons for suspecting various people, in turn, but each time his further investigations reveal so much to their credit that he comes to doubt his first conclusions.

One might well have expected that Robert Louis Stevenson (1850—1894), who was so keenly aware of the trends of his day in popular fiction, and whose best work so often skirts the very fringe of the detective story, would have produced an outstanding novel of this type. An interesting comment in *The Wrecker* (which he wrote in collaboration with his stepson, Lloyd Osbourne) reveals that he gave serious consideration to the subject, but finally rejected it because of the artistic limitations from which such fiction inevitably suffers.

'We had long been at once attracted and repelled by that very modern form of the police novel or mystery story, [. . .] attracted by its peculiar interest when done and the peculiar difficulties that attend its execution; repelled by that appearance of insincerity and shallowness of tone, which seems its inevitable drawback. For the mind of the reader, always bent to pick up clues, receives no impression of reality or life, [. . .] and the book remains enthralling, but insignificant, like a game of chess, not a work of human art.'[1]

In *The Wrecker*, which appeared in 1892 but may have been written some years earlier, the authors set out to write a 'police novel,' but their attempts to give it 'life' and 'reality' made it a tale of adventure, rather than a detective story. In detective fiction, the background is usually familiar to the reader, and the clues are such that he can at least hope to interpret them from his own general knowledge. *The Wrecker*, however, is a tale of the Marquesas Islands and the blue Pacific; of sabotage and salvage, piracy, murder and opium smuggling; money-making schemes involving bankruptcies and fraudulent insurance claims. The landsman-reader knows so little about the world of sailing ships that he can scarcely follow, much less anticipate, the conclusions of the men who investigate the various plots and counterplots. He cannot, for instance, determine for himself whether *The Flying Scud* was really wrecked or deliberately beached. He has no idea of the normal stores of a brig, or what articles a skipper invariably takes with him if he has to abandon ship. The reader, therefore, is not equipped to deduce the solution of the mystery, as he hopes to do when entertaining himself with such fiction, and *The Wrecker* fails, as a detective story, not because it lacks a well worked out detective theme, but because its setting, its clues and arguments, are too remote from the general knowledge of the average reader.

Stevenson and Lloyd Osbourne had already published a detective novel written in a rollicking, humorous vein. *The Wrong Box* (1888), its original title being *A Game of Bluff*. In it, two penurious nephews take the utmost care of their aged uncle because, if he lives a little longer, he will inherit a fortune that

[1] *The Wrecker*, Cassell, 1892, pp. 425-426.

they hope to acquire in due course. After a railway accident they find a body which they believe to be that of their uncle, and determine that no one shall suspect his death. (Actually, the old gentleman is unhurt, but has seized the opportunity of escaping from his irritating nephews). The unfortunate victim is never identified, but his body, concealed first in a water-butt and then in a locked piano, is sent from place to place, by train, delivery van or carrier's cart, in complete defiance of all probability, as well as of the normal canons of decency and decorum, until at last the cart is stolen, together with its incriminating load, and never heard of again.

This 'piece of judicious levity,' as the authors term it in their preface, is clearly a parody of contemporary detective stories, and, as such, is informative concerning the currently accepted view of this type of fiction, in particular that it was of French origin. All through *The Wrong Box* one character or another makes some facetious reference to 'French police fiction' or to its authors, in particular to Fortuné du Boisgobey. One young man in the story, 'inspired by the muse who presides over the police romance, a lady, presumably, of French extraction,' is himself the author of a detective novel called *Who Put Back the Clock?*,[1] in which the investigator bore the would-be apposite name of Robert Skill.

> 'To readers of a critical turn, Robert appeared scarce upon a level with his surname, but it is a difficulty of the police romance that the reader is always a man of such vastly greater ingenuity than the writer.'[2]

Just at the time when *The Wrong Box* was published, detective fiction was at a critical juncture in its history. There was a good deal of truth in the view expressed by Stevenson and Lloyd Osbourne that it was 'enthralling but insignificant,' and after a long period of popularity it had reached the dangerous point when it was beginning to be laughed at, parodied and made to

---

[1] This title may well have been an allusion to the central mystery in Du Boisgobey's *Le Coup de Pouce*, published in English translation by *Routledge's Railway Library*, 1884.
[2] P. 185 in the edition consulted, Longman, Green, 1895.

seem ridiculous. An American writer, T. B. Aldrich, much read in this country as well as in his own, had dealt detective fiction a shrewd blow in *The Stillwater Tragedy* (1880). It begins by following, quite seriously, the customary train of events. The crime is committed and discovered; the detective, Mr. Taggett, appears on the scene, carries out his investigations with meticulous thoroughness, and in due course reveals his discoveries and deductions. Unfortunately, they are all wrong! There is more than a hint of burlesque in such clues as Mr. Taggett's discovery of a half-burned match at the scene of the crime, and a box of similar matches in the room of his suspect. He counts them carefully, decides there is one missing and concludes it must be the one he has found, quite overlooking the fact that the matches have been in regular use since the 'fatal night,' if only to light the bedroom candles mentioned in the text.

Another American author, Ambrose Bierce (1842—1914?) in a volume of short stories, *Can Such Things Be?* (1893) wrote an even more broadly humorous example with the title 'My Favourite Murder' told by the dead man's nephew, who concludes his account with the 'surprise ending': — "Altogether, I cannot help thinking that, in point of atrocity, my murder of Uncle William has seldom been excelled."

Developments along such lines as these, with the central figure shown as a bungler or the subject treated humorously, would inevitably have brought the popularity of detective fiction to an end. Indeed, the vogue for the sensational 'police romance in the French manner,' fell sharply out of favour at this time. That the downward trend was halted, and that detective fiction entered, instead, on a new era of popularity, was almost entirely due to the work of Conan Doyle, who infused the *genre* with new vigour and gave it greater prestige than it had ever enjoyed. One particular feature of his stories had a far-reaching and immediate effect. In spite of the example of Poe and of Gaboriau, no English writer before Conan Doyle had created a detective-hero who appeared in a series of different tales. When *The Adventures of Sherlock Holmes* delighted English readers in the 1890's, they set a fashion for well-planned, well written short stories, with the same central figure displaying his detective skill in each of them.

Several writers quickly followed Conan Doyle's lead in this respect. The most prolific was "Dick Donovan," (Joyce Emmerson Muddock, 1843—1934), who from 1888 onwards related an almost interminable number of his own investigations in short stories that appeared in popular magazines, many of them in the *Strand*, which for some years published a 'Dick Donovan adventure' in almost every issue. Most of his comparatively simple mysteries concern the activities of sinister secret societies, or crimes committed unknowingly by people under the influence of drugs or of 'mesmerism.' Some long novels written in the third person, such as *The Man From Manchester* (1890), give his energies wider scope, but whatever their length the tales are generally trivial and unconvincing. "Dick Donovan" seldom displays any genuine aptitude for detection, and his reports of his own successes inevitably make him appear insufferably conceited.

In striking contrast is the work of Arthur Morrison (1863—1945) a distinguished journalist who was for a time on the staff of the *National Observer*. Side by side with his realistic, penetrating studies of crime and social conditions in London's East End, *Tales of Mean Streets* (1894) and *A Child of the Jago* (1896), he wrote a number of short detective stories around the activities of Martin Hewitt, a gentlemanly hero, once a solicitor's clerk, who displayed such skill in collecting evidence for his employer's clients that he started in business on his own account as a private consultant. His methods, and the cases he investigates, are less spectacular than those of Holmes, and he 'has no system beyond a judicious use of ordinary faculties,' but the stories related by his journalistic friend, Brett, show Martin Hewitt to be more akin to Sherlock Holmes than were any other detectives of the period. A circumstance that may have stressed this similarity in the eyes of contemporary readers is that the Martin Hewitt stories, which first appeared in the *Strand Magazine* between March and December, 1894, were illustrated by Sidney Paget, the artist who had already illustrated Conan Doyle's *The Adventures*

146

of Sherlock Holmes, published in the same magazine a year or so earlier. Arthur Morrison's stories were quickly re-issued in volume form, *Martin Hewitt, Investigator* in 1894, *The Chronicles of Martin Hewitt* in 1895, and *The Adventures of Martin Hewitt in* 1896.

There remains, in nineteenth century fiction, one other outstanding figure, the most remote and erudite detective of all, the high-born Russian exile, Prince Zaleski. He was created in the book of that name by Matthew Phipps Shiel, who had been studying surgery at Bart's Hospital and has related how he became 'sickened of knifing and gave it up, and lying idle one day, gazing at the sky, was given the idea to write my *Prince Zaleski.*'[1] The volume, published in 1895, presents three of Zaleski's investigations, or, rather, his flights of inductive reasoning, for in only one of them does he leave his couch. The atmosphere of the tales, their background of exotic grandeur fallen into disuse and decay, is much more in tune with the Tale of Terror of a hundred years earlier than with the practical work-a-day world of Sherlock Holmes or Martin Hewitt. Prince Zaleski is more of a recluse than Dupin (and of still more exalted birth) more out of touch with normal living, more pre-occupied with strange learning gleaned from distant ages and long-dead civilisations.

Shiel has acknowledged his debt to Edgar Allan Poe. As we have noticed earlier, he was probably also influenced by Eugène Sue, for the similarities between Sue's Prince Rodolphe, or his Prince of Hansfield, and Shiel's Prince Zaleski seem too striking to be due entirely to chance. But many of Zaleski's eccentricities may well be due to a desire on Shiel's part to make him as different as possible from Sherlock Holmes, who was in the first flush of his popularity when *Prince Zaleski* was written. Except that they shared an addiction to drugs, the contrast between the two men could scarcely be greater than it is. Holmes loves the busy streets of London; Zaleski buries himself in a solitary retreat. Holmes is a 'scientist' whose knowledge is applied to practical purposes; Zaleski's studies are so vague and abstruse as

[1] M. P. Shiel, *Science, Life and Literature,* Williams & Norgate, 1950, pp. 19-20.

to be almost beyond human understanding. The detection of crime is Holmes' most absorbing interest; Zaleski considers any such problem as an unwelcome interruption, and turns his mind to it only as a favour to his one personal friend, the anonymous narrator. Every detail of Holmes' face and figure is familiar to the reader; Prince Zaleski's appearance is nowhere described, and thus he remains a remote, unreal personality, who mingles prophecies with his detective deductions, for he possessed 'the unparalleled power not merely of disentangling in retrospect, but of unravelling in prospect, able to relate coming events with unimaginable minuteness of precision.' A further point of difference is that whereas Conan Doyle, and almost every other writer of detective fiction, uses plain, realistic language, Shiel's prose is ornate and polysyllabic, designed to conjure up an atmosphere of strange, unreal beauty, rather than to tell a straight-forward tale.

The stories themselves are equally remote from reality. In the first, *The Race of Orven,* Zaleski's knowledge of the symptoms of hereditary insanity may be accurate, his interpretation of psychological reactions may be convincing, but his grasp of practical matters is not invariably sound. It is, for example, inconceivable that the police who searched the earl's mansion would have missed a series of holes cut through floors and ceilings, or the bloodstains caused by the accident to the maid. Such discrepancies would hardly have been overlooked by readers who had learned from the Sherlock Holmes stories to expect a precise and feasible interpretation of the evidence.

Another feature which is at variance with the normal pattern of detective fiction is the haughty, class-conscious snobbery which, though possibly natural to a Russian prince like Zaleski, is completely out of place in a story of this type. Even if, in view of Zaleski's royal blood, we are prepared to overlook his contemptuous reference to 'the yokels, jabbering uncouthly together,' or his savage scorn of the hard-working ill-used maid— 'that poor specimen of humanity, a peering, hysterical caricature of a woman, we cannot accept his smooth generalisation that 'Earls' sons do not, in fact, go about murdering people,' for

Lord Randolph is an unscrupulous, dangerous and brutal criminal. When a villain of this calibre figures in a detective story, the reader expects him to be brought to justice, and does not find satisfying an ending which merely hints at this event.

The second story, *The Stone of the Edmundsbury Monks,* is more in the tradition of detective fiction, and concerns the mystery of a missing baronet. From a scrutiny of his diary, Zaleski discovers the reason for his disappearance and predicts his death at a specified time and place. In the third story, *S.S.,* the mystery is more horrifying, and the urgency so intense that, for the first time, Zaleski leaves his retreat and returns to the outside world. Only by the most intense mental concentration does he fathom the secrets of the Society of Sparta and bring to an end their schemes for mass murder, without, however, taking any steps to inform against those responsible. It is, apparently, a sufficient triumph for Zaleski that the Society will plan no further crimes.

There is no one quite like Zaleski. He is the quintessence of the inductive, analytical reasoner, a student with an immense store of learning, created for readers capable of grasping clues derived from a Latin quotation, a couple of words in Greek, or some inconsistency in a sketch of mythological figures. He is the detective for the intelligensia, the greatest possible contrast to Nick Carter, who is the detective of the uneducated. Each of them could appeal only to a limited section of the reading public, and neither could compare in popularity with their illustrious contemporary, Sherlock Holmes, who attracted readers of all classes of society and every educational level.

Several factors encouraged the remarkable growth of English detective fiction during the closing decades of the nineteenth century. The great scientific discoveries made at this time, particularly in the fields of chemistry, bacteriology and medicine (many of them concerned with preserving life and health or improving living conditions, and therefore of special interest to the general public) aroused lively admiration for men who were clever at finding things out, whatever their sphere of activity. The materialism of the period also had its effect, public opinion ranging itself increasingly strongly on the side of those whose function was to protect society from the depredations of criminals. A further point is that the changing economic conditions of the later nineteenth century created a vast, hard-worked, often poorly-paid section of the community, city dwellers for the most part, who looked to the Free Libraries then springing up in all large towns, or to the many cheap magazines of the day, to provide entertainment for their brief leisure, an escape from the narrow realities of their daily life, an escape which the detective story most readily supplied.

A further explanation for the rapid growth of the detective story during the 1890's lies in 'the cult of the individual' which manifested itself everywhere in English fiction at that time. Detective fiction is a medium that lends itself particularly well to expressing this 'individualism,' and it was precisely at this period that English writers began to place special emphasis upon the personality of their detective heroes, all of them amateurs, not members of an organisation, and therefore free to act as individuals. It was the figure of Prince Zaleski, Martin Hewitt, Sherlock Holmes, or even Dick Donovan, that monopo-lised the reader's interest, the plot of each story being devised to give one more instance of the hero's amazing powers of detection.

The individuality of the author himself acquired a new signi-ficance. Earlier in the nineteenth century, English writers of popular fiction were prone to conceal their names from their readers, and the title page of a novel might simply state, for example, *"A Secret of the Sea,* by the author of *In The Dead of Night,"* or *"Done in the Dark,* by the author of *Recommended to Mercy."* Even a writer as well-known as Miss M. E. Braddon observed the same convention, and the numerous romances that followed her first success were all described as being "by the author of *Lady Audley's Secret."* By the 1890's, however, this near-anonymity had become outmoded, and the writer's name, with very few exceptions, not only appeared on his work but also served to identify the specific type of story of which he was the inventor and sole producer. A "Fergus Hume story," an

"Arthur Morrison story," or a "Conan Doyle story," implied a tale of a particular pattern already familiar to the reader, and though Conan Doyle occasionally produced fiction of a different type, the general public expected "a Conan Doyle story" to be a tale about Sherlock Holmes.

At this period, perhaps to a greater degree than ever before, readers of popular fiction tended to limit their reading to whatever types of story best satisfied their individual preferences. For many people, then and later, their enjoyment of fiction depends largely upon the extent to which they can identify themselves mentally with the leading character, and this they may do more readily with a detective hero, particularly an amateur detective, than with almost any other type of hero, because the qualities on which his success is shown to depend, his powers of observation, deduction and intelligence, are precisely those which most people believe they themselves possess. Once the individuality of the detective had become the central point of interest, the individuality of the reader could find a special satisfaction by sharing in spirit his problems and his ultimate triumph.

Striking changes came about in detective fiction during the period reviewed in this chapter. At the beginning of the 1870's, when Sheridan Le Fanu's *Checkmate* appeared, few English novels gave an important place to a detective theme, and those that did made the investigator one of the normal characters in the story, who undertook the enquiry for personal reasons, on a single occasion only. In the 1890's, detective fiction was being produced in great quantity, and though some excellent novels of this type were written, for example Israel Zangwill's *The Big Bow Mystery* (1891), one of the best of the 'crime in a sealed room' problems, the great majority of detective stories were short. The chief, often the only, interest was the theme of detection; the detective himself, in that capacity, was the dominating figure in a series of 'cases,' and a recognisable pattern had been evolved which was followed almost without variation for the ensuing quarter of a century.

CHAPTER
IX

WOMEN WRITERS OF DETECTIVE
FICTION IN THE NINETEENTH CENTURY

When the outcry against 'Sensation Novels' was at its height in the 1850's and 1860's, contemporary critics were considerably disturbed because many of them were written by women. In spite of the notable precedent set by Mrs. Radcliffe at the end of the eighteenth century and the popularity of her Tales of Terror, mid nineteenth century publishers seemed to feel there was something peculiarly indelicate about tales of crime or criminals being written by a woman, and were reluctant to print them, though stories of social or domestic life were readily accepted.

Elizabeth Cleghorn Gaskell (1810—1865) was among the first contributors to Charles Dickens's *Household Words,* which published *Cranford* between December, 1851, and May, 1853. Her next work, a comparatively short tale, appeared in the Christmas number of *Household Words* for 1853, with the title *The Squire's Story,* and deserves special notice for its discreetly-handled detective interest. The wealthy stranger who has settled in a small country town regularly leaves home for a few days "to collect his rents," but the reader is given clues suggesting that he is really a notorious highwayman, and his riches are derived from armed robbery. During one of his expeditions he commits murder. and though there seems nothing to connect him with the crime, suspicion is aroused by indicative trifles, evidence is gathered exactly as in a detective story, until he betrays guilty knowledge of details not reported in the newspapers and is arrested. It is a neat little tale of crime and detection, though presented as a social commentary, thus escaping the stigma of 'sensationalism.'

Most of the melodramatic novels written by women during the latter half of the nineteenth century were of little value in themselves or for our purpose, except that they maintained the popularity of a background against which certain types of detective theme could show to advantage. In brief, they prepared the way for what may be called 'the domestic detective story,' in which the reader becomes acquainted with the normal daily life of the characters before the *motif* of a mysterious crime is introduced.

A few such novels did more than prepare the way. They travelled some distance in that direction, and enlivened the domesticity or social intrigues of their plot with a sensational crime, leading to investigations along detective lines, if not to the creation of a detective.

Of the hundreds of short stories and some forty novels written by Mrs. Henry Wood (1814—1887), scarcely more than one is instantly called to mind whenever her name is mentioned—*East Lynne*. It appeared as a serial in *Colborn's New Monthly Magazine* between 1860 and 1861, but its appearance in volume form was delayed by publishers' prejudice against 'sensation novels,' and it was rejected three times. Yet, when it was at last accepted and published by Richard Bentley, it was received with such enthusiasm that more than a million copies were sold during the author's lifetime.

Within the extensive framework of this romance is a well-constructed murder mystery. The problem is difficult, for years have elapsed since the crime, and an innocent man was, at the time, convicted on circumstantial evidence. New information is gradually discovered, an alias penetrated and an alibi proved false. Material witnesses must be traced before the case can be re-opened and the truth established. More interest is focussed upon the drama of these developments than upon the process of detection which brings them about, yet that process is clearly and logically followed through to a successful conclusion, and an orderly array of evidence is placed before the court at the trial which forms the culmination of this detective theme.

A point which links Mrs. Henry Wood with many later writers of detective fiction is her appreciation of what constitutes evidence, her accurate knowledge of the law. Her son commented on this detail in his biography: —

'The science and mystery of the Law had always possessed great charm and attraction for her. She followed out the points of any intricate case that might be going on with clearness and insight—in trials of mystery and complication quickly forming her opinion, which seldom proved wrong.'[1]

When *East Lynne* was published, the *Saturday Review* noticed this feature of the novel with considerable surprise: —

'What is more remarkable is that the legal proceedings taken when the murderer is finally discovered are all, or almost all, right. There is a trial with its preliminary proceedings, a real summing up, and a lively cross-examination. Mrs. Wood has an accuracy and method of legal knowledge which would do credit to many famous male novelists.'

Perhaps the most important of the many favourable reviews of *East Lynne* was that which appeared in the *Times* on January 25th, 1862. Very few current works of fiction were similarly honoured, and the novel at once became known throughout the English speaking world. A French translation quickly followed, and versions in other European languages were soon available. America gave the story an even more enthusiastic reception than it received in this country, both as a novel and as a play. Though none of Mrs. Wood's later works equalled *East Lynne* in popularity or in detective interest, one or two of her *Johnny Ludlow* stories gave some place to crime mysteries, and in *The Story of Charles Strange,* published posthumously in 1888, she wove together no fewer than five distinct problems and dealt skilfully with their ultimate solution.

The success of *East Lynne* had an immediate effect on the status of women fiction-writers, and also influenced 'sensation novelists' in general, especially in respect of plot construction. Many could, and did, imitate Mrs. Wood's descriptions of family affairs in aristocratic circles, with details of great estates, devoted servants, eccentric relatives and brilliant social events. Nor was it difficult to introduce a mysterious crime, with enough complications to fill three or even four volumes. But it required abilities of another calibre to create and develop a convincing

[1] C. W. Wood, *Memorials of Mrs. Henry Wood*, Bentley, 1894, p. 241.

detective theme, and most writers were content to reveal the explanation of the mystery through the confession of the guilty person, who forthwith committed suicide.[1] It is patent that in such a plot there is little or no room for a detective, and the great majority of these novels are outside our present scope, but one or two women writers of the period approached the *genre* sufficiently closely to merit consideration in this connection.

In the same year which saw the publication of *East Lynne*, there appeared another extremely popular novel of somewhat similar type, *Lady Audley's Secret* (1861). It was the first successful work of a young writer, Mary Elizabeth Braddon (1837—1915), who was to become even more prolific than Mrs. Henry Wood, for she published her eightieth (and last) full length romance, *The Green Curtain*, in 1911, when she was seventy-four. It was to Wilkie Collins's *The Woman in White* that Miss Braddon owed her inspiration for *Lady Audley's Secret*,[2] a melodramatic tale of bigamy, blackmail, murder and attempted murder. It contains nothing comparable to the detective theme in Collins's novel, but it deserves mention here because in it Miss Braddon devised an original method of presenting the story. Lady Audley enjoys an honourable social position and the complete trust of her elderly doting husband, but almost from the opening pages the reader is made aware of her real character. He suspects her of past crimes, watches her plan and carry out new ones, and his mounting suspense arises out of his uncertainty as to whether her schemes will succeed, and how, if at all, her guilt can be proved. Eventually she meets retribution through the efforts of a former victim, whose success is due to coincidence and good luck, rather than to any detective skill.

As one romance after another flowed from Miss Braddon's pen, she placed more emphasis upon the steps whereby the guilt of her villains is discovered. Her plots are conventional in the sense that evil-doers are all brought to justice, while the virtuous

[1] So general did this pattern become that literary critics freely commented upon it. Cf. *inter alia* the *Athenaeum*, June 12th, 1875, ' Our modern novelists have abolished the gallows, and suicide is almost invariably the penalty '.

[2] Cf. her discussion with Joseph Hatton, Editor of *The Gentleman's Magazine*, related in his *Old Lamps and New*, Hutchinson, 1890, p. 213.

invariably triumph in the final chapters. The central mystery always concerns a secret crime—blackmail, fraud, or murder—and various characters do their best to solve whatever part of the problem affects them personally, but Miss Braddon never makes it the function of one particular figure to view the puzzle as a whole, or to collect and co-relate evidence in the manner of a detective.

Miss Braddon was a solicitor's daughter, and, like Mrs. Henry Wood, had a good working knowledge of English law. Perhaps her greatest influence upon detective fiction lies in the use she made of that knowledge, for she showed remarkable ingenuity in devising highly original ways of breaking the law, making the technique of crime so interesting that she was savagely attacked by contemporary critics as the most dangerous of the sensation novelists, and accused of encouraging criminals. But her appreciative public held a different opinion, and her novels were so popular that for almost three decades she was described in current periodicals as 'The Queen of the Circulating Libraries.'

Several of her later books give more place to the detection of crimes than to their sensational or technical aspects. In *A Strange World* (1875) the hero falls under suspicion in the first volume, and the reader is entertained by the conflicting attemps at detection by the hero and concealment by the villain until the final chapters of the third. *An Open Verdict* (1878) shows the heroine suspected of having caused her father's death. Her innocence is at last established, though the detective work that clears her of suspicion is overshadowed by her plans for punishing those who doubted her. The balance swings in the other direction in *Just As I Am* (1880), the love story of Morton Blake and Dulcie being less important to the plot than the mysterious crime and the detection of the murderer.

In *Willard's Weird* (1885) there are two love affairs and two strange crimes. Evidence has to be discovered in Paris, and Miss Braddon unravels the sensational clues in a manner very reminiscent of Gaboriau or Fortuné du Boisgobey. In so doing, she may have had in mind a wish to please her wide circle of French readers, for she was proud of the success of French translations of her novels, and was in close touch with literary circles in Paris. *Like and Unlike* (1887) tells of a bloodless murder that nearly succeeds in baffling detection, and the young nobleman who so carefully plans 'the perfect crime' is finally proved guilty. Almost without exception Miss Braddon's later novels deal with ingenious crimes and the circumstances that lead to the punishment of the criminal, and though she did not produce a detective hero, she certainly made some contribution to the detective fiction of the 1870's and 1880's.

Only one or two other women writers in England at this period followed Miss Braddon's lead in this respect, but there are points of special interest in *The Land of the Leal* (1878), by Miss Helen Mathers (1853—1920). The volume contains two comparatively short and unconnected tales (an innovation in itself) and in the first of them, *As He Comes up the Stair*, Miss Mathers used a technique which does not seem to have been employed before that time. The story is told retrospectively, from the condemned cell, by a woman wrongly convicted of murdering her husband and his gipsy sweetheart. The husband has, in fact, been poisoned by the gipsy, and the wife shows considerable detective skill in discovering the truth, but falls under suspicion herself. Miss Mathers shows remarkable perception in depicting the thought-processes of the unfortunate woman, and for this alone the story deserves notice. The trial is related in detail, rather inadvisably in view of Miss Mathers' inaccurate impressions of judicial procedure. The same handicap mars the second tale, *Stephen Hatton*, in which a man is convicted on circumstantial evidence and executed, after which his supposed victim is found alive. Contemporary reviewers, who were beginning to expect writers of such fiction to have accurate legal knowledge, pointed out with some care just how far Miss Mathers was in error in her presentation of these matters.

Miss E. S. Drewry, in *The Death Ring* (1881) created a clever private detective, and this work could be considered an exciting detective novel if only the writer had not revealed, far too early in the story, details which would have been better concealed until the end. But Miss Drewry not only chose a title that disclosed the means, and indicated the identity of the murderer in the opening chapters, she went so far as to quote in her Preface an extract from the *Standard* describing an ancient ring lately discovered in Paris, which would inflict a poisoned scratch, causing death. It is by no means unusual for detective stories to be based upon such items found in newspapers, but by giving the explanation before the puzzle Miss Drewry sacrificed the element of mystery and deprived her readers of what could have been an entertaining problem.

A far clearer conception of how a detective novel should be constructed is shown in the work of an American writer, Anna Katharine Green (1846—1935), who exercised a considerable influence upon detective fiction in her own country and in England. She was the daughter of a distinguished defence lawyer of Brooklyn, and almost her first attempt at fiction, *The Leavenworth Case* (1878), achieved a remarkable success. She was the first woman to write a full-length detective story, and she described *The Leavenworth Case* in that way on the title page. Early in 1879 the book was re-issued in London, and her later novels were published more or less simultaneously on both sides of the Atlantic. While ostensibly obeying the contemporary convention that a full length novel should consist of several volumes, she made each 'volume' short enough to allow the whole story to be contained within one pair of covers. Almost without exception, the novels we have considered earlier were first issued in serial form, but *The Leavenworth Case* made its first appearance in the form of a complete detective novel in one volume.

In some respects Miss Green's novels resemble those of Mrs. Henry Wood and Miss Braddon in their introduction of such melodramatic features as guilty secrets behind a façade of wealth and luxury, unjust suspicions, dramatic revelations and noble reconciliations, but Miss Green uses them merely to provide a background and create the mystery. The paramount interest is clearly the theme of detection, and all her stories of this type are constructed upon a fairly uniform plan. A sensational puzzle is placed before the reader at the earliest possible moment; one enigma leads on to others even more baffling; false trails and temporary setbacks delay the investigations, but in the final chapters the detective triumphantly unmasks the criminal, generally someone quite unsuspected until that moment. Dickens had made a special explanatory chapter the culmination of the detective theme in *Bleak House;* Collins had done much the same in *The Woman in White* and *The Moonstone;* Le Fanu had gone much further in *Checkmate,* but in none of these does the detective theme monopolize the reader's attention so completely as in Miss Green's novels, and in her work we can discern for the first time, in its entirety, the pattern that became characteristic of most English detective novels written during the following fifty years.

Anna Katharine Green certainly knew the detective stories of her fellow-countryman, Edgar Allan Poe, and one of her shorter tales, *The Mayor's Wife,* contains a cryptogram worked out in the same way as the one in *The Gold Bug.* In *The Leavenworth Case,* the murderer needed to dispose quickly of two incriminating items, a letter and a key, and he reasoned in precisely the same way as the Minister D—— in *The Purloined Letter:* —

'Hide them? I would not try to. Instead of that I would put them in plain sight, trusting to that very fact for their being overlooked. Making the letter into lighters, I carried them into the spare room and placed them in a vase. The key I placed within the ornamental metal-work of the gas-bracket.'[1]

Like Poe, Miss Green generally constructed her mysteries around a sensational murder, and worked out the explanation step by step, in logical sequence. Dupin (and also Lecoq) had figured in a series of different tales, and Miss Green followed this example, making her Mr. Gryce the central figure in several novels. But she did not give him an admiring friend to chronicle his exploits, nor did she begin her tale by relating anecdotes to illustrate his detective powers, as Poe did for Dupin, and as Conan Doyle did in later years for Sherlock Holmes. In this respect, and in making her detective a police officer, Miss Green was more akin to Gaboriau, whose tales of M. Lecoq had been well known in

[1] *The Leavenworth Case,* London, Nicholson, 1879, p. 241.

America for some ten years before she began to write in similar vein. His influence is also reflected in other aspects of her work, particularly in her concentration on intricately woven plots and in making her secondary characters 'types,' rather than individuals. In one or two points she improved upon Gaboriau's technique, for she kept her plots well within the bounds of probability, and contrived to reduce to a minimum the tiresome, but almost inevitable, passages relating the past histories of those concerned in the crime.

The Leavenworth Case opens dramatically when news of Mr. Leavenworth's murder is brought to his lawyer, Everett Raymond, who relates the story. The plot is unfolded skilfully with steadily increasing tension, and the atmosphere of the novel is so modern that little touches which reveal its period are encountered almost with a sense of shock. For example, the fact that Mr. Leavenworth had installed gas lighting in one or two of his private rooms is considered an ostentatious extravagance, the rest of the house being lighted 'in the ordinary way, with paraffin candles.' The police and the coroner cannot understand why a business man should employ a private secretary, for 'such an office in this country is not a common one.'

Mr. Ebenezer Gryce, 'one of our city detectives,' is introduced very early in the story, and at once assumes the leading rôle, by virtue of his personality as well as his official position. He is a quiet, competent, middle-aged man, quite unlike Dupin or Lecoq, and far more akin to Charles Dickens's Detective-Inspector Bucket. Miss Green's comment on Mr. Gryce's first appearance shows clearly that a popular conception of a fictional detective already existed in the minds of American readers, and, like so many detective-heroes, Mr. Gryce was to be as different as possible from that conception.

> 'He was not the thin, wiry individual with a shrewd eye that seems to plunge into the core of your being, and pounce at once upon its hidden secret, that you are doubtless expecting to see. Mr. Gryce was a portly, comfortable personage with an eye that never pounced . . .'[1]

[1] *Ibid.*, p. 10.

His reputation precedes him, and Mary Leavenworth at their first meeting greets him thus: —

> 'Sir, I hear that you have great talents: that you can ferret out the real criminal from a score of doubtful characters, and that nothing can escape the penetration of your eye.'[1]

Mr. Gryce is sagacious, patient and imperturbable, with a mild, gentle manner that wins him the confidence of women in particular. He is hard-working rather than brilliant, and when at a loss he likes to arrange dramatic surprises for his suspects which usually prove informative. He is a pleasant, likeable human being, convincing as a detective and not lacking in strength or dignity. He believes, however, that his profession carries a social stigma, and discusses his difficulties in this respect with the young lawyer whose assistance he hopes to gain, commenting frankly that neither he nor any of his colleagues can ever hope to 'pass for a gentleman.[2]

In this regard, Mr. Gryce is certainly not a descendant of Poe's detective, the Chevalier C. Auguste Dupin, who was on visiting terms with the illustrious Minister D——, nor of Detective-Inspector Bucket or Sergeant Cuff, men of modest social status as private individuals, but fully capable, in their official capacity, of talking on equal terms with people of the highest rank. The memoirs of that most famous of all American detectives, Allan Pinkerton, do not convey the impression that in the democratic United States, during the 1870's, competent police officers suffered under such handicaps as Mr. Gryce describes. It may be that in exclusive Brooklyn, Miss Green's home, social distinctions were more rigidly observed, but it seems far more probable that, having little or no personal knowledge of the police of her own country, she was simply reflecting an impression she had gained from Gaboriau, possibly also from Balzac and from Dumas, about the position of the police in France.

However, just as Dumas' M. Jackal was assisted by Salvator, Mr. Gryce solves his difficulty by enlisting the help of the gentlemanly

[1] *Ibid.*, p. 61.
[2] Cf. *Ibid.*, p. 82.

Mr. Raymond, while the less dignified detective work falls to the lot of Gryce's subordinate, "Mr. Q.", a young man who rushes energetically here and there, following clues and collecting information for his chief, stooping on occasion to methods which are questionable, as, for instance, when he clambers over roofs to peer into windows, or searches rooms which he has no legal right to enter. With Mr. Raymond's co-operation in exalted spheres and the help of Mr. Q. in more menial researches, Mr. Gryce manages the case efficiently. He can talk as familiarly of firearms as of the 'science of probabilities'; has a good technical knowledge of such matters as the various grades of writing paper, and the distinctive ash that each type would form if burned; and knows business routine as well as he understands human nature.

In *The Leavenworth Case*, Anna Katharine Green not only made her detective the leading figure and formulated a plan of construction that later became conventional. She also introduced characters and incidents that were new in her day, though they have since become familiar in novels of this type: the rich old man, killed when on the point of signing a new will; the body in the library; the dignified butler with his well-trained staff; detailed medical evidence as to the cause and estimated time of death; the coroner's inquest and the testimony of expert witnesses; the authority on ballistics who can identify the gun that fired the shot. Miss Green even included a sketchmap of the scene of the crime and a reproduction of the torn-off fragment of a letter, not unlike the one that later occupied Sherlock Holmes's attention in *The Reigate Squires*. It is rather remarkable to find such an assemblage of characteristic features in the first novel of this young American writer of detective fiction.

There followed a long sequence of novels from her pen, among the best of them being *A Strange Disappearance* (1879), *The Mill Mystery* (1886) and *Behind Closed Doors* (1887). *The Doctor, his Wife and the Clock* (1893), though originally published as a slim volume, is little more than a short story in which Mr. Gryce personally relates one of his earliest cases, scarcely a successful one. A mysterious murder has been caused through an error made by a blind doctor, and though Gryce's enquiries lead him to suspect the truth, he fails to prevent or even to foresee the tragic *dénouement*.

That Affair Next Door (1897) is a long novel in which Mr. Gryce figures with some prominence, his detective work being at first handicapped and later assisted by a woman amateur detective, Miss Amelia Butterworth, who probes the mystery from motives of curiosity. It is possible that, before creating this character, Miss Green may have read a small book published in London in 1861, *The Experiences of a Lady Detective*, the author hiding behind the coy pseudonym of 'Anonyma.'[1] The heroine of these slight tales was a Mrs. Paschall who darted busily here and there to solve various fairly simple problems, and was distinguished by her regard for 'ladylike conduct' and her personal appearance, rather than by any detective skill.

Miss Green created a far more entertaining and perspicacious amateur detective in Amelia Butterworth, a spinster of good family, uncertain age and enquiring mind who narrates the story of *That Affair Next Door*. When the body of an unknown girl is discovered in the house next to her own, she determines to learn for herself all the circumstances behind the mystery. She soon finds herself in disagreement with Mr. Gryce, the officer in charge of the police investigation, but their initial antipathy develops into mutual respect, and she helps him by pointing out clues he would not have noticed himself—the dead woman's 'indoor shoes that had recently been acquainted with the pavement,' and her hat which, though soiled and crushed, was nevertheless being worn for the first time, since it had only once been pierced by a hatpin. Miss Butterworth, through her social contacts, obtains information to which Mr. Gryce has no access, and though they are often at cross purposes they each contribute materially to the eventual solution of the problem.

In a later novel, *Lost Man's Lane* (1898), Mr. Gryce seeks Miss Butterworth's help to fathom the mystery surrounding the disappearance, one after the other, of several visitors to a small

---

[1] Charles H. Clarke was either the editor or publisher. Michael Sadleir, in an essay on ' Yellow-Backs ', (*New Paths in Book Collecting*, Constable, 1934, p. 159) mentions that ' Anonyma ' was probably a syndicate, for a long series of cheap volumes ' by Anonyma ' had appeared by 1864.

country town. The suspense is fostered by such Radcliffiana as a gloomy mansion with vast, neglected rooms and hidden trap-doors; sinister bloodstains on the floor of a locked apartment; a secret midnight burial; even a 'phantom coach,' later accounted for rationally. But the chief interest lies in the detective work carried out with intelligence and courage by Amelia Butter-worth, who shows herself a worthy forerunner of those shrewd observers Miss Marple, Miss Climpson and Hildegarde Withers, of half a century later.

There have been very few convincing women detectives in fiction, and Amelia Butterworth, notwithstanding her occasional prim fussiness, is a pleasing member of that small group, and one of the earliest.

Almost at the end of her long life, Miss Green created in *The Golden Slipper* (1915) another, far less competent, woman detective, Violet Strange, whose successes were largely due to her remarkably sagacious bloodhound. The tale follows much the same plan of construction as Miss Green's earlier novels, but the volume is of minor interest, except as showing that a manner of presentation and a style of writing that were new in 1879 had become old-fashioned, almost antiquated, by 1915, so greatly had detective fiction changed between those dates, particularly in England.

These changes began to make themselves felt far earlier, and were sweeping in their effect. It was not only that the 'domestic' background for fiction of this type, so much used between the 1860's and 1880's, had fallen almost completely out of favour by the closing decade of the nineteenth century, and did not become popular again until the second quarter of the twentieth. The full-length detective novel itself suffered a similar, though less prolonged, eclipse, for the magazine reading multitudes of the 1890's preferred short stories. Even Sherlock Holmes failed to surmount this intangible barrier when he was first introduced in the novels *A Study in Scarlet* (1887) and *The Sign of Four* (1889), but when he became the hero of a series of short detective stories in the *Strand Magazine* in 1891, he was at once received with tremendous acclaim.

The great and growing demand was for short stories presenting a sequence of individual 'cases,' all dealt with by the same
'specialist-consultant' on detective problems. An immediate
result of this trend was that the detective himself became the
real centre of interest. The 'cases' varied, but the familiar, dominant figure remained the same, greeted by the reader as an
old friend whom he greatly admired. The popular detective hero
of the period was not only a brilliant analytical reasoner, but
could also draw upon an almost inexhaustible fund of specialised
technical knowledge about such matters as the varieties of
tobacco ash, the principles of ballistics or the workings of
machinery. Above all, he tended to become more and more of a
'scientist,' seeking evidence in a test-tube or under the lens of a
microscope. Such a hero could be convincingly portrayed only
by a writer who possessed scientific knowledge, and at that time
the path to a scientific education, particularly in medicine, was
still closed to women.

At the turn of the century and for some years later, many of
the notable writers of detective fiction in English were men with
long years of specialised training and experience in science, often
in medicine. Doctor Arthur Conan Doyle created Sherlock
Holmes while waiting for patients to arrive at his surgery.
Richard Austin Freeman was a surgeon with a distinguished
professional career, before he began writing of Doctor John
Thorndyke, the specialist in medical jurisprudence. Such men
were familiar with the facilities of a laboratory, and could often
describe scientific experiments—chemical analysis of material
clues, for example, or tests to identify poisons—with an accuracy
born of knowledge. Women at that time could not, and it is
therefore hardly surprising that the advent of the 'scientific'
detective brought to an end the period during which this type
of fiction was first influenced by women writers.

The writers considered in this chapter, who were eagerly read
by thousands of their contemporaries, influenced the development of the detective novel, rather than the shorter detective
story, and though their effect was interrupted in the 1890's for
almost two decades, yet it made itself felt later. The success of

the detective investigations related in their novels depended upon a shrewd application of common sense to a puzzling problem, an urge to satisfy curiosity, and a quick eye for such informative details as sudden changes in household routine, an unusual choice of items on an invalid's breakfast tray, or the talk of a frightened child. Their skill lay in assessing the implications of an odd circumstance or an unexpected human reaction, and thus they played some part in fore-shadowing the non-scientific, 'intuitional' or 'psychological' detectives of the twentieth century, such as Chesterton's Father Brown, who appeared when the popularity of the purely scientific detective had begun to wane.

It is noticeable that there is no Frenchwoman among the authors considered here, though during the same period there were in France many outstanding women writers of other types of fiction. Was this because of national differences in temperament, in education, in social or cultural background? A different assessment of the purpose and scope of fiction? There must be reasons to account for this discrepancy, and they may be the same reasons which explain why, though detective fiction was appreciably gaining popularity in England and America before the end of the nineteenth century, in France it was not recognised as an acceptable literary *genre* until the second quarter of the twentieth, a matter which will be considered in a later chapter.

CHAPTER
X

SHERLOCK HOLMES

There are in literature certain characters who have come to possess a separate and unmistakable identity, whose names and personal qualities are familiar to thousands who may not have read any of the works in which they appear. Among these characters must be included Sherlock Holmes, who has acquired in the minds of countless readers of all nationalities the status of an actual human being, accepted by many in the early years of the twentieth century as a living contemporary, and still surviving fifty years later with all the glamour of an established and unassailable tradition, the most convincing, the most brilliant, the most congenial and well-loved of all the detectives of fiction. Interest in Sherlock Holmes still persists, and has, indeed, become a cult that has been carried to rather remarkable lengths.

From internal evidence in the stories, putative and inferential rather than explicit, the date of his birth has been taken as January 8th, 1854. On January 8th, 1954, the B.B.C. broadcast a special programme 'in honour of his hundredth birthday,' with 'reminiscences' of Sherlock Holmes by 'one of his old school friends,' and by 'his old German teacher of the violin.' 'Lord Peter Wimsey' related that, as a child of eight, he himself had consulted the great detective about a lost kitten. Each speaker expressed a hope that the master, celebrating his birthday in his quiet Sussex home, was himself listening to the broadcast. Has any other character in fiction been so widely accepted as a living celebrity? The Sherlock Holmes Society of London, feeling that the evidence as to the date of January 8th was not entirely

GENERAL FOOTNOTE—When reference is made to Sir Arthur Conan Doyle's stories of Sherlock Holmes, a footnote will indicate the page on which the appropriate passage appears in one of the two Omnibus Volumes: *The Sherlock Holmes Short Stories*, Murray, 1928. and *The Sherlock Holmes Long Stories*, Murray, 1929. An initial S. indicates a reference to the first of these, and an initial L. a reference to the second. The title of the particular story will also be given.

conclusive, held their 'centenary' celebration dinner on the 15th, but their New York counterparts, 'The Baker Street Irregulars,' agreed with the B.B.C. in accepting the 8th as the true anniversary.

All the world knows the famous consulting rooms at No. 221b, Baker Street, Marylebone, where the troubled and the perplexed brought their problems to be solved by Sherlock Holmes and preserved for posterity by his fellow-lodger, friend and chronicler, Dr. Watson. When plans were being considered for the Festival of Britain in 1951, the St. Marylebone Borough Council debated whether to mark the occasion by a display showing municipal progress in the borough, or by a Sherlock Holmes Exhibition, 'to honour their most distinguished resident.' The latter plan was triumphantly carried out, to the great delight of thousands of enthusiasts who flocked to a restored 'No. 221b Baker Street,' to see with their own eyes the consulting room of the great detective who 'kept his cigars in the coal-scuttle, his tobacco in the toe end of a Persian slipper and his unanswered correspondence transfixed by a jack-knife into the very centre of his wooden mantelpiece.' There, too, were his dressing gown, deer-stalker cap and Inverness cape; his newspapers, test-tubes and retorts, his magnifying glass and that treasured companion of his introspective hours, his Stradivarius.

Later writers have attempted to add to the sixty-odd cases related by Sir Arthur Conan Doyle,[1] but to enthusiasts of Holmesiana the detective himself provides an even more entertaining problem, and a fresh field for ingenuity has been found in interpreting, by Holmes' own methods of analytical reasoning, the casual comments that occur in the stories as to his ancestry, his immediate relatives, his education and personal background.

---

[1] Cf. (*inter alia*) *The Misadventures of Sherlock Holmes*, by ' Ellery Queen ', 1944. *Two Unrecorded Adventures*, ' Christmas Eve ', and ' The Strange Case of the Megatherium Thefts ', included in a volume by S. C. Roberts, (Vice Chancellor of Cambridge University and Master of Pembroke College), *Holmes and Watson*, Oxford University Press, 1953.
The Exploits of Sherlock Holmes, Adrian Conan Doyle and John Dickson Carr, first published as a series of short stories in the *Evening Standard*, January 1954, re-issued in volume form, London, John Murray, 1954; New York, Random House, 1954.

Several authors, among them some of the best known detective fiction writers, have exercised their powers of deduction in producing his 'biography'; in placing his recorded cases in chronological order (a highly controversial matter) and in examining certain aspects of his personality and career.[1]

But this popularity did not begin as soon as the first Sherlock Holmes story was written, and though Conan Doyle had confidence in his hero from the start, even he was almost frustrated by the obstacles that hindered the first appearance of the great detective's name in print. Arthur Conan Doyle (1859—1930), after studying at Edinburgh where he gained his M.B. in 1881 and his M.D. in 1885, was struggling to establish himself in medical practice at Southsea when he began writing in order to occupy his over-abundant leisure. By 1886 he had already published several short stories, many of them anonymously, and had completed a full-length novel. *The Firm of Girdlestone* which was consistently rejected by every publisher to whom it was sent. To quote Sir Arthur Conan Doyle's own comment: —

'I felt now that I was capable of something fresher and crisper and more workmanlike. Gaboriau had rather attracted me by the neat dove-tailing of his plots, and Poe's masterful detective, M. Dupin, had from boyhood been one of my heroes. But could I bring an addition of my own? I thought of my old teacher, Joe Bell, of his eagle face, of his curious ways, of his eerie trick of spotting details. If he were a detective he would surely reduce this fascinating but unorganised business to something nearer to an exact science. I would try if I could get this effect.' [. . .] It is all very well to say that a man is clever, but the reader wants to see examples of it, such examples as Bell gave us every day in the wards. The idea amused me. What should I call the fellow? [. . .] First it was Sherringford Holmes then it was Sherlock Holmes.

[2] Cf. Father Ronald Knox, ' Studies in the Literature of Sherlock Holmes ' included in a volume of *Essays in Satire*, 1928. S. C. Roberts: *Life of Sherlock Holmes*, O.U.P., 1930, and *Life of Dr. Watson*, London, Faber, 1931. Both these are included with other essays on Sherlock Holmes in *Holmes and Watson*, O.U.P., 1953. Guy Warrack, *Sherlock Holmes and Music*, London, Faber, 1947. *Baker Street, Studies* (Edited by H. W. Bell), London, Constable, 1947, which includes ' Holmes ' College Career ', by Dorothy L. Sayers. ' The Mystery of Mycroft ' by Ronald V. Knox, and ' Sherlock Holmes and the Fair Sex ,' by S. C. Roberts.
Gavin Brend, *My Dear Holmes: A study in Sherlock*, Allen & Unwin, 1951.

He could not tell his own exploits, so he must have a commonplace comrade as a foil. [. . .] A drab, quiet name for
this unostentatious man. Watson would do. So I had my
puppets and wrote my *Study in Scarlet*.'[1]

To his disappointment, this book also failed to please the publishers to whom he sent it, until at last Messrs. Ward Lock
offered him £25 for the copyright if he would agree to a delay
of some fifteen months before publication.

Certainly the offer was not attractive, but it was at least an
offer, and it might well not have been made at all. The chief
editor of Messrs. Ward Lock, Professor G. T. Bettany, passed
the manuscript to his wife, who was herself a writer and critic
and found the story very much to her taste. In deference, then,
to a woman's opinion, and remembering, no doubt that a large
proportion of fiction-readers are women, the firm accepted the
story, the size of their offer and the delay in publication indicating their estimate of its importance. Had the tale not chanced
to be placed in Mrs. Bettany's hands, had her views not carried
weight, or had Conan Doyle himself refused the suggested terms,
then *A Study in Scarlet* would almost certainly have joined *The
Firm of Girdlestone* as 'a dishevelled mass of manuscript at the
back of a drawer,' and English detective fiction would have
missed the outstanding figure whose adventures entertained the
whole civilised world.

A Study in Scarlet duly appeared as *Beeton's Xmas Annual*
for 1887 and in 1888 was published as a novel. It received some
favourable comment, but was not recognised by critics in this
country as having any significance. It did, however, attract the
attention of an American publishing firm, and Conan Doyle was
invited to write a novel for *Lippincott's Magazine,* which in 1889
published his second tale of Sherlock Holmes and Dr. Watson,
The Sign of Four.[2] The work was produced in volume form in
London during 1890,[3] and it is interesting to note that the personality and original methods of the chief character made so

[1] Sir Arthur Conan Doyle, *Memories and Adventures,* Hodder & Stoughton, 1924,
   p. 74.
[2] Conan Doyle's original title was *The Sign of the Four.*
[3] By Stephen Blackett.

slight an impression on at least one eminent literary critic that he reviewed the book in terms of moderate approval without mentioning Sherlock Holmes at all![1] A second edition of the novel did not appear until 1892, after the first series of short stories in the *Strand Magazine* had made this detective the most popular figure in current fiction.

Sir Arthur Conan Doyle himself did not regard his detective stories as having any special importance. Indeed, he said in 1924: "I believe that if I had never touched Holmes, who has tended to obscure my higher work, my position in literature would at the present moment be a more commanding one."[2] As early as 1887 he was devoting his energies to writing historical novels, which seemed to him the one way of combining 'literary dignity' with 'scenes of action and adventure.' *Micah Clarke* was published in 1889, followed in 1890 by *The White Company*, but these, though moderately successful, did not provide Conan Doyle with a sufficient financial reward. Accordingly he thought of the idea of offering to the *Strand Magazine* a series of short detective stories, each of them relating a separate 'adventure' of the same central figure, Sherlock Holmes.

This was a brilliant plan of construction, far more effective than a sequence of disconnected tales, and maintaining all the advantages, with none of the disadvantages, of the serials upon which most monthly magazines of the period relied as a means of keeping up their regular circulation. The danger of a serial lay in the fact that a reader who missed even one instalment almost inevitably lost the thread of the story, and consequently his interest. By visualising each 'instalment' as a complete short story about the same hero, Conan Doyle brought up to date, and improved upon, the method first adopted by Edgar Allan Poe.

Conan Doyle greatly admired Poe and had studied his work, in particular the construction of his Dupin stories, all of them short, with the same detective-hero in each, though too few in number to constitute a 'series' such as Conan Doyle now had

[1] Cf. *The Athenaeum*, Dec. 3rd, 1890, p. 773.
[2] Cf. *Memories and Adventures*, p. 81.

in mind. The short story had been slow to appear as a distinct literary form in England, where the long three-volume novel had, almost from the beginning of the century, been the only popular type of fiction. Sir Walter Scott and Charles Dickens each included notable short stories within the framework of full-length novels, usually presenting them as tales told to relieve the tedium of a journey, or to pass an hour of leisure around a fire at the end of the day, but such brief narratives, if given a separate existence, found no favour with the general public until the late 1880's, when the number of successful magazines, which could use short stories, began to increase rapidly.

Yet there is much to be said for the strength and artistic completeness of the short story, as Poe had pointed out: —

'If any literary work is too long to be read at one sitting, we must be content to dispense with the immensely important effect derivable from unity of impression, for if two sittings be required, the affairs of the world interfere, and anything like totality is at once destroyed.'[1]

The detective story, perhaps more than any other type of story, gains an additional force if it can maintain this 'unity of impression,' for its subject matter is in essence episodic. It is to Conan Doyle's influence, and the examples provided by his *Adventures of Sherlock Holmes,* that the sudden immense popularity of the short detective story in the 1890's must be attributed.

He found that the plan he had conceived was by no means easy to carry out.

'The difficulty [. . .] was that every story really needed as clearcut and original a plot as a longish book would do. One cannot without effort spin plots at such a rate. [. . .] I would not write a Holmes story without a worthy plot, and without a problem which interested my own mind.'[2]

To have devised a 'worthy plot' and an 'interesting problem' for some sixty tales of Sherlock Holmes is a truly remarkable achievement. How did Doyle find the material from which to

[1] In his essay on ' The Philosophy of Composition ', *The Works of Edgar Allan Poe,* London, Chatto & Windus, 1872, p. 662.
[2] *Memories and Adventures,* p. 97.

create so many original stories with little if any duplication? His memoirs tell us very little on this point, except as to his having based Sherlock Holmes upon 'my old teacher, Joe Bell.' But this well-known Edinburgh surgeon disclaimed most of the credit, protesting that his own powers of observation and deduction fell far short of those displayed by Holmes, and commenting, "Doyle's genius made a great deal out of very little, and owes much less than he thinks to, yours truly, Joseph Bell."[1]

It is precisely this ability to 'make a great deal out of very little' that explains Conan Doyle's versatility in plot construction. Each tale is built around one ingenious idea; a harmonious setting is skilfully devised; emphasis is laid upon everything that could suggest an erroneous answer to the puzzle; and finally Holmes gives the true explanation, explaining his reasons. A simple formula, once the vital 'idea' has been found! One at least of the stories, *The Copper Beeches,* was based upon a suggestion made by Doyle's mother. A friend's reference to a Dartmoor legend resulted in *The Hound of the Baskervilles.* The idea for one of his most ingenious tales was almost certainly inspired by a brief papagraph in the *Strand Magazine,* a periodical with which he was closely in touch. In the May number, 1903, there appeared a letter from a correspondent, with a photograph of two ancient horse-shoes recently found in the moat at Birtsmorton Court, near Tewkesbury.[2] One of them was so contrived as to make the imprint of a child's foot; the other counterfeited the mark of a cloven hoof. Here is the kernel of the mystery in *The Priory School,* published a few months later. One can readily imagine the train of thought prompted by this curious item of information, more particularly by the second horse-shoe. Where might similar relics be found? How might they be used with a criminal purpose, and what sort of man could employ them? How could their use be detected? The answers to these questions provide the main features of the plot; —'the museum at Holdernesse Hall, where such shoes had been

---

[1] Dr. Bell's letter to an interviewer on the staff of the *Strand Magazine* appeared in the volume July-Dec., 1892, p. 188.
[2] The *Strand Magazine*, Vol. XXV (1903), Jan.-June, p. 596.

dug up from the moat'; the child kidnapped without trace; the morose keeper of the lonely inn with its little smithy in the corner of the yard; the deserted moor with its miry paths, along which there could be enough undisturbed tracks for Holmes to recognise their characteristic sequence.

But the search for plots did not present any difficulty when Conan Doyle first visualised his Sherlock Holmes stories, for he meant to write a short series only. Six tales were completed and sent to the *Strand*, where the first of them, *A Scandal in Bohemia*, appeared in July, 1891. They at once attracted a great deal of attention, and the editor asked for more, but Conan Doyle refused. His mind was full of plans for a new historical novel, and he was reluctant to turn aside from it, even briefly. By October, when the fourth tale appeared and public interest was still growing, Conan Doyle found it difficult to withstand the editor's persistence, so he asked a price which he hoped would be refused. It was at once accepted, so the historical researches were laid aside while six more adventures of Sherlock Holmes were written. Discussing their subject matter in a letter to his mother, his shrewdest critic and most devoted reader, Conan Doyle remarked: "I think of slaying Holmes in the last, and winding him up for good and all. He takes my mind from better things." The suggestion appalled her. "You won't! You can't! You mustn't!" she stormed in reply.[1] So, instead, this series ended with Holmes alive and at the top of his form in *The Copper Beeches*, but Conan Doyle kept his original intention in mind.

One particular circumstance which added considerably to the appeal of the stories, and gave readers a vivid, unforgettable visual impression of Holmes and Watson, was that the *Strand* illustrations for *The Adventures* were created by a brilliant young artist, Sidney Paget. The two earlier novels about Holmes had also been illustrated, *A Study in Scarlet* by several drawings from the pen of Conan Doyle's father, Charles Doyle, and *The Sign of Four* with a frontispiece by Charles Kerr. Sidney Paget

---

[1] Cf. Conan Doyle's letters, given by John Dickson Carr in *The Life of Sir Arthur Conan Doyle*, Murray, 1949, pp. 87-88.

made no attempt to follow the work of these earlier artists, or even the descriptions given by the author himself, but followed his own ideas and succeeded in producing illustrations which harmonised so perfectly with the spirit and atmosphere of the stories that from the moment they appeared they were accepted as exact portraits, and have been so regarded ever since, particularly in the case of Holmes.

If Conan Doyle thought that twelve of Holmes's adventures were enough to satisfy his readers, he was mistaken. "They have been bothering me for more Sherlock Holmes tales," he wrote to his mother in February, 1892. "Under pressure I offered to do a dozen for a thousand pounds, but I sincerely hope they won't accept it."[1] His terms were agreed without hesitation, and so the second series was begun, *The Memoirs of Sherlock Holmes,* in which the great detective reached new heights. This time, however, the author carried out his earlier threat and concluded the series with *The Final Problem,* in which a heavy-hearted Watson recorded Holmes's fatal struggle with Professor Moriarty at the Reichenbach Falls. Doyle was amazed at the public outcry. He was deluged with letters of protest from grief-stricken readers and heard of many who wept, while sober London business men took to wearing mourning bands.[2] The *Strand* hastened to reassure its subscribers: —

> 'There will be only a temporary interval in the Sherlock Holmes stories. A new series will commence in an early number. Meanwhile, powerful detective stories will be contributed by other eminent writers.'[3]

But the tales by other writers merely whetted the public's appetite without satisfying it. Sherlock Holmes was now an international favourite, and readers in every civilised country, especially in the U.S.A. and France, waited anxiously to hear of him again. Letters reached Conan Doyle from all over the world,[4] but for almost ten years he steadily refused to reverse his decision.

Early in 1901, Conan Doyle was intrigued by a friend's con-

[1] Carr, *Op. cit.,* p. 91.
[2] Cf. *Memories and Adventures,* p. 99.
[3] The *Strand Magazine,* July, 1892, p. 82.
[4] Cf. *Memories and Adventures,* pp. 108-109.

versation about Dartmoor, its craggy wastes and treacherous bogs, the swirling mists, the bleak, grey prison, the local legends, especially one about a spectral hound. The plot for *The Hound of the Baskervilles* at once began to take shape in his mind, and he wrote it at white heat, in the intervals of exploring on foot the actual setting of the novel. Originally, he did not visualise making it a Sherlock Holmes story, but as the plot took shape it called for one dominant central figure, and Holmes was the obvious answer. The story appeared as a serial in the *Strand* between August, 1901 and April 1902. Though it was presented as occurring 'in the eighties,' and therefore prior to the tragedy at the Reichenbach Falls, it was a new Sherlock Holmes story, and the hope grew that others might follow. At last, in the spring of 1903, Doyle consented to restore Holmes to life, and immediately a fever of anticipation gripped the reading public. On June 8th, 1903, the *Evening News* reported that he proposed to 'spend the summer at Montauk, New York, in order to revive Sherlock Holmes in a series of mysteries of American origin,' but there were still many baffling problems for Holmes to solve in London, and the new series showed him still working in his old familiar background.

When the opening story, *The Adventure of the Empty House*, appeared in the October number of the *Strand*, 1903, Newnes could not print copies fast enough. and long queues formed in Southampton Street to buy them straight from the presses. "The scenes at the railway bookstalls were worse than anything I ever saw at a bargain sale," wrote one lady who vividly remembered the occasion.[1] From that time on, Sir Arthur Conan Doyle continued to create new problems for Sherlock Holmes at frequent intervals, producing another long novel, *The Valley of Fear* (1915) and thirty-three more short stories, the last appearing in 1927, only a few years before his death.

Thus, from his early days as a struggling, unknown writer till the end of his long literary life as a world famous figure, he returned again and again to the great detective with whom his name will always be identified. He himself did not regard

[1] Cf. Carr, *Op. cit.*, p. 202.

Holmes as a hero he was proud of inventing, and he placed a greater value upon his historical novels; his treatises on the Boer War[1] and on the Submarine Menace in 1914; his devotion to psychic research in his later years. But the world remembers him almost solely as the man who created Sherlock Holmes, and so brought the detective story to the forefront of English fiction.

The reasons for the immense popularity of Sherlock Holmes are not hard to establish, and lie chiefly in Conan Doyle's inspired blending of two contrasting elements, the old and the new; mingling familiar, almost by that time traditional, features of the *genre* with startling, even sensational innovations. The time was exactly right in the 1890's for the appearance of a fresh detective hero of outstanding individuality, and to create him Doyle took the most notable characteristics of earlier fictional detectives and added to them the very qualities that the late Victorian general public admired most. Sherlock Holmes not only possessed far greater mental brilliance than his predecessors, but also a good social and cultural background, perfect respectability and integrity, the status of a 'scientist,' and an international reputation as a celebrity in his own field. Above all, he was an Englishman, while for the past fifty years, indeed ever since the time of Vidocq, all the celebrated detectives of fiction—Dupin, Père Tabaret, Monsieur Lecoq, Rocambole—had been French.

Sherlock Holmes's skill in following a trail is a legacy from the Three Princes of Serendip, inherited through Voltaire's *Zadig*, a novel which Conan Doyle acknowledged as one of his sources of inspiration. The same faculty characterised the Indian trackers of Fenimore Cooper and of his successor in the same sphere, Captain Mayne Reid, who was Doyle's favourite author in his boyhood days. Sherlock Holmes could perform even more masterly feats of tracking, deriving remarkable information from footprints on a garden path or a snow-covered

[1] Dr. Conan Doyle wrote two books in defence of British action in South Africa, *The Great Boer War* (1900) and *The War in South Africa; its Causes and Conduct* (1902). He served as registrar of the Langman Field Hospital in South Africa, and was knighted in 1902.

lane, the wheelmarks of a cab, or the traces left by a small bare foot on a windowsill. Holmes's kinship with the Redskin hunters is also apparent from his habit of silent laughter, his ability to go without food or rest when on the trail, and that 'immobility of countenance' which made Dr. Watson more than once compare him to a Red Indian.

Like the almost legendary Vidocq, Holmes is a master of disguise, an accomplished actor and a man of great physical strength. They both have a sound grasp of criminal psychology and an encyclopaedic knowledge of criminal history which serves them well. Holmes once referred disparagingly to Dupin, calling him "a very inferior fellow, [. . .] showy and superficial," yet Dupin is the literary ancestor whom he most closely resembles. Like Poe's hero, Holmes is 'unemotional,' reasons with 'ice-cold logic' and regards detection as 'an exact science'; has a brilliant mind stored with all sorts of technical information; sometimes uses a newspaper advertisement to bring a suspect within his reach; can break in upon a friend's train of thought with an apropos remark after a quarter of an hour's silence. Both detectives express the opinion that when all impossibilities have been eliminated, what remains, however improbable, must be the truth; that an article is best hidden when left in full view; that an 'abstract thinker' is the most formidable of all opponents, especially if he is a mathematician; that the more grotesque a mystery seems, the easier it will be to explain, while an apparently commonplace problem is the most difficult of all. They are both heavy smokers, take long walks through city streets at night, and hold a poor opinion of the police, whom they assist on occasion with brilliant deductions or inspired advice. Both are men of good family, bachelors with no interest in the opposite sex, and very little in their fellowmen, except as factors in a problem calling for the exercise of their analytical powers.[1]

[1] Many later detectives of fiction take this same limited view, though others, especially in the twentieth century, show a broader interest in human nature. This trait shown by Dupin and Holmes may be simply a reflection of certain inherent limitations in detective fiction, which is more concerned with facts, details or material clues that can be isolated and regarded individually, than with differences in character, which can not.

They have their individual eccentricities, and while Poe comments on Dupin's "Bi-part soul," Dr. Watson meditates on Sherlock's "dual nature."

Both Dupin and Holmes are fortunate in having a faithful, long-suffering companion to chronicle with unfailing amazement and delight their various activities, their discourses on detective topics, but whereas Dupin's friend reveals little or nothing of his own individuality, Dr. Watson conveys his own character as clearly as he does the temperament and perspicacity of his famous colleague. He plays an active, if secondary, rôle in almost every story, serving not only as a foil to his brilliant friend but also as a figure with whom the reader feels a comforting comradeship when he, too, "sees but does not observe," and needs to have the implications of a clue explained. Dr. Watson, with his sturdy common sense and sincerity, his patient cheerfulness and instant readiness to face any danger beside his friend, stands almost as high as Holmes in the reader's affection. *The Lion's Mane*, which lacks his presence, has lost an appreciable part of the characteristic savour, even though it is related by Holmes himself. The important part played by Watson, so different from the minor rôle of the narrator in Poe's tales of Dupin, is one of Conan Doyle's most pleasing innovations.

In spite of the similarities between Dupin and Holmes, the contrast between Poe and Conan Doyle, as writers of detective stories, could hardly be more striking than it is. Poe's tales are purely analytical discussions of the science of detection, argued out like a geometric theorem with no irrelevant detail. Though the subjects may be sensational, in their treatment we find little excitement and less romance. The characters, other than Dupin himself, are so lightly drawn that they have no personality, often not even a name, and the interest lies not in the people but in the things that have happened to them and the bonds of logic that link cause and effect. Of action or normal conversation there is practically none. Dupin moves in logical steps from the stated problem to its solution, and he is never wrong, never at a loss, never misled by a false clue. Doyle's stories are full of movement and animation. Men and women bring their personal troubles to Holmes (as they never did to Dupin) and the reader shares their dramatic moments, for much of the action takes place before his eyes. Sherlock Holmes is not merely an abstract logician, and is sometimes baffled, if only temporarily, or misled by conflicting evidence, even by unforeseen human reactions. On some occasions, as in *The Yellow Face,* he is completely in error, but he loses no prestige thereby, his mistake making him seem still more convincingly human, and serving also to throw his almost invariable success into stronger relief. Poe was unfamiliar with Paris, and the French background he gave to his Dupin stories had no special significance in the plot. Victorian London, which Conan Doyle knew so well, gives its own characteristic atmosphere to the tales of Sherlock Holmes, so much so that the mere thought of that hero conjures up the great metropolis of the period, with its November fogs and August heat, its hansom cabs and gaslight, the docks and railway stations, the dignity of Westminster, the humdrum suburbs, the squalor of an East End opium den.

Conan Doyle admired Gaboriau for 'the neat dove-tailing of his plots,' and in his first novels of Sherlock Holmes (as distinct from the short stories) he followed Gaboriau's example of plot-construction, and found himself in the same technical difficulty, needing to break the thread of the detective interest to interpolate a long account of events that had taken place at some distant time or place. In *A Study in Scarlet* it is so abruptly done as to seem the opening of an entirely different story. In *The Sign of Four* it comes about more naturally, in the form of Jonathan Small's confession of his share in looting the Agra treasure during the Indian mutiny. Only once more, in *The Valley of Fear,* written a quarter of a century later, does Conan Doyle follow the same plan of construction, and this time he carefully reassures his readers, before transferring his story to America, that in due course they will 'return to those rooms in Baker Street' for the conclusion of the tale. In this novel Doyle improved upon Gaboriau, and took an original step by making the interpolation another complete detective story with a different hero, 'one of Pinkerton's best men, Birdy Edwards'.

At the time when Conan Doyle began to write, detective fiction consisted mainly of two distinct groups, each designed to appeal to very different types of reader. The great majority of such stories were sensational, written for the uncritical general public, and seldom able to be read with interest a second time, once the secret was known. Side by side with these there was a growing popularity among more intellectual readers for the closely reasoned, more abstruse detective stories of Poe, which were repeatedly issued in new editions in this country and in France, as well as in his own country, especially from 1875 onwards. Conan Doyle contrived to combine the best features of both groups, and, by restraining the sensational within acceptable limits and explaining Holmes's deductions in such entertaining fashion, he evolved a new kind of detective story that pleased both types of reader. Sherlock Holmes's exploits are not simply tales of crime, nor mere puzzles that lose their interest as soon as they are solved. They can be read over and over again with renewed, even increased, appreciation for Holmes's detective acumen and the artistry with which the tale is unfolded.

When the reading public came to appreciate Holmes's powers in the *Adventures* they accorded him an affection that has scarcely diminished with the passing of more than half a century. If, now and then, a plot contained some debatable statement, as, for example, Holmes's interpretation of the bicycle tracks in *The Priory School,* or his inaccurate impressions of the rules of horse-racing in *Silver Blaze,* Conan Doyle quickly learned about these discrepancies from readers' letters, or even from articles in the Press, but such comments did not ruffle his robust good humour. It is characteristic of well-written detective fiction that it stimulates the reader's mind almost equally to intelligent participation and analytical criticism. Mental effort on his part is essential to full enjoyment of the story, and he likes to increase his pleasure by exercising inductive reasoning upon the incidental details, provided always that the tale itself is sufficiently absorbing. The Sherlock Holmes stories quickly evoked this responsive interest, an interest which they still arouse in many critical minds seeking diversion.

Conan Doyle was singularly well equipped to produce fiction of this type. His prose was clear and factual, and he was mentally in tune with the spirit of sensational romance, for he loved action, adventure and tales of exciting quests. When little more than a youth, being troubled by religious doubts, he formulated for himself the rule: "Never will I accept anything which cannot be proved to me,"[1] and he made it his guiding principle through life, a principle that might well have served as a motto for Sherlock Holmes. Conan Doyle's love of justice and his appreciation for truth are evident from his championship of those friendless prisoners, George Edalji and Oscar Slater, whom he believed, after studying the evidence given at their trials, to have been wrongly convicted, and whose innocence he finally established. His long training in medicine enriched his mind in ways that had an important bearing on his work as a writer of detective fiction, giving him an intimate knowledge of all types of men and women and sharpening his inductive skill, his perception of the vital importance of *minutiae*. It also gave him, in the person of Dr. Joseph Bell, a prototype for the new 'scientific' detective he was to create.

Holmes is introduced to the world as an expert in chemical research, a choice of profession very much in tune with the spirit of an age that was reaching out into scientific fields. On the historic occasion when Dr. Watson meets Sherlock Holmes for the first time, in the chemical laboratory at Bart's Hospital, Holmes has 'just discovered a re-agent which is precipitated by haemoglobin and nothing else.' "Practical?" cries Holmes in response to Watson's comment, "It is the most practical medico-legal discovery for years. Don't you see that it gives us an infallible test for bloodstains?"[2] The same note is struck repeatedly. We hear of Holmes 'spending seven weeks working out a few experiments in organic chemistry'[3]; 'settling down to one of

---

[1] Cf. *Memories and Adventures*, p. 33.
[2] *A Study in Scarlet*, L. 10.
[3] *The Gloria Scott*, S. 380.

those all-night researches which he frequently indulged in, [. . .] stooping over a retort and test-tube'[1]; 'spending months on research into the coal-tar derivatives'[2]; or discovering the decisive clue to a murder by testing a solution with litmus paper.[3]

But it was not yet time for the appearance in fiction of a really scientific detective, such as Dr. Thorndyke and other specialists in this field who came later, for the average reader in the 1890's was scarcely able to appreciate chemical analysis as evidence. In spite of this flourish of test-tubes in the background, Holmes's experiments do little more than create the ilusion of a scientific approach. He does not reason as a scientist in the cases related in detail, or make use of chemistry to solve the problems that form the framework of the plots. In *A Study in Scarlet* he believes that Enoch Drebber was murdered by poison, but he does not analyse the pills found later by the police. He tries them on his landlady's dog, and the little terrier's instant death satisfies the reader that the drug was lethal. The actual identification of the poison is a superfluous detail to him, as it is to Holmes.[4] When, in *The Devil's Foot*, Holmes at last comes to suspect that the burning of a mysterious brown powder has killed Brenda Tregennis and driven her brothers insane, he does not turn to his test-tubes, or, since he was on holiday in Cornwall at the time, send the powder to a local analyst. Instead, he arranges a rough and ready experiment to discover how the fumes would affect himself and Dr. Watson, with all but fatal results—a dramatic, rather than a scientific course of action.

In his early days of research at Bart's Hospital, Holmes was once seen "beating the subjects in the dissecting room with a stick, to verify how far bruises may be produced after death," but he is nowhere reported as using such knowledge, or, indeed, examining a body in a mortuary. The public was not yet ready for the detective with a scalpel, or for post mortem investigations such as were later performed so brilliantly by Sir Bernard Spils-

[1] *The Copper Beeches*, S. 284.
[2] *The Empty House*, S. 569.
[3] *The Naval Treaty*, S. 500.
[4] *A Study in Scarlet*, L. 67-68.

bury in real life and Reginald Fortune in fiction. Holmes found his famous magnifying glass sufficiently informative for his purpose in most cases, though he sometimes used a microscope, as other detectives had done before him.[1] He was, however, the first fictional detective to use a microscope for examining the dust extracted from his suspect's clothing, and this is perhaps his closest approach to 'scientific detection.'[2]

In most cases, his successes depend far less upon science than upon his wide general knowledge, his quick perception of informative trifles, and in such matters the average reader can grasp his arguments with full appreciation. It needs no scientific training to perceive (or to agree) that a man writing on a wall usually does so at his own eye level, thus indicating his height; that only a strong man with special training could drive a harpoon through a human body; or that there is something sinister about a coffin which "took longer to make, being out of the ordinary." No one will deny that there are grounds for suspicion when a first-class workman accepts a job at half the usual wages, or when a governess is offered a situation at three times the normal salary. All through the series it is such clues as these, placed in passing before the reader, that enable Holmes to solve apparently inexplicable mysteries. Doctor Watson once exclaimed: "I had heard what he had heard, I had seen what he had seen, and yet from his words it was evident that he saw clearly not only what had happened, but what was about to happen, while to me the whole business was still confused and grotesque!"[3] The reader feels the same mingling of frustration and curiosity, and not until he learns just where and when he has failed to notice the clues can he put the story down.

Holmes once discussed with Watson[4] the Bertillon system for the identification of criminals from certain unvarying measurements of parts of the human frame, and expressed enthusiastic admiration for the work of that eminent French anthropome-

---

[1] Dupin referred to ' the microscopes of the police ' in *The Purloined Letter* (1842).
[2] Cf. *Shoscombe Old Place*, S. 1300-1301.
[3] *The Red-Headed League*, S. 46.
[4] *The Naval Treaty*, S. 522.

trist.[1] But he showed considerable pique when Dr. James Mortimer tactlessly, but quite rightly, placed him second to Bertillon as a 'precisely scientific mind,'[2] and he made no use of Bertillon's findings, nor, which is even more surprising, of the discoveries of Sir Francis Galton concerning fingerprints, which attracted wide attention in England at the time when Holmes's popularity was reaching its zenith.[3]

It seems odd that Sherlock Holmes, who scrutinized footprints with such minute care on so many occasions, was so contemptuous of fingerprints—an indication that the Red Indian outweighed the scientist in him! In only one of his cases, *The Norwood Builder*, is a fingerprint mentioned in any detail, and then it is a forgery, misleading to the police but not to Holmes, who 'writhes with inward merriment' before explaining how simply such a print could be counterfeited. On a later occasion, in *The Three Gables*, a pompous Inspector presumed to advise Holmes "never to pass anything, however trifling. There is always the chance of fingermarks or something." The remark was coldly ignored, and apart from these disparaging references there is scarcely a hint in all the Sherlock Holmes stories of this method of identification, and none of that familiarity with and respect for the work of fingerprint experts which became such a generally accepted feature in later detective fiction.

Conan Doyle, whose love for France was deep-rooted and sincere, repeatedly linked Sherlock Holmes with that country. His faculty of observation and deduction may have been inherited, he says, from his French grandmother, 'the sister of Vernet, the French artist.' Holmes was often engaged with French cases which are referred to in passing, that of the unfortunate Mme Montpensier, for example, or of Huret, the boulevard assassin, 'an exploit which won for Holmes a letter of thanks from the French president and the order of the Legion of Honour.'

[1] Alphonse Bertillon's treatise on this subject was published in Paris in 1893, and in 1894 the English Government sent a special committee to Paris to investigate and report on Bertillon's methods.
[2] *The Hound of the Baskervilles*, L. 282.
[3] Francis Galton's works on the importance of this means of identification in connection with police work were published in England between 1892 and 1895.

Holmes frequently worked closely with the French police, and Dr. Watson records that one eminent French detective, François le Villard, was so impressed with Sherlock Holmes's many monographs on technical aspects of detection that he translated them into French for the benefit of his colleagues.

The English police also valued Holmes's advice, and throughout his long career his services were available to help the professionals with any difficult case, from *A Study in Scarlet* (1887) to *The Retired Colourman* (1927). He had no great opinion of 'the Scotland Yarders,' in spite of their 'quickness and energy,' considering them 'shockingly conventional,' 'lacking in imagination,' sometimes even 'obtuse to the point of imbecility,' but he appreciated their persistence and their powerful organisation, and eventually found it a great convenience to be able to say: "Thanks to the telephone and the help of the Yard, I can usually get my essentials without leaving this room."[1]

The numerous police officials who worked with him in turn, always began by distrusting his 'far-fetched theories' and unconventional methods, but quickly came to value his co-operation, especially since he wanted no publicity, and never identified a criminal to them without at the same time giving them such clear proofs of his guilt that they ran no risk of losing their case in court. On occasion, however he deliberately refrained from revealing the entire truth to the police, reserving the right to with-hold information when he saw fit, though he never hampered or misled the official force. In *The Devil's Foot* he was scrupulous in leaving every clue for the police to find, if they could, but decided that in view of the special circumstances he was 'not called upon to interfere.' In *The Abbey Grange,* also, he kept silence from similar motives, and never did Holmes let the police know that he and Watson had actually been present when a certain noble lady shot the blackmailing Charles Augustus Milverton.

In other murder cases when Holmes identifies the murderer, the guilty man may die of some long-standing disease, as in *A Study in Scarlet* and *The Boscombe Valley Mystery*, or by some

[1] *The Retired Colourman*, S. 1325.

avenging stroke of Fate, as in *The Speckled Band* or *The Hound of the Baskervilles*. If he is to stand trial, the story closes with his arrest, and no more is heard of him. Apart from one brief newspaper report of an inquest in one of the early stories there are no court-room scenes, no dramatic trials such as had been popular in earlier detective fiction and would be so again; no attempt to follow a murderer along the sombre paths that lead from arrest to conviction and on to execution, that harrowing, inevitable sequence in the administration of justice which has disturbed the peace of mind of many sensitive investigators, from Walter Lester in *Eugene Aram* to Lord Peter Wimsey in *Busman's Honeymoon*. While recognising that some readers might wish to know what happened to the criminal, Watson dismissed the matter with the brief comment: —

> 'It has been difficult [. . .] to give those final details which the curious might expect. Each case has been the prelude to another, and, the crisis once over, the actors have passed for ever out of our busy lives.'[1]

Most of Sherlock Holmes's problems, in any case, are not concerned with murder but with less sensational crimes—burglary, fraud, blackmail, or the theft of important documents. Some of the most interesting do not treat of crime in the legal sense at all, but with human perplexities outside the scope of the law. Conan Doyle is unique among writers of detective fiction in the skill with which he so repeatedly weaves a fascinating mystery around some personal dilemma brought to Holmes by a distressed client—a missing fiancé, for instance, a husband's worry about his wife's health, or the disappearance of a rugby footballer on the eve of an important match. The reader finds additional pleasure in Holmes's frequent, intriguing little impromptu deductions about irrelevant matters, Dr. Watson's watch or Grant Munro's pipe, Dr. Mortimer's walking stick, or the profession of a casual passer-by; and a further savour is provided by the many tantalising hints of other mysteries which, for reasons of discretion, cannot yet be told, such as 'The Case of the Two Coptic Patriarchs,' 'the truth about the Amateur

---

[1] *The Solitary Cyclist*, S. 660.

Mendicant Society,' or 'the dreadful business of the Abernetty family.'

In every story of Sherlock Holmes, the reader's interest is captivated not only by the detective's 'unique methods,' but perhaps to an even greater degree by 'the singular personality of this remarkable man.' Discussing his family link with Vernet, the French painter, Holmes commented that "Art in the blood is liable to take the strangest forms," and it may well have accounted for more than that hereditary aptitude for perception and deduction which he shared with his elder brother, Mycroft. There is artistry in his sense of the dramatic and in his skill as an actor. His impersonations deceive even his closest friend, and the reader is as amazed as Dr. Watson when Sherlock Holmes's voice is heard from a figure that till that moment has been fully accepted as a French workman, an elderly lady, a rough looking groom or a venerable Italian priest.

Dr. Watson was at pains to present Holmes as unemotional, but in this he did his friend less than justice, for the great detective was often warm-hearted and impulsive, moved to indignation, amazement or frenzied delight, to profound sympathy with human suffering. He was patient and courteous to his women clients and was even prepared to attach some value to feminine intuition, though he with-held his confidence. "They are never to be entirely trusted." declared this wary investigator, who in his first short adventure, *A Scandal in Bohemia*, had been outwitted by a woman. Yet those who brought their problems to him were as impressed by his kindness as by his cleverness, and he often showed a sympathetic understanding of feminine psychology, as, for instance, in his dealings with Mary Sutherland, Violet Hunter, Hatty Doran and Violet de Merville. Although Holmes smilingly told Watson: "The fair sex is your department," it was Sherlock, and not the doctor, who correctly diagnosed the mental stress that troubled Lady Hilda Trelawney Hope, and the real cause of Mrs. Ferguson's illness. When Watson attempted to conduct an enquiry, it did not occur to him to seek information from "the girl at the post-office, the wife of the green-grocer or the young lady at the Blue Anchor," until Holmes, who could follow such a course with singular success, advised him to do so.

Sherlock Holmes had many interests outside his professional activities, philology, for instance, and his study of ancient manuscripts or the music of the Middle Ages. He was an ardent lover of music, a composer as well as a capable performer, and the author of scores of treatises on abstruse subjects. Rather surprisingly, he was 'one of the finest boxers of his weight,' and it is a tribute to Conan Doyle's mastery of convincing detail that the reader can without hesitation accept Holmes in all these widely differing capacities. He had his eccentricities, his habit of countering boredom with cocaine, and now and then, like some of his French predecessors, he allowed his thoughts to stray to the other side of the fence. One of his particular hobbies was the opening of safes, and in idle moments he would remark: "I have always had an idea that I could have made a highly efficient criminal," or "Burglary was always an alternative profession had I cared to adopt it." Yet his honour remained clear, and if, once or twice, he did break the letter of the law when all other means of achieving his purpose had failed, his motive was always to further the ends of justice, and he could say in all sincerity, "In over a thousand cases I am not aware that I have ever used my powers upon the wrong side."

The popularity of the Sherlock Holmes stories inevitably inspired many imitations and even burlesques, in none of which is the central character more than a puppet without life or personality, lacking everything except eccentricity. Such productions attested the vogue for detective fiction without affecting its development and they need not be examined here, though one which Conan Doyle himself enjoyed, calling it "the best of all the numerous parodies," may be noticed in passing. It was written for fun to Conan Doyle by Sir James Barrie, after the failure of a comic opera which the two men had amused themselves by writing together.[1] Barrie called it *The Adventure of the Two Collaborators,* and after giving a short humorous version of their experiences in this venture the skit ends with

[1] Cf. *Memories and Adventures, pp.* 103-105.

Holmes slowly dissolving into smoke, exclaiming to Conan Doyle: —

> "Fool, fool! I have kept you in luxury for years! By my help you have ridden extensively in cabs, where no author was ever seen before. Henceforth you will ride in buses!"

The point of this parting shot is that Barrie's parody was written in 1892, the year in which Doyle, despite the attractive offers of his publishers, had, as he thought, finally disposed of Holmes in the Reichenbach Falls.

James Barrie never wrote a detective story, but this spritely *tour de force* reveals a definite aptitude, and it is interesting to recall that in 1889, while Sherlock Holmes was little more than a character in an 1887 Christmas Annual, Barrie produced *A Window in Thrums,* in which the second chapter, 'On the track of the Minister,' and the fourteenth, 'Visitors at the Manse,' are perfect, sustained examples of detective reasoning from observation and deduction. The subject is far removed from the sensational or the criminal, and concerns nothing more sinister than the gratification of a lively curiosity about the personal affairs of neighbours, but Holmes himself could hardly have improved upon the shrewdly-reasoned conclusions that Libbie and her mother drew so accurately from tiny, informative clues. Possibly the analytical thought processes of the Scottish surgeon Joseph Bell, who inspired Conal Doyle to create Holmes, were more of a national characteristic than has been realised!

Sherlock Holmes is a focal point in the evolution of the detective hero. He not only embodied the characteristics of his most notable predecessors, but also became the ancestor of almost all the outstanding twentieth-century detective heroes in English fiction, who reflect one or more of the varied facets of his personality, widely though they differ from him, and from each other, in other respects. Father Brown, with his intuition and his psychological flair; the scientist, Dr. Thorndyke, specializing in chemical analysis; Poirot, that neat little Belgian, and the burly French official, Hanaud, who so much enjoyed mystifying their friends, Captain Hastings and Mr. Ricardo, and arranging a dramatic denouement; Lord Peter Wimsey, who collected rare volumes and was a skilled musician; Reginald Fortune, enigmatic and sarcastic, who loved to work on his own and keep the regular police in suspense; all these and many others have a certain kinship with Sherlock Holmes.

With Conan Doyle, the detective story came at last to full fruition. His sincerity, his great skill as a writer, gave it a new distinction and won for it a wider, almost universal, acceptance as a literary form. It was by no means his only, or to him his most important, work, but the reading public of his generation recognised him as unquestionably a master of this type of fiction, which in his hands became a force potent enough to influence world trends in popular literature. For the first time, English detective fiction, which had received so much in earlier years from American and French sources, repaid that debt fully and created a new standard for developments in the twentieth century.

CHAPTER
XI

THE EARLY TWENTIETH CENTURY

In the closing years of the nineteenth century, English detective fiction suffered from the absence of Sherlock Holmes, who had disappeared via the Reichenbach Falls, leaving behind him in the hearts of the magazine reading public an aching void which several writers attempted to fill with the adventures of other detective heroes.

Arthur Morrison continued his pleasant, unsensational tales of Martin Hewitt, the final story in the series, *The Red Triangle,* appearing in 1903. It is workmanlike and entertaining, but cannot compare in literary quality with his better known novel *The Hole in the Wall* (1902), an unforgettable picture of crime and squalor in London's Dockland and the old Radcliffe Highway, a murder thriller rather than a detective story. *Michael Dred: Detective* (1899) by Robert and Marie Connor Leighton, has some interest as being perhaps the first novel of this type to be written jointly by husband and wife, and the first in which the detective himself is the murderer. Headon Hill, whose volume of short stories *Clues From a Detective's Camera* (1893) had met with some success, followed it with several novels planned on similar lines, *Zambra, the Detective* (1894) *Guilty Gold* (1896), *Tracked Down* (1902), *Her Grace at Bay* (1906), *Links in the Chain* (1909) and *The Comlyn Alibi* (1918).

M. McDonnell Bodkin, Q.C., whose *Paul Beck, the Rule of Thumb Detective* appeared in 1897, invented a 'ladylike sleuth' in *Dora Myrl* (1900), but she was by no means as efficient a detective as her predecessor, Miss Green's Amelia Butterworth, and no more clever than her near-contemporaries, Loveday Brooke and Dorcas Dene.[1] She was, however, much more charm-

---

[1] Caterina Louisa Pirkis, *The Experiences of Loveday Brooke, Lady Detective* (1894); George R. Sims, *Dorcas Dene, Detective* (1897).

ing, and McDonnell Bodkin had the original idea of arranging her marriage to the detective-hero of his earlier novel in *The Capture of Paul Beck* (1909).

M. P. Shiel created no new detective of the calibre of his Prince Zaleski, and of his later novels *The Man-stealers* (1900) comes nearest to being a detective-adventure story. It tells of the almost successful attempt by a band of French fanatics to kidnap the Iron Duke from his English home, in revenge for the capture of Napoleon and his exile on St. Helena. Shiel collaborated with Louis Tracy in writing several light novels with some detective interest, under the pen name of "Gordon Holmes,"[1] but it is doubtful whether Shiel contributed to all five of the novels published under this pseudonym.[2] They are not particularly satisfying as detective stories, and each of these authors produced better work alone. Tracy wrote at least three well-constructed detective novels under his own name, creating, in contrast to the popular amateurs of the period, an efficient police detective, Inspector Furneaux, who first appeared in *The Strange Disappearance of Lady Delia* (1901), followed by *The Silent House* (1911) and *The Case of Mortimer Fenley* (1915).

Perhaps the only fictional character to rival Holmes in popularity at the dawn of the twentieth century was Raffles, the

---

[1] *A Mysterious Disappearance* (1905).   *The Arncliffe Puzzle* (1906).
   The Late Tenant (1907).   *By Force of Circumstances* (1909).
   The Feldisham Mystery (1911).

[2] John Gawsworth (in *Ten Contemporaries*, Benn, 1932, p. 194) says ' Of these five, on re-reading, Shiel now declares he had a hand in but two, *The Late Tenant* and *By Force of Circumstances*. . . . The *Arncliffe Puzzle* is obviously Tracy's work alone, since he introduces into it his celebrated character, the detective Furneaux '. In that event, Louis Tracy must presumably have been using this pseudonym himself, before his collaboration with Shiel began. It is, however, pertinent to note Shiel's own comment in his essay ' Of Myself ', (originally issued as an advertising pamphlet by Gollancz, 1929, and included in *Shiel's Science, Life and Literature*, Williams & Norgate, 1950). On p. 24 of the latter volume Shiel says :—
   ' I was in with Louis Tracy, with whom I wrote several " books " under a pen name, he having " the idea ", I concocting the plot, writing the first half, he the second, in a wildly different style! I can't think now with what motive I so wasted myself.'
' Several books ' certainly seems to imply more than two. Shiel's final sentence suggests that he was not likely to remember them with any special satisfaction, and the details may possibly have escaped his memory, for all five of these novels were published twenty years or more before Shiel made the comment quoted by John Gawsworth.

'gentleman-burglar,' created by Conan Doyle's brother-in-law, E. W. Hornung (1866—1921), who preceded Doyle as a contributor to the *Strand Magazine*, where two of his stories of life in the Australian bush had appeared before the first of Sherlock Holmes's "Adventures" was published in that periodical in July, 1891. Besides numerous tales of criminals in Australia, Hornung also produced a few detective novels. *Dead Men Tell No Tales* (1899) is almost wholly melodrama, with some intervention by a private investigator and by the police. *The Shadow of the Rope* (1902) gives rather more importance to various attempts at detection, but the eventual explanation of a mysterious murder is revealed only through the confession of the guilty man. *The Crime Doctor* (1914) is a group of short stories in which fairly simple problems are solved by 'psychological' methods. It is, however, as the creator of Raffles that Hornung's name is still remembered.[1]

Before writing *Raffles, the Amateur Cracksman* (1899), Hornung discussed with Conan Doyle his plan for making Raffles 'a kind of inversion of Sherlock Holmes, Bunny playing Watson.' Doyle, whose scorn for dishonesty in word or deed is apparent in everything he wrote, strongly advised against this 'dangerous suggestion,' urging "You must not make the criminal a hero."[2] Nevertheless, Hornung carried out his idea, dedicating the book to Conan Doyle, and constructing his tales somewhat in the manner of the Sherlock Holmes stories, with Bunny, more blindly loyal, more easily led than Watson, and Raffles as dominating and reticent as the great detective himself. The problem of 'how it was done' is expected to baffle the reader until the hero reveals the answer in the final paragraphs, but whereas for Holmes 'success' means that he has fathomed a mystery contrived by others, for Raffles it means merely that he has carried out a cunning plan he had formulated himself.

Raffles is presented as a celebrated cricketer of good social position, and apparently wealthy, but his income is derived from

---

[1] Horning may have borrowed the name of his hero from Conan Doyle's story *The Doings of Raffles Haw* (1892), a tale about a scientist whose discovery of how to transmute metals by electricity brought him wealth and disillusion.

[2] Cf. *Memories and Adventures*, p. 259.

the daring burglaries he carries out whenever he is short of cash, or when the odds against bringing off a successful coup are so high that sheer bravado leads him to attempt 'Art for Art's sake.' There is a limit to the ways in which an author can portray the career of a romantic adventurer such as Raffles without losing the reader's sympathy. Some of Raffles's escapades are farcical; others, such as *The Fate of Faustina* and its sequel, are 'thrillers'; and in one or two, *Nine Points of the Law*, for example, or *To Catch a Thief*, Raffles comes to function more or less as a detective, as most fictional rogue-heroes do sooner or later, Rocambole, for instance, or Arsène Lupin, or The Saint in more recent times. Raffles's career, however, was comparatively short, and the first volume of his adventures was followed by only two more, *Raffles* (1901) and *A Thief in the Night* (1905), concluding with his death as a soldier in the Boer War.

In France, translations of the Sherlock Holmes stories were very popular indeed, even among the more cultured readers who had hitherto despised *romans policiers*, and the tales of Raffles, though more limited in their appeal, also met with considerable success. Two French writers were quick to follow these examples and produce stories in similar vein. They were Maurice Leblanc, creator of Arsène Lupin, and Gaston Leroux, whose Rouletabille was almost equally celebrated.

Maurice Leblanc (1864—1941), a journalist and the author of half a dozen light romances, was, in 1906, asked by the editor of *Je Sais Tout* to write a crime story for that periodical. He produced *Arsène Lupin, gentleman-cambrioleur*, which was published in volume form in 1907, and in English translation as *The Seven of Hearts* (1908). In addition to his descriptive title, Leblanc's hero may owe something to Raffles, whose success certainly indicated that the public still liked reading of an attractive rogue. But Lupin is essentially French, a re-incarnation, not of Raffles, but of Rocambole—the Paris *gamin* who loves flouting the conventions and the police, the gay, adventurous leader of a gang of thieves. Like Rocambole, Lupin has a fancy for masquerading as a prince, a duke, or a Spanish Grandee, and both rascals are young, handsome, supremely self-confident, incredibly daring and quick-witted. Rocambole once captured an English detective, Simouns, and impersonated him at Scotland Yard. Lupin caps these achievements by kidnapping an important government official, Daubrecq, and having him secretly conveyed from Switzerland to Paris in a trunk on the roof of a cab. For four years, Lupin, posing as Lenormand, *chef de la Sûreté*, takes charge of the police investigations into his own activities!

Leblanc makes frequent use of neo-gothic features that had been popular in *feuilletons* from the time of the *roman noir*, ruined castles, subterranean passages, secret trap-doors and other outmoded contrivances, and his plots are, for the most part, borrowed from Ponson du Terrail, or from Gaboriau and his imitators. 'Scientific' methods of detection play little if any part, and, even when attempted, are inaccurate. The detectives who challenge Lupin—Guerchard, or Isadore Beautrelet, even the Prefect of Police himself, Louis Prasville, cannot be compared with the 'scientific' detectives who were popular in English fiction of the same period.

Leblanc certainly had English detectives in mind in his second story in the series, *Arsène Lupin contre Herlock Sholmès* (1908),[1] a heavily sarcastic parody in which Lupin outwits 'the great detective.' Herlock Sholmès, slow and ponderous, with red hair and a moustache, is totally unlike Doyle's hero, while his friend and biographer, Wilson, prone to over-indulge in whisky and fond of a brawl, bears no resemblance to Watson. Leblanc borrowed both figures from the 'comic' Englishmen of French vaudeville, fifty years earlier. After this regrettable lapse, the saga of Lupin was resumed in *L'Aiguille Creuse* (1909), *813* (1910), *Le Bouchon de Cristal* (1912), *Les Confidences d'Arsène Lupin* (1914), *Les Trois Crimes d'Arsène Lupin* (1917), other volumes appearing at short intervals until the 1930's.

Throughout his long career, Lupin is, first and foremost, the 'master-brain' behind a succession of burglaries which completely

---

[1] An English translation was published by Grant Richards in 1909, but Leblanc's title, with its awkward accent, presented a difficulty. The First English title was *The Fairhaired Lady*, from the chief tale, and a later translation was issued as *Arsène Lupin versus Holmlock Shears*.

baffle the police. In *Le Bouton de Cristal* his rôle begins to undergo the inevitable change, and he agrees to assist the police, though for his own reasons. Other adventures follow, most of them short stories or episodic novels, with Lupin either correcting the blunders of the police without their knowledge, or putting them on the right track when it suits him to do so. His later exploits, *Les Dents du Tigre* (1920), and especially *Les Huit Coups de l'Horloge* (1922), show him openly engaged in detective investigations, but shorn of most of his earlier glamour. He is far better at evolving brilliant schemes of his own than in fathoming the plans of others. His explanations are not always sound, and minor problems are left unsolved. His daring and his quick perceptions stand him in good stead, but his inability to resist a joke or a love affair, his fondness for the melodramatic, and his sympathy with the criminals among whom he once reigned supreme—all these handicap his efforts as a detective, and he is most convincing as originally created, the resourceful, irresistible gentleman-burglar.

Gaston Leroux (1868—1927), like Leblanc, was well-known as a journalist and writer of popular fiction before he began writing detective stories. He was for some years a special correspondent to *Le Matin*, contributing reports of notable trials, an experience which gave him an invaluable familiarity with judicial procedure that he turned to good account in his first, most notable, detective novel, *Le Mystère de la Chambre Jaune*. It first appeared as a serial in *L'Illustration* in 1907, and on completion was at once re-issued in volume form. An English translation, *The Mystery of the Yellow Room*, was published in New York by Bretano as 'the book of the month' (August, 1908), and described as 'the most extraordinary detective story of recent years.'[1] In England it was issued as No. 54 of the *Daily Mail Sixpenny Novels* series (1908), and a slightly different version appeared in a more permanent form in 1909, published by Edward Arnold.

The plot, a variation of that ever-popular theme, 'a crime in a sealed room,' is largely borrowed from Israel Zangwill's *The*

[1] Cf. *The Bookman*, New York, Dodd, Mead, Aug. 1908, pp. 603-604.

Big Bow Mystery, but an original feature of Leroux's presentation is that he is clearly challenging the detective skill of the reader. Clue after clue is revealed, but no sooner has the reader begun to guess than he is confronted with some new and baffling complication which upsets his theories. For fully three-quarters of the novel, all the evidence suggests that the assassin is the American doctor, Arthur Rance. The surprise ending reveals that Frédéric Larsan, the detective in charge of the case, is in fact the desperate criminal Ballmeyer in disguise, already wanted for murder by the police of two continents. He is unmasked by the young reporter, Joseph Rouletabille, who is 'covering' the mystery for his paper, *L'Epoque*.

Other newspapermen had acted as detectives in earlier French and English fiction, but none of them can rival the precocious Rouletabille, who systematically eliminates one suspect after another, and has such remarkable aplomb that at the age of sixteen or so he could interrupt a criminal trial and virtually take over its direction. As Holmes had his Watson, so Rouletabille has his admiring friend, Sainclair—a partnership which is rare in French detective fiction, though not unknown. The eventual explanation of the mystery owes much to coincidence, and, indeed, the probabilities are severely strained throughout, though this is scarcely perceived while reading, so rapidly does the exciting story carry one along.

In the sequel, however, *Le Parfum de la Dame en Noir* (1907) the long arm of coincidence is stretched beyond all credibility, and the old-fashioned conventions of earlier French fiction— family scandals, endless disguises, melodramatic, exclamatory dialogue—are once more brought into play. Later stories by Leroux, presenting Chéri-Bibi and Hardigras, are even more sensational, and never again did he reach the heights he attained in *Le Mystère de la Chambre Jaune*.[1]

Meanwhile, detective fiction had become recognised in England as an acceptable literary *genre*, and writers already distinguished

[1] Leroux adapted *Le Mystère de la Chambre Jaune* as a play, which was presented in 1912 at the Ambigu with Jean Coquelin in the cast, and was very well received.

in other fields began to experiment in this new medium, among them Arnold Bennett (1867—1931), whose *The Grand Babylon Hotel* (1902) contained a detective theme, and Godfrey Benson (1864—1945) who became Lord Charnwood in 1911, and whose *Tracks in the Snow* (1906) is a well constructed tale of detection by Serendipity. Robert Barr (1850—1912), author of innumerable light romances and humorous tales, also wrote a series of short detective stories, *The Triumphs of Eugène Valmont* (1906), interesting because of the personality of his hero, a natty little Frenchman with sublime self-assurance, a quick, Gallic wit, and a poor opinion of the English police. Even his friend, Spenser Hale of Scotland Yard, is, in his view, slow and ponderous compared with himself. Most of Valmont's exploits reveal no great ability, however, and the tale by which he is generally remembered today is *The Absent-minded Coterie*, in which he uncovers a fraudulent hire-purchase arrangement.

Eugène Valmont, popular in his day, was the first French detective-hero in English fiction (Dupin, of course, being created by an American) and he was presented as a humorous, almost a ridiculous, figure. The two points are not unconnected, and for some decades English writers who introduced a French detective followed Barr's lead and made him amusing, sometimes even comic, almost as a matter of course. Chesterton made 'the famous French detective, Aristide Valentin' perform absurd antics in *The Blue Cross*, and even Hercules Popeau, Mrs. Belloc Lowndes's imposing and elderly detective, loses his dignity on occasion. Agatha Christie's Hercule Poirot, though a Belgian, has all Valmont's conceit, and is equally amusing in his finicky mannerisms and misuse of English, while A. E. W. Mason's Hanaud sometimes indulges in school-boy buffooneries.

Gilbert Keith Chesterton (1874—1936) was one of the first distinguished men of letters to champion detective fiction, in his 'Defence of the Detective Story' (1901) and his essays on Sherlock Holmes which appeared in the Daily News in 1901 and 1907. In 1905 he produced *The Club of Queer Trades*, a series of tales somewhat in the manner of Conan Doyle, with Chesterton him-self playing the part of Watson, while the rôle of the great detective is undertaken by Basil Grant, an ex-judge whose unconventional exuberance has driven him from the Bench. The mysteries to be unravelled are due to the apparently inexplicable activities of certain individualists who have devised highly original ways of earning a living.

The Man Who Was Thursday (1908) is presented as a detective novel, but in its final pages reveals itself as an allegory. Gabriel Syme, a 'poet of respectability' and an amateur detective, becomes a member of a wonderful new police force consisting of Philosophical Policemen, whose function is to outmanoeuvre a group of anarchists called The Supreme Council of Seven. The framework of a detective story, however, is not well adapted to the purposes of allegory and social criticism, and after these tentative efforts Chesterton devoted himself to a less unconventional application of the *genre*, creating his famous detective-cleric, Father Brown, who appeared in a series of fifty tales.[1] Chesterton's irrepressible originality expressed itself by evolving a completely new type of detective story, with a new kind of hero, who owes nothing to the footrule, the microscope or the laboratory, and everything to a profound insight into human nature, to that special acquaintance with the ways of evil-doers which is gained by a churchman rather than by a policeman.

It would be almost impossible to imagine a greater contrast to Sherlock Holmes than Father Brown, a little Roman Catholic priest whose 'conspicuous quality was not being conspicuous,' his face 'round and dull,' his 'eyes as empty as the North Sea.'[2] This mild, unobtrusive figure goes quietly about his priestly duties with unsuspected vigilance and intelligence, viewing the criminal not as an enemy of society to be uncovered and brought to justice, but as a soul to be saved; an evil-doer whose sin must be brought to light for his own good. For Father Brown, problems of crime are problems of character, and his skill lies in

---

[1] Collected in five volumes :—*The Innocence of Father Brown* (1911); *The Wisdom of Father Brown* (1914); *The Incredulity of Father Brown* (1926); *The Secret of Father Brown* (1927); and *The Scandal of Father Brown* (1935).

[2] In his *Autobiography* (Hutchinson, 1949, pp. 321-322), Chesterton comments that he based Father Brown's intellectual and spiritual qualities, but not his external appearance, upon ' my friend, Father John O'Connor, of Bradford '.

his understanding of human nature, his perception and appraisement of an incongruous circumstance. He is scarcely concerned with the police, who may (or may not) take over when Father Brown departs.

To throw the personality of Father Brown into stronger relief, Chesterton introduced two characters, each drawn flamboyantly 'larger than life,' and each a traditional figure of earlier French, not English, detective fiction. The first of these is Aristide Valentin, 'Head of the Paris Police and the most famous investigator of the world,' 'unfathomably French,' whose successes have all been gained by 'plodding logic.' His greatest ambition is to arrest his fellow-countryman, Flambeau, the second stock-figure and a typical rogue-hero, a colossus of crime, who, like his predecessors, possesses incredible daring, fantastic physical strength, the agility of an acrobat and a robust sense of humour.

Between these two gigantic figures steps the unassuming Father Brown and vanquishes them both, though in different ways. His sympathy lies entirely with the sinner, Flambeau, and after recovering the jewelled cross stolen from his church he allows the thief to go free, whereupon Flambeau repents and reforms. In sharp contrast is Chesterton's (and Father Brown's) attitude towards Valentin, the conventional police official, who receives no sympathetic understanding, no practical assistance, certainly no admiration. In the second story, Valentin is driven to commit a murder that he ingeniously contrives to render almost undetectable, and when Father Brown uncovers his secret crime the Chief of Police commits suicide. The repentant Flambeau, however, embarks on a new career under the guidance of his priestly mentor, setting himself up in business as a private detective-consultant, as Vidocq and Rocambole had done before him. Soon he is celebrated enough to be called in to assist Inspector Craven of Scotland Yard, and before the end of the first series he has opened a grand London office, where, with Father Brown's detective powers always at his disposal, his success is assured.

In endeavouring to make a detective story convey a spiritual message, Chesterton is going outside the normal function of the *genre*, and, as the long sequence continues, he carries this design to considerable lengths. In many of the later stories the circumstances are improbable, the detective arguments slight and overshadowed by moral or philosophical teachings, paradox is emphasised to excess. Nevertheless, Chesterton's detective stories have a special importance not only because his Father Brown is one of the unforgettable heroes of detective fiction, but also because in these tales the criminal, who in contemporary fiction was often a mere cipher, is a human being with good as well as bad impulses, and Father Brown, the antithesis of the 'scientific' detective, was less concerned with examining his footprints or his cigar-ash, than with fathoming the psychological causes that led him into crime.

It is interesting to note the changing viewpoint of writers themselves, towards the detective story during the first decade of the twentieth century. Conan Doyle never ceased to feel that Holmes 'took his mind from better things,' and might cause the reading public to identify him with what he regarded as 'a lower stratum of literary achievement.' Bennett, Benson and other English writers of good standing produced a single detective novel, as if to see whether they could. But Chesterton turned again and again to writing detective stories for fun, without in any way feeling that he was thereby descending to a lower level of literary endeavour. and he took a rollicking pleasure in devising and working out his tales of Father Brown.[1]

One of Chesterton's closest friends, Edmund Clerihew Bentley (1875—1956) also imagined it would be good fun to write a detective story. He enjoyed working out his ideas for the plot, but he found the labour of actually writing the book so exhausting that 'he meant never to attempt a detective novel again,' and therefore decided to call it *Philip Gasket's Last Case*. The original publishers, the Century Company of New York, suggested changing the hero's name to Trent and the title to *The Woman in Black*, and with these alterations it was published in America in 1912. In March of the following year it was issued in England, by Nelsons, with the title that it has borne ever since, *Trent's Last Case*.

[1] Cf. his *Autobiography*, Ch. XVI.

Mr. Bentley, a distinguished journalist, at one time on the staff of the *Daily News* and later with the *Daily Telegraph,* has set down in detail how this remarkable first novel came to be written. From boyhood he had delighted in Sherlock Holmes, but came to dislike his eccentricities and his 'extreme seriousness.' He disliked even more the seriousness of Holmes's imitators, and thought it ought to be possible to create a detective who was a human being, 'not quite so much the "heavy" sleuth.' Accordingly, he drew up a list of 'things absolutely necessary to an up-to-date detective story,' added 'a crew of regulation suspects,' and decided to introduce two original features, a love interest and the idea of 'making the hero's hard-won and obviously correct solution of the mystery turn out to be completely wrong.'[1] Having worked out the plan in his mind, he wrote the last chapter first, thus following, perhaps unconsciously, the method used by many of his notable predecessors, from William Godwin onward.

Trent's Last Case, unlike most detective fiction of the period, gave an important place to character drawing. the creation of credible portraits of human beings with their changing thoughts and emotions. The detective himself is a cultured man of leisure, a successful painter with an analytical habit of mind, who once solved a murder mystery simply by studying newspaper reports of the case, just as Poe had done in the matter of Mary Rogers. When the great financier, Sigsbee Manderson, is found murdered, Trent is called in, unofficially, to find out what he can of the circumstances.

His deductions are at first based upon his observation of detail —footprints in the garden, clothing and other personal possessions of the dead man and his associates—on 'Serendipity,' in fact, with nothing more scientific than a fingerprint or two. He gains further information from studying the individual characteristics of his suspects, their background, hobbies, casual conversation, even the habitual expression of their features. Intuition, which served Father Brown so well, does nothing to help

---

[1] Cf. E. C. Bentley's autobiography, *Those Days,* London, Constable, 1940, pp. 249-254.

Trent reach his conclusions. It does, however, restrain him from making those conclusions public. Although his perceptive and logical brain has built up what seems a completely water-tight proof, he feels there is something wrong somewhere, as indeed there is. E. C. Bentley had planned *Trent's Last Case* to be 'not so much a detective story as an exposure of detective stories,' and the same note is struck in the closing lines of the novel itself: —

> 'The Manderson affair shall be Philip Trent's last case. His high-blown pride at length breaks under him. I could have borne everything but that last revelation of the impotence of human reason.'

But this attempt at 'exposure' did no disservice to detective fiction. What Bentley had, in fact, done was to devise a new method of presenting a detective story. He had broken the convention inherited from Poe, that such a tale must move in ordered sequence like a proposition in Euclid, from 'Given' and 'Required to Prove,' to the logical steps that end with Q.E.D. In *Trent's Last Case* the detective's soundly argued conclusions, which normally form the end of such a story, are given when the tale is little more than half told. What he has proved is true, but not the whole truth. He has discovered facts with great cleverness, but is wrong in the construction he places on those facts. Thereafter, veil after veil is lifted by other hands, still leaving veil after veil behind, until the complete surprise that explains the crux of the mystery is sprung on Trent, and on the reader, in the final pages.

Trent's Last Case, a novel written at a period when the short detective story was still the most popular form of the *genre,* brought to fiction of this kind a more spacious atmosphere, time to consider and reconsider the implications of the evidence, and a new literary excellence. It is that rare thing, a detective story that can be read with pleasure even when the secret is known, for the skill with which the puzzle is devised and concealed, and for qualities that are less frequently found in detective fiction, its sensitive study of character and its delightful prose.[1]

[1] Later stories with the same hero, *Trent's Own Case* (1936) and *Trent Intervenes* (1938) cannot rank with *Trent's Last Case.*

Meanwhile, side by side with these newer conceptions of detective fiction, the Sherlock Holmes tradition continued to flourish, particularly since the new stories of that hero which appeared from time to time whetted the appetite of the reading public for still more in the same vein. One or two new detectives began to win favour, each of them a specialist who polished to a greater brilliance one or other of the facets of Holmes's genius— his powers of mental concentration, his skill as a scientist, or his ability to 'sense' a situation.

"He was," said Watson of Holmes, "the most perfect reasoning and observing machine that the world has seen." Much the same idea of what a detective should be must have been in the mind of Jacques Fūtrelle (1875—1912), an American writer whose best known books were published in this country as well as in his own. His detective, known as 'the thinking machine,' who first appeared, almost casually, towards the end of an adventure novel, *The Chase of the Golden Plate* (1906), was Augustus S. F. X. Van Dusen, a distinguished professor at an un-named university, whose degrees and honours fill many lines of small print. He excels at the instant application of pure logic to any mystery; he is concerned only with facts; and the speed with which he reduces any problem to its simplest terms ensures that the reports of all his cases are short stories. These were collected in two volumes, *The Thinking Machine* (1907) and *The Thinking Machine on the Case* (1908), the first collection being re-issued in 1918 with the title of *The Problem of Cell 13*, the first tale in the group and Futrelle's best known work. It tells how Van Dusen, for a wager, succeeded in escaping from the condemned cell in a strongly guarded prison, a most ingenious *tour de force*. Van Dusen has a brilliant brain, but a brusque, unfriendly personality, a disregard of common courtesy to his associates, and indirectly to the reader, and he cannot be considered one of the popular detectives of fiction.

The scientific skill attributed to Sherlock Holmes was displayed far more efficiently by Dr. John Thorndyke, the leading figure in a long sequence of detective stories by Dr. R. Austin Freeman (1862—1943). Like Conan Doyle, Freeman turned from a medical career to become an extremely popular fiction writer, and based his hero upon one of his medical school instructors, in this instance Dr. Alfred Swayne Taylor, a specialist in medical jurisprudence, as was his fictional counterpart. From the moment of his first appearance in *The Red Thumb Mark* (1907), Dr. Thorndyke is unquestionably an expert whose findings bear the stamp of authenticity. He carries with him at all times a special despatch case, a miniature laboratory containing everything he may need for making an immediate examination of a material clue, and though readers may have to wait for enlightenment, his tests are eventually described in minute detail and his conclusions are convincing beyond all doubt. Indeed, Mr. Freeman personally carried out in his own laboratory every experiment he proposed using in his stories, and Dr. Thorndyke's cases have not only delighted readers for several decades, but have provided the police themselves with new detective methods.

Almost as famous as Dr. Thorndyke himself are his two assistants, his friend, Jervis, and that highly-skilled technician, Polton, both as different from the amiable, obtuse Watson as Dr. Thorndyke is from Sherlock Holmes, but equally devoted to their chief, patiently enduring periods of bewilderment until the master-mind chooses to make all plain. The second volume, *John Thorndyke's Cases* (1909), was followed by *The Eye of Osiris* (1911) and *The Mystery of 31 New Inn* (1912). In *The Singing Bone* (1912). Austin Freeman made an interesting experiment with a new technique of plot construction. When a detective story begins with the discovery of a murder, as so many do, one of the fundamental difficulties is the almost inevitable need to interrupt the progress of the story at some point to relate the events that led up to the crime. This can cause a tiresome break in continuity, yet unless the reader learns why, as well as how and by whom, the crime was committed, the tale is not fully told. Gaboriau made various attempts to overcome this artistic difficulty. Chavette handled the problem rather differently, without, however, finding a smooth way round. Even Conan Doyle, a master of technique, found the point a stumbling block, and in three of the four novels of Sherlock Holmes the recapitulation sharply disrupts the action.

In *The Singing Bone* Austin Freeman tried a new method of approach. First of all, the reader meets the criminal-to-be in his ordinary daily life, before the crime has even been thought of. Then the events that led to the murder are related, with all the circumstances placed before the reader. Finally, Dr. Thorndyke begins his investigation, gathering evidence here and there until his proofs are complete. This method leaves no room for 'red herrings,' and eliminates almost completely the valuable elements of surprise and mystification. Instead, the reader enjoys the novelty of knowing more than the detective; his attention is concentrated on the processes of detection, rather than on what is discovered. As a result, stories told in this manner—*The Echo of a Mutiny*, for instance, or *The Case of Oscar Brodski*— have a special atmosphere of their own, with the detective playing the rôle of Nemesis. Freeman did not repeat this experiment, and his next work, *A Silent Witness* (1914) reverts to the more conventional technique which he followed in the later tales of Dr. Thorndyke that continued to appear at fairly regular intervals until Austin Freeman's death in 1943. In most of these tales, the reader, though his interest and curiosity are adroitly kept at a high pitch of excitement, has no hope of solving the mystery for himself, unless he is skilled enough to deduce Dr. Thorndyke's line of enquiry from the type of experiment he employs, or possesses some highly-specialised knowledge of, for instance, the craft of making Japanese shadow-mirrors. Dr. Freeman's literary life extended almost to the middle of the twentieth century, but the leisurely, unsensational atmosphere of his stories, the romantic sentimentality of his strong, silent heroes and gentle, ladylike heroines, the courteous manner of the cultured investigator himself, all are typical of the period before the first World War, and Dr. Thorndyke's comfortable chambers in King's Bench Walk belong to much the same world as Sherlock Holmes's gas-lit rooms at 221b Baker Street.

One other noteworthy detective who belongs in spirit to this pre-war period appeared in *Max Carrados* (1914) by "Ernest

Bramah" (1869?—1942). The 'private enquiry agent' nominally in charge of the various investigations in this series is Louis Carlyle, but the central figure is his blind friend, Max Carrados, whose sensitive touch and keen hearing are supplemented by his intuitive understanding of human reactions and his delightful sense of humour. Carlyle relies on Carrados in much the same way as Flambeau depended upon Father Brown, and the amicable partnership continues through the later series, *The Eyes of Max Carrados* (1923) and *The Max Carrados Mysteries* (1927).

As a single, complete contrast to the city-dwelling populaɪ detectives of the time, it is worth remembering a very different figure created in *November Joe* (1913) by Hesketh V. H. Pritchard, (1876—1922) an English explorer, sportsman and novelist. 'November Joe,' a delightful Red-Indian guide, brought his mastery of woodcraft. to assist the North American Police in investigating mysterious crimes committed in lonely backwoods.

Women writers of this period, still handicapped in any attempt to create a scientific detective, found various solutions to their particular problem. Mrs. L. T. Meade (1854—1914) collaborated with a male colleague, "Clifford Halifax," and together they wrote a series called *Stories from the Diary of a Doctor,* which appeared in the *Strand* simultaneously with *The Adventures of Sherlock Holmes* in 1891. These tales are only slightly concerned with detection, dealing mainly with sensational mysteries encountered by the doctor in his professional career, but when the Sherlock Holmes series came to an end a second group of tales by Mrs. Meade and "Clifford Halifax" began in the *Strand* with the same title as before, and this series is much more closely allied to detective fiction, presenting investigations into cases of murder.

With a second collaborator, "Robert Eustace,"[1] Mrs. Meade produced another group of stories, published in volume form as *The Sanctuary Club* (1900), in which the detective interest is much more definite. The hero, Mr. Bell, is called in to investigate 'haunted houses' and deaths attributed to supernatural

---

[1] 'Robert Eustace' was also the pseudonym of Dorothy L. Sayers's collaborator in *The Documents in the Case* (1930).

causes, usually finding that the phenomena are due to human agency, though in one tale, *The Felwyn Tunnel,* two railwaymen, said to have been struck down by a ghostly hand on a haunted stretch of line, are proved to have died accidentally, poisoned by "choke damp, that is, carbonic acid gas." *A Handful of Ashes,* in the same series, shows how evidence to prove murder was obtained by analysing the ashes of the victim after cremation. Both these stories give the explanation at the end in the form of a little lecture on chemistry, similar in spirit, if not in quality, to Dr. Thorndyke's more learned dissertations a few years later.

Mrs. Belloc Lowndes (1868—1947) made no attempt to compete with the 'scientific' detectives of contemporary English fiction, and in her handful of short detective stories she made the hero a Frenchman, Hercules Popeau, a benign and dignified figure whose mild successes are almost wholly due to his knowledge of human nature and his access to all the facilities of the *Sûreté.* Mrs. Lowndes did more notable work in volume form, bringing a clever, psychological approach to problems of mysterious crime. *A Chink in the Armour* (1912) is presented from the viewpoint of the unsuspecting intended victim of a murder plot, an unusual and interesting technique with which Wilkie Collins experimented in his *Mr. Lepel and the Housekeeper.* In the following year, Mrs. Belloc Lowndes began that series of fictional reconstructions of actual, sensational murder mysteries for which her name is now most widely remembered. *The Lodger* (1913) reproduces the atmosphere of suspense and terror that surrounded the Jack-the-Ripper crimes, as it affected the homely, suburban landlady who came to suspect that her new lodger might be the elusive murderer. Other subtle studies of murder cases appeared at intervals, including her fascinating *Lizzie Borden: a Study in Conjecture* (1939), but Mrs. Belloc Lowndes's importance in the realm of crime fiction rests chiefly upon *The Lodger,* possibly also upon her sensitive and convincing short story *An Unrecorded Instance,* based on the 'Brides in the Bath Murders.'

Emmuska, Baroness Orczy (1865—1947), a Hungarian of noble

birth, came to this country as a young girl to study Art, knowing practically no English, but quickly making herself happily at home in London, where she married an English painter, Montagu Barstow. Her fame as a writer depends chiefly upon her popular stories of 'The Scarlet Pimpernel,' produced with her husband's collaboration, but she also has a place among writers of detective fiction. In her autobiography[1] she has related how the idea came to her while fog-bound on a London horse-omnibus, close to the gloomy waters of 'The Cut.' She and her husband both enjoyed reading detective stories and had idly wondered whether they would be difficult to construct. While waiting for her bus to move, Baroness Orczy caught sight of a placard advertising the latest tale of Conan Doyle's popular hero, and suddenly decided that she would herself write a series of 'stories of crime and detection,' which should be 'built round an original character whose personality must in no way be reminiscent of Sherlock Holmes.' The first six stories appeared in the *Royal Magazine* in 1901, with such success that a further six were called for, the whole group being re-issued in volume form in 1909, with the title *The Old Man in the Corner*.

The 'old man' is completely insignificant in appearance, and his name is an unimportant detail that never crops up. He is to be met only by chance in a certain A.B.C. shop, where, over a cup of coffee, he falls into casual conversation with Miss Polly Burton, a reporter attached to the *Evening Standard*, and discusses with her certain recent crimes which have baffled the police. He is not, strictly speaking, a detective at all, either official or amateur, for his sympathies are all on the side of 'the criminal who is clever and astute enough to lead our entire police force by the nose.' "Crime," he says, "interests me only when it resembles a clever game of chess, with many intricate moves which all tend to . . . checkmate the antagonist, the detective force of the country," a sentiment already expressed years earlier by Count Fosco, in *The Woman in White*.

He loves 'to reason out a case for the love of the thing,' purely to satisfy his curiosity, as Caleb Williams did before him. Like

[1] Cf. Orczy, *Links in the Chain of Life*, London, Hutchinson, 1947, pp. 85-86.

Dupin, and like Sherlock Holmes, he considers the regular police conspicuously lacking in intelligence, and he reserves his only word of praise for 'the French detectives who are acknowledged masters of their craft, and never proceed till after they have discovered the feminine element in a crime.' (Thus does he paraphrase M. Jackal's watchword in Dumas' *Les Mohicans de Paris*—"Cherchez la femme").

In addition to the features he shares with earlier investigators he has certain unique characteristics of his own—his habit of fiddling endlessly with a piece of string; the disparity between his shabby anonymity and his self-satisfaction; his assiduity in attending inquests or visiting the scene of various crimes, simply to exercise his perspicacity and enjoy the discomfiture of the police; especially his ability to produce from his pockets at a moment's notice all the relevant newspaper cuttings, copies of letters, photographs of everyone concerned, to place before Miss Burton's astonished eyes. "As I conceived him," said Baroness Orczy, "he was in no way reminiscent of any other character in detective fiction,"[1] and as far as these details are concerned, that is certainly true.

But his methods of detection are seldom original, and not always sound. Sometimes his deductions are brilliant and convincing, as in *The Regent's Park Murder*, but more often the enigmatic figure simply states his explanation of the mystery and slides out of his corner seat in the tea shop, leaving the reader in much the same state of mind as Miss Burton, who longs in vain for a chance to ask him "What were his proofs, his facts?" The final story in this series, *The Mysterious Death in Percy Street*, conveys more than a hint, in its surprise ending, that 'the old man in the corner' has himself committed the murder which he describes in such detail and attributes to 'one of the most ingenious men of the age, who will never be caught.'

These, and Baroness Orczy's later short stories of detection, all belong unmistakably to the early twentieth century in their atmosphere and manner of treatment, even though some of them were actually written after the first World War. Her *Lady Molly*

[1] *Ibid.*, p. 87.

of Scotland Yard (1910) introduced one of the least convincing 'fair sleuths' of fiction, who relied more upon good luck and intuition than on any sound grasp of detective technique. A further group of cases discussed by 'the old man in the corner' appeared in 1925, with the title *Unravelled Knots,* and in *Skin o' my Tooth* (1928) Baroness Orczy invented another unconventional investigator, 'the eminent lawyer, Mr. Patrick Mulligan,' whose exploits, related by his confidential clerk, show that legal expert going to quite unprofessional lengths to clear his clients of whatever charges they were facing, in much the same way as did Anthony Gilbert's popular detective Arthur Crook, a decade or two later.

Another woman writer of detective fiction who first became celebrated in the early twentieth century (and is still writing popular novels almost fifty years later), was Mrs. Mary (Roberts) Rinehart, born in Pittsburg in 1876. She produced many sentimental romances of contemporary American life, with rich 'socialites' owning oil wells or cattle ranches; cowboys performing miracles of horsemanship on the range or at the rodeo; inscrutable, revengeful Indians in their reservations. She has also written many humorous tales, but she is chiefly associated in the public mind with her murder mysteries, cleverly devised to pile suspense on suspense, and remarkable for the technical skill that makes the reader share the emotions of those who investigate the mystery. Her best known works in this field are her earliest, *The Circular Staircase* (1908), later dramatised as *The Bat* and played with immense success during the nineteen twenties in this country and in America, and *The Man in Lower Ten,* serialised in 1907 and published in volume form in 1909.

The plo· of *The Circular Staircase,* typical of Mrs. Rinehart's crime mysteries, is in many respects reminiscent of the pattern created by Anna Katharine Green almost thirty years earlier, with two lines of detective enquiry being followed, separately and often at cross purposes, by a police official and the strongminded, inquisitive. kind-hearted elderly spinster who narrates the story. Miss Rachel Innes, in *The Circular Staircase,* is largely a re-incarnation of Miss Green's Amelia Butterworth in her personal qualities, social position and habits of thought, her relationship with her long-suffering maid, her sympathy with young lovers, as well as in her detective methods and her facility for 'happening' to discover important information by accident. Mrs. Rinehart, however, handles this plot technique with greater literary skill than her predecessor, and her first crime novels are particularly interesting because they owe nothing to French or English influences, and represent the emergence of a new vein of purely American detective fiction, with an authentic background of characteristically American social conditions. Mrs. Rinehart is still actively engaged in literary work, and her novel *The Wandering Knife* (1952) once again introduces an efficient detective, Mary Adams, who appeared in earlier stories, but the mysteries she has written in recent decades, though entertaining, are not outstanding, and Mrs. Rinehart's greatest impact on the American detective novel, her influence upon its development, was made in the early part of the twentieth century.

Carolyn Wells, another American writer, must be noticed for her prolific production of detective novels, most of them relating the activities of Fleming Stone, who first appeared in *The Clue* (1909) and was still regularly solving fresh mysteries more than thirty years later. Fleming Stone is not one of the cleverest detectives of fiction, but he is pleasantly entertaining, and his record of almost eighty 'cases' has seldom been eclipsed, except, of course, by his much less reputable fellow-countryman, Nick Carter. Miss Wells, in addition to writing detective stories, was one of the earliest authors to publish a study of the construction, purpose and limitations of such fiction in *The Technique of the Mystery Story* (1913)[1] and to collect examples of these tales in anthologies, with an analytical introduction.

One other American writer of detective stories before the first World War was Arthur B. Reeve (1880—1936) who studied Law before becoming a distinguished journalist. After writing a series of articles on scientific crime detection he turned his attention to fiction conceived in the same vein, and his popularity, though

---

[1] Published at Springfield, Mass., by the Home Correspondence School. A revised edition was issued in 1929.

comparatively short-lived, was intense while it lasted. His hero, Professor Craig Kennedy, was presented as a 'scientific detective,' following the vogue for similar figures in English fiction of the period, and first appeared in a series of short stories published in the *Cosmopolitan Magazine* during 1910, re-issued in 1912 in volume form with the title *The Silent Bullet*. For some years Reeve produced a long sequence of tales of Kennedy's successful exploits, but the spontaneity and real detective interest of the earlier groups was not maintained. Craig Kennedy's achievements depended more and more upon his use of newly-invented mechanical contrivances, such as the Maxim silencer, or his own special 'lie-detector,' and in the later stories he became a manipulator of apparatus, a reader of dials, rather than a detective whose investigations the reader could share. His name became famous in England, as well as throughout America, because of the popular, melodramatic serials that Arthur B. Reeve wrote for the screen, when the cinema was in its infancy as a mode of entertainment. Thousands who saw *The Exploits of Elaine, The Romance of Elaine*, or finally, *The Triumph of Elaine* in the troubled years between 1914 and 1918 retained a vivid, visual impression of 'Craig Kennedy, the American scientific detective,'[1] working, white-coated, in his laboratory, or dashing forth with unfailing regularity to rescue the heroine from the astonishing perils that loomed over her week by week. The screen is not the most satisfying medium for presenting detective themes. It cannot portray analytical thought, and therefore almost invariably tends instead towards the melodramatic, but the popularity of the Craig Kennedy films created a public for the stories in volume form, and brought about the first real vogue in England for contemporary American detective fiction.

Despite these new developments coming from America, and the activities of Arsène Lupin or Rouletabille in France, it was in England that the growth of detective fiction was most strongly

---

[1] As a measure of Craig Kennedy's ' scientific ' accuracy it may be remembered how he explained the ' invisibility ' of ' The Clutching Hand '. This villain habitually concealed himself in a cloak of ' absolute black ', which ' reflected no light whatever, and therefore could not be seen '. This, however, did not explain why furniture and other objects could be seen *through* it.

rooted in the early years of the twentieth century. But the surge of popularity that had begun in 1890 was by 1914 largely spent, and the first great formative period in this country came to an end with the declaration of war, when readers of popular fiction turned from the detective story to 'adventure thrillers,' tales of foreign spies or of sinister arch-criminals in the manner of Edgar Wallace.

The influence that dominated this pre-war period, and can be almost exclusively identified with it, was Sherlock Holmes, for though his adventures continued to appear at intervals until 1927, their atmosphere was by that time out-of-date, the great detective being associated in the public mind with the era of gas lamps and hansom cabs, as, indeed, he still is today. Those investigators who grew up beside him during the first decade of the new century were all in some way indebted to him, for his example inspired their creation, his prestige helped them to secure the attention of the reading public. Because of their need to be in some way different from Conan Doyle's hero, fictional detectives of the time were forced to strike out upon some original line of their own, making their career in some specialised field of operation, or in stories of a particular type. As a result, they initiated certain clearly differentiated groups which persisted and retained their individuality when the golden age of detective fiction began in the post-war years.

Dr. Thorndyke was the progenitor of the scientific detective story, depending for its solution upon an accurate, impersonal examination of material clues, generally through a microscope or in a test-tube; the victim, the motive, even the criminal himself, being of merely incidental interest, important only in that they created a puzzle to challenge the detective's skill. In direct contrast to Dr. Thorndyke, Father Brown originated what may be called the 'intuitional' school of detectives. The non-scientific story in which these appear takes little note of material clues, giving much more importance to personal considerations. The character of the criminal and his motives for the crime receive detailed examination, because deductions will be drawn from the emotions he reveals and the thoughts he expresses, as well as from his actions. If the crime is murder (and in this type of story it frequently is not) sympathy is seldom extended to the victim, who generally remains relatively unimportant. The man who was killed by Chesterton's Aristide Valentin, for instance, was scarcely more than a name!

One consequence of the popularity of these two types of hero, the scientific detective on one hand and the intuitional detective on the other, was that the earlier convention of 'fair play' between writer and reader tended to fall into disuse, and in its place there grew up a new technique of presentation, which expected the reader to be satisfied when the detective announced dictatorially, at the end, "The guilty man is X, because I say so." It was largely as a reaction from this technique, attributed in this period to amateur detectives, that the post-war years brought about a return to the professional police officer, and methods of detection which the reader could follow as the story unfolded.

One other type of amateur detective, however, persisted from the pre-war period to later decades, the gentleman of leisure who undertakes an occasional investigation for the pleasure of solving a puzzle—Philip Trent and his lineal descendants, Colonel Gore, Anthony Gethryn, Lord Peter Wimsey and others. Stories with such heroes give some regard to 'fair play,' and the victim, for a change, is of considerable importance in the story. His personality, his way of life, his past history, the plans he has in mind, may all play a part in the working out of the plot, to disclose possible motives for his murder (the crime with which such stories are generally concerned) or to provide a shoal of 'red herrings.' Often enough the investigator becomes convinced that the person compromised by the evidence, usually a woman, is in reality innocent, and an element of romance, or at least of chivalry, is thus introduced. The detective is then no longer simply an impartial enquirer whose intellectual faculties are brought to bear on the problem with 'ice-cold logic.' The drama tends to involve him personally, appealing to his emotions, and his affections may be deeply engaged, as Trent's were by Mabel Manderson, Gethryn's by Lucia, and Lord Peter's by Harriet Vane.

Side by side with these three main groups which developed during the first decade or so of the twentieth century, and may be identified respectively with Dr. Thorndyke, Father Brown and Philip Trent, there still persisted two much older types of story. The romantic rogue-hero found a fresh popularity in the tales of Raffles and of Arsène Lupin, both of whom acted as detectives on occasion; and, though almost all the popular detectives of this period were amateurs, one or two writers made their hero a police officer, thus giving fresh life to a group which stemmed from the days of Detective-Inspector Bucket, Sergeant Cuff and Monsieur Lecoq, and, beyond them, from the memoirs of Vidocq and other professionals. Only two official policemen of any note emerged in the fiction of this first decade, Louis Tracy's Inspector Furneaux, and A. E. W. Mason's Hanaud, who first appeared in *At the Villa Rose* (1910), but whose career extended so far beyond this period that he can more properly be considered in our next chapter.

In the 1920's the Detective Novel entered upon an era of fresh and far more prolific growth. Indeed, the 'modern detective story' is sometimes said to have originated in that decade, and it is certainly true that since then the *genre* has progressively exploited new scientific discoveries, new methods of communication, new ways of living, to give broader scope to the puzzle-device and exciting variations in the techniques of detection. But many distinctive features that had originated in the nineteenth century still persisted—planning the clues and the solution before the rest of the story; giving the explanation in the form of a dialogue between a clever character and one who is less perceptive; presenting the story from the viewpoint of several different characters, of the victim himself, or even from that of the murderer; and particularly the convention of 'fair play' between writer and reader. In addition to these old-established techniques, detective fiction since the 1920's has retained those clearly distinguishable groups—the 'scientific,' the 'intuitional,' the 'psychological' and the 'straightforward' or 'pure' detective story, which first took shape in the formative years we have considered in this chapter.

CHAPTER
XII

THE GOLDEN AGE

Volumes have been written about the flood of detective fiction which began to pour forth in England and America after the first World War and has continued almost unabated until the present day. A work such as this, primarily concerned with placing the Detective Novel in historical perspective, can give only a somewhat general view of these developments, noting more particularly those writers who originated new trends, gave fresh life to old ones, or in other ways contributed materially to the growth of the *genre*.

In 1918, Joseph S. Fletcher (1863—1935), a Yorkshireman who had already written one or two reasonably entertaining detective novels, produced his best work, *The Middle Temple Murder*,[1] which not only made his name celebrated in England but had the good fortune to be enjoyed and praised by President Woodrow Wilson. As a result, this novel and Fletcher's later stories were published in the States as well as in England, though of them all only *The Charing Cross Mystery* (1923)[2] can compare with his earlier achievement. In general, Fletcher's detection is plodding rather than brilliant, but his tales contain pleasing descriptions of English scenery and country life, and they are well written. Their regular appearance in America, beginning at a time when the *genre* there was at a rather low ebb, had a useful two-fold effect. It gave a stimulating contrast to the 'fluttering spinster' detectives in the novels of Mary Roberts Rinehart and of Isabel Egenton Ostrander (1885—1924), who continued in the Anna Katharine Green tradition. It also provided some support, possibly a flattering comparison, for the tales of Uncle Abner, the most entertaining detective of the day in American fiction.

GENERAL NOTE:—In this chapter, dealing for the most part with works still in print, references to American and English publishers, when applicable, will be given with other notes, in the general bibliography, pp. 258-259.

This rugged Virginian squire, responsible for maintaining justice and good order in his own remote community, was created by Melville Davisson Post (1871—1930), whose short stories of that hero appeared in magazines from 1911 onwards, the best of them being re-issued in volume form as *Uncle Abner: Master of Mysteries* (1918).[3]

In England, too, the detective story had reached a stage when its future seemed uncertain, but in 1920 there began to appear in quick succession a whole constellation of new stars, in particular Freeman Wills Crofts, Agatha Christie and H. C. Bailey, followed by Dorothy L. Sayers, G. D. H. & M. I. Cole, Philip Macdonald, Anthony Berkeley and that eminent churchman who brought such erudition to the *genre*, Monsignor Ronald A. Knox.

Freeman Wills Crofts[4] (1879—1957), Dublin born, spent long years as a railway construction engineer before he began writing detective fiction, and his first book, *The Cask* (1920), marked a return of the professional police detective-hero, in this instance Inspector Burnley. In this, as in almost all his many novels, Crofts made the central interest depend upon the slow, methodical destruction of an 'unbreakable alibi,' a matter in which he made amazingly good use of his professional knowledge of railway routine, not only in this country but also on the continent. Much of the action in *The Cask* takes place in Paris, and the famous *Sûreté* once more figures in English fiction, with M. Chauvet and his staff giving the fullest co-operation to their old friend from Scotland Yard. Crofts wrote three more detective novels before introducing to the world his most famous police officer, Inspector Joseph French, with whom his name will always be linked. The title *Inspector French's Greatest Case* (1925) rather suggests that the author had not envisaged a sequence, but French's success was so immediate and so demanding that most of Croft's later works concern that ever-popular figure.

Agatha Christie (189?———),[5] surely the best-loved, most prolific detective fiction writer of our time, was working as a V.A.D. in a Torquay hospital, reading detective novels that she found 'excellent to take one's mind off one's worries,' when she decided to write such a story herself, and produced *The Mysterious Affair at Styles,* published in 1921. It introduced her most inspired creation, M. Hercule Poirot, the precise little Belgian with his waxed moustaches and his 'little grey cells,' who since that time has achieved at least one new success each year. In her gentle little Miss Marple, Agatha Christie made a notable addition to the small group of credible, pleasing women detectives of fiction, all of whom owe their astonishing insight to their quick eye for informative detail and their shrewd appraisement of human reactions. One other character who appears in several stories and sometimes takes a hand in the investigations is Mrs. Ariadne Oliver, a writer of detective novels, whose revealing commentaries on her own methods of composition are particularly interesting, in view of their original source.

Of all Mrs. Christie's novels, perhaps the best known, still the most widely discussed, is *The Murder of Roger Ackroyd* (1926), with its staggering but perfectly legitimate surprise ending. If in recent years Mrs. Christie's plots have tended to become repetitive, if Hercule Poirot's little mannerisms have lost some of their freshness, nevertheless her stories remain outstanding for their lightness of touch, their masterly skill in misdirection, the clearcut differentiation of their characters, the broad geographical range of their settings and their world-wide appeal. Mrs. Christie is one of the very few writers who have successfully brought detective themes to the theatre, notably with those currently celebrated productions *The Mouse Trap* and *Witness for the Prosecution.* Her fiftieth novel, *A Murder is Announced* (1950) is one of the most entertaining of Miss Marple's 'cases,' and *The 4.50 from Paddington* (1957) relates a further investigation handled by that gently ruthless sleuth, while M. Poirot has continued his saga of success in *Dead Man's Folly* (1956).

Henry Christopher Bailey (1878———)[6] began writing detective stories as a relief from the strain of his work as a war correspondent of the *Daily Telegraph,* his first group of collected tales appearing as *Call Mr. Fortune* (1920). Though the current English trend strongly favoured the long novel, and Mr. Bailey had already written historical romances in that form, he very wisely chose the short story framework in which to present

Reginald Fortune. The highly individual qualities of that bland yet pungent young doctor, his distinctive combination of science and intuition, his erudition, the caustic wit he employs on occasion to goad his slower-thinking associates to fresh endeavours, his conversational style, all show to better advantage in a relatively small compass. Like Chesterton's Father Brown, whose adventures were still appearing in the 1920's, Reggie Fortune often relies too much upon his ability to 'sense' evil, persisting in his conviction despite rational indications to the contrary until events finally prove him right. After a long series of short stories, collected in some ten volumes, Dr. Fortune appeared in a few novels, notably *Black Land, White Land* (1937) and *The Life Sentence* (1946).

In 1930, H. C. Bailey created an entirely different kind of investigator in his Joshua Clunk, a subtle, sanctimonious, hypocritical old lawyer who initiates enquiries for his own devious purposes, most of the actual detective work being carried out by his confidential clerks under his direction. Joshua Clunk appeared in long novels only (no smaller space could contain the highly involved, beautifully constructed plots) the first of them, *Garstons* (1930) being followed by others, culminating in *Shrouded Death* (1950). Joshua Clunk, however, has never won quite as firm a hold on the affections of the reading public as his creator's exuberant Dr. Reginald Fortune.

Dorothy Leigh Sayers (1893—1957),[7] scholarly and meticulous, with her sparkling imagination and her love of literature, has exercised a remarkable influence upon the detective fiction of recent decades. Her first detective novel, *Whose Body* (1923), introduced the hero with whom her name will always be associated, Lord Peter Wimsey, the detective-minded aristocrat whose special aptitudes were shown in a long series of novels and short stories. His cases related in *Clouds of Witness* (1926), *Unnatural Death* (1927), *The Unpleasantness at the Bellona Club* (1928) and *Lord Peter Views The Body* (1928) are entertaining, but not outstanding, examples of well-written detective stories. At that point, however, Miss Sayers became fascinated by the *genre* as a literary medium, probed its origins, examined notable nineteenth century examples, and devoted herself to preparing, first one, and eventually three anthologies of the finest examples of the *genre* then in existence. A few years earlier, a small collection of detective stories had been published, with a somewhat tentative introduction by E. M. Wrong, but D. L. Sayers set about the matter in far greater detail, giving two of her anthologies an illuminating Introduction that revealed the wide scope of her research into the techniques and historical background of this kind of fiction. Thereafter, the detective novel in her hands began to bridge the gap which had, for more than half a century, separated it from the 'literary' novel.

In the Introduction to her first anthology, Dorothy L. Sayers gave her opinion that *"The Moonstone* is probably the very finest detective story ever written, . . . and comes about as near perfection as anything of its kind can be."* In her next novel she borrowed Collins's technique of telling the story by means of letters and reports, in *The Documents in the Case* (1930), written in collaboration with "Robert Eustace," to whom, doubtless, is due the authoritative presentation of scientific laboratory detection. Technically, this novel is superb, but it lacks the stimulating presence of Lord Peter Wimsey, who makes a welcome return in *Strong Poison* (1930), in which he meets Harriet Vane, a prisoner awaiting re-trial on a charge of murder. Harriet is a detective novelist, whose lively comments upon the technique of her art give Lord Peter an entertaining variant from his immediate problem of proving her innocence, and his longing to make her his wife, an ambition he eventually achieves in *Busman's Honeymoon* (1937). In the intervening years, however, Dorothy L. Sayers's most famous novels were to be written, *Murder Must Advertise* (1933), *The Nine Tailors* (1934) and *Gaudy Night* (1935).

Here, also, Miss Sayers followed an example set by certain nineteenth century novelists who derived interesting material from the inner workings of various trades or professions, e.g. Thackeray's *Pendennis,* with its background of the Press; Surtees' rollicking tales of Mr. Jorrocks, the fox-hunting grocer; Trollope's series of novels dealing with clerical life. Miss Sayers, who had earned her living as a copy-writer in an advertising firm (and had, indeed, already written a few short detective stories about an enterprising commercial traveller, Montague Egg) created from her experience a completely convincing setting for *Murder Must Advertise;* her own early life at her father's vicarage in the Fen country, plus her knowledge of campanology, gave her the greater part of *The Nine Tailors;* and her years as a student at Somerville provided her with the background, and most of the action, of *Gaudy Night.* In attempting a 'literary detective novel' there is, however, a grave risk that the detective theme may be forced into a subordinate position, instead of remaining the centre of interest. This disturbance of balance is just avoided in *Murder Must Advertise* and *The Nine Tailors,* which are among the finest in the *genre,* but in *Gaudy Night,* with its well-sustained portrayal of college life and its acutely-reasoned discussions of intellectual integrity and psychological problems, there is scarcely sufficient real detection to sustain even a short story.

George Douglas Howard Cole (1889———)[8] and his wife Margaret Isabel, both distinguished authorities on History and Economics, collaborated in writing detective novels (and a few short stories), the first in the series, *The Brooklyn Murders* (1923) being followed by *The Death of a Millionaire* (1925) and a new volume almost every year for more than two decades. Their detective, Superintendent Henry Wilson, began his fictional career as one of the leading lights of Scotland Yard, but after a certain unfortunate brush with a Home Secretary he resigned his official position and set up in private practice. Novels such as those of G. D. H. & M. I. Cole, with a detective in the Inspector French tradition, tend to suffer from a serious handicap. Once the crime is discovered, the police official embarks upon a series of interviews with everyone in any way connected with the house or family, and all this often wearisome, repetitive 'evidence,' most of it chaff with a very occasional grain of wheat, has to be sifted and assessed, a slow and tedious process. In spite of this over-load of detail, the novels of G. D. H. & M. I. Cole do not invariably keep the reader fully informed on material points.

One writer with the skill to avoid these defects was Philip Macdonald (189?——)[9] who reduced such interviews and 'statements' to a minimum, and found ways of imparting information with scrupulous fairness in the midst of action and excitement. His semi-official detective, Colonel Anthony Gethryn, made his *début* in *The Rasp* (1924) and continued his brilliant career in a long series of novels, among which the most notable are *The White Crow* (1928), *The Link* (1930), *Murder Gone Mad* (1931), *R.I.P.*, (1933) and *The Nursemaid Who Disappeared* (1938). After a break of some years, Macdonald returned to detective fiction with a particularly fine short story, *The Green-and-Gold String,* presenting a completely new type of private investigator, the crystal-gazing Doctor Alcazar.

Alfred Edward Woodley Mason (1865—1948),[10] whose *At The Villa Rose* (1910) had introduced that great detective, Hanaud, wrote two more novels with the same hero, *The House of the Arrow* (1924) and *The Prisoner in the Opal* (1929), all of them set in France, and all as remarkable for their delightful character studies as for the credibility of their breathlessly exciting plots. They follow the same unusual pattern with a strong vein of chivalry. Crimes have been committed, and Hanaud will in due course capture the criminals, but his more immediate concern is to rescue the next intended victim, for whom he shows a gentle solicitude, 'like a big St. Bernard dog.' Hanaud, with his love of mountains, a habit of talking with his colleagues in the darkness of a cinema, his affection for his puzzled English friend, Mr. Ricardo, his ruthless efficiency and his irrepressible humour, is one of the most human detectives of fiction.

Major Cecil John Charles Street (1884——), who under his own name wrote works on international politics, biographical studies and a scholarly reconstruction of a famous crime, *The Case of Constance Kent* (1928),[11] also produced a large number of detective novels under the pseudonym of "John Rhode,"[12] some of his earliest being still the best known, *The Paddington Mystery* (1925), *Dr. Priestley's Quest* (1926), *The Ellerby Case* (1927) and especially *The Murders in Praed Street* (1928). Dr. Priestley represents a return to an earlier type of popular detective, and is not only a scientist but an enthusiastic criminologist who tackles a crime mystery as though it were a problem in astronomy or higher mathematics, with the human characters relatively unimportant.

Detective fiction owes a great debt to Monsignor Ronald A. Knox[13] (1888—1957), not so much for his first detective novel, *The Viaduct Murder* (1925), a light-hearted, improbable fusion of the railway-timetable alibi and the secret passage *motif*, or even for *The Body in the Silo* (1933), *Still Dead* (1934) and *Double Cross Purposes* (1937), as for his many sound examinations of technique. His 'Studies in the Literature of Sherlock Holmes,' which appeared in his *Essays in Satire* (1928) opened up new vistas, and in the following year, as a Preface to a new anthology of "Best Detective Stories" which he edited in collaboration with H. Harrington, he discussed the whole question of plot construction, formulating Ten Rules that the author of such stories must not break. Other critics have since added to that decalogue, but few have done more to shape the *genre* in recent decades than Father Ronald Knox.

The strong revival of public interest at this time inspired the publication of anthologies in America also, where one of the first, *The World's Great Detective Stories*, (1927), was edited, with a far-sighted, informative Introduction, by Willard Huntington Wright (1888—1939),[14] a literary figure of considerable stature as an editor, journalist and art critic. For his own 'fictional sleuthing' he adopted a pseudonym based on 'an old family name, Van Dyne.' Whether the spelling was changed by design or accident, it was as "S. S. Van Dine" that he became the most widely read writer of his day, and brought to American fiction a new kind of amateur detective in his immensely popular novels of Philo Vance. Vance is a languid, scholarly hero, with "a tremendous flair for the significant under-currents of the so-called *trivia* of life," and a tiresome habit of holding up the action by his long discourses on extraneous subjects. In his 'intuitional' methods, his sensitiveness to psychological clues, he is sometimes faintly reminiscent of Reginald Fortune, but he lacks the saving graces of modesty and a sense of humour. In startling contrast to the personality of Philo Vance is the tone of the stories in which he appears, crammed as they are with every form of melodramatic violence. 'S. S. Van Dine' introduced two special features that were later much used by other writers; his technique of eliminating all the obvious suspects, one after the other, by making them victims of the unknown killer, the suspense mounting as the circle narrows[15]; and his adoption of a form of title that came to serve almost as a signature for his work. The words "murder case" appear in the titles of all twelve of his novels, of which the best are among his earliest, *The Benson Murder Case* (1926),[16] *The Greene Murder Case* (1928), *The Bishop Murder Case* (1929) and *The Dragon Murder Case* (1933).

Earl Derr Biggers (1884—1933),[17] whose first mystery novel, *Seven Keys to Baldpate* (1913) was enjoyed in a dramatised form on both sides of the Atlantic during the war years, is today chiefly remembered for his blandly imperturbable Chinese-Hawaiian sleuth, Charlie Chan, who pursued his official investigations, ashore and afloat, through several novels which were serialised in the *Saturday Evening Post* before appearing in volume form —*The House Without a Key* (1925), *The Chinese Parrot* (1926), *Behind That Curtain* (1928) and *Charlie Chan Carries On* (1930). Charlie Chan's adventures were widely portrayed on the screen, as were those of the almost equally well-known Japanese detective-hero created in the following decade by John Phillips Marquand (1893——)[18] in *Thank You, Mr. Moto* (1936), *Think Fast, Mr. Moto* (1937), *Mr. Moto Is So Sorry* (1938) and *Last Laugh, Mr. Moto* (1942), all with soundly constructed plots. Mr. Moto, however, lacked Charlie Chan's urbane charm, and conveyed a more subtly sinister atmosphere of oriental cunning.

Frances Noyes Hart (1890——)[19] wrote several mystery novels that found an appreciative public, in particular *The Bellamy Trial* (1927) in which the detective theme is conveyed through the day-to-day evidence in court. Her *Hide in the Dark* (1929) returns to the setting of a country house party, over-familiar in contemporary American mystery novels, and *The Crooked Lane* (1934) brings nothing new to the *genre*. Mrs. Hart did not create a detective-hero, but her plots are intricate and well-devised, her characters subtly drawn. Her popularity was eclipsed by a new vogue for over-emphasis, a cult of exaggerated realism, that suddenly dominated American detective fiction in the 1930's through the influence of Dashiell Hammett and his successors. Before passing on to this new generation of writers, however, it will be worth while to glance at certain developments that made themselves felt in the Old World as the third decade opened.

In France, where detective fiction had for so long been represented almost solely by melodramatic *romans policiers* or by translations of English authors (Conan Doyle in particular) there was a sudden burst of popularity for a Belgian writer, Georges Sim (1903——), "Georges Simenon,"[20] who presented with considerable literary skill the activities of Inspector Maigret, a fresh type of police-detective-hero, as realistic as Lecoq was theatrical. Maigret is sometimes brilliant, sometimes tedious, as he plods, smoking his pipe, through the slums, cheap cafés and railway stations of France and the Netherlands, awaiting with monumental patience the moment for the lightning stroke. Simenon in no way glorifies the work of detection, whether carried out by Maigret himself; by a poor shopkeeper torn between curiosity, cupidity and fear; or perhaps by some heartsick relative of an innocent prisoner, handicapped by shyness and inexperience, who yet somehow manages to uncover the truth. The characteristic savour of the stories lies in their stark realism, their tacit acceptance of the darker sides of human behaviour as normal, their picture of the shifts and indignities whereby the very poor contrive to scrape a living. Crime causes little surprise. There is perhaps a shrug of pity for the victim or the bereaved; pity and a deeper understanding for the criminal, hard driven by circumstances and inevitably doomed. The central puzzle is never merely an ingenious plot-device, always a poignant human problem. In Simenon's tales, detection lacks the exhilaration so familiar in English or American fiction of this type, and becomes routine police work with a sigh for the sorrows of humanity.

The series began in 1930, a time when anything fresh in the *genre* could command a hearing, and translations of seven

Maigret stories were published in England between 1932 and 1934, two of them being quickly reprinted in cheap editions.[21] In America they met with little favour until 1940, when an enterprising publisher, realising that most of them were too short for the novel-reading public, hit upon the idea of combining two to form a volume of more acceptable length, and in this form twenty-four of Simenon's best stories, to date, met with considerable, if belated, appreciation from American readers.[22]

By 1930, the output of detective fiction in England had become so vast that it stood at a crossroads, in danger of losing its distinctive qualities, its very individuality, in the mass of its own production. Was it to shrink to the limited compass of the sensational crime thriller, produced so prolifically by Edgar Wallace (1875—1932)?[23] Detection played some part in most of his hundred-odd works, though seldom as soundly as in the series: *The Mind of Mr. J. G. Reeder* (1925), *Red Aces* (1930), and *Mr. J. G. Reeder Returns* (1933). In general, his detection is facile, his plots intricate but stereotyped, his writing hasty, his characters little more than puppets.

Was the detective novel to become merged with the Adventure Novel, following the lead given by John Buchan (1875—1940) in *The Thirty-Nine Steps* (1915) and its sequels, with the 'detective' a high-ranking Army officer and enemy spies substituted for criminals—a lead already followed by "Francis Beeding"[24] in a long sequence of novels? An alternative type of popular adventure story also offered an opening for detective themes, as in the 'Bulldog Drummond' tales by "Sapper," (H. C. McNeile, (1888—1937)) or the exciting quests for hidden treasure devised by "Dornford Yates," (Cecil William Mercer, 1885——).

Should the detective story follow another inviting avenue that opened at this moment, and sink its own identity in tales of a rogue-hero, a gay adventurer flouting the conventions, trickster and detective by turns? Leslie Charteris (1907——)[25] had created just such a re-incarnation of Rocambole in his wildly popular Simon Templar, "The Saint," whose fascinating career began in *Enter The Saint* (1930) and is still continuing with undiminished zest.

That detective fiction followed the right road at this juncture was due in no small measure to the influence of a group of distinguished detective story writers who realised the immense potentialities of the *genre,* provided it maintained and improved its own standards. With this purpose in view they founded in 1929 The Detection Club of London, an august body whose first President was G. K. Chesterton, followed in that office by E. C. Bentley and later by Dorothy L. Sayers. Members admitted to this Club—a coveted honour—are sworn to respect the King's English, and to observe with meticulous care certain rules formulated to ensure 'fair play' between writer and reader, a technique that had been too long neglected. The outcome of this authoritative guidance, this inspired encouragement to new writers, was the Golden Age of detective fiction that dawned in England in the early 1930's.

One of the prime movers in the formation of The Detection Club was Anthony Berkeley Cox (1893———),[26] who, under his pseudonym "Anthony Berkeley," has produced many fine detective novels since his first, *The Layton Court Mystery* appeared in 1925. In his Preface to *The Second Shot* (1930) he expressed his conviction that the 'days of the old crime puzzle, pure and simple' were gone, and that the future lay with the more literary novel, dealing with 'a puzzle of character, rather than a puzzle of time, place, motive and opportunity'; a conviction amply borne out in his own works. His detective, Roger Sheringham, appears at his best in *The Poisoned Chocolates Case* (1929), though his exploits fill several volumes. Under a second pseudonym, "Francis Iles," A. B. Cox wrote a small group of novels of a different type, *Malice Aforethought* (1931), *Before The Fact* (1932) and *As For The Woman* (1939). The detective interest, particularly strong in *Malice Aforethought,* is inverted, and the tales are studies of criminal psychology, or, in their author's words, of 'murder as a natural out-growth of character.'

Meanwhile, a new note had been struck in America. Samuel Dashiell Hammett (1894———)[27] learned his detection the hard way, working for eight years as a Pinkerton's man, and knew at first hand the world of guns and gangsters portrayed in *Red*

Harvest (1929) and *The Dain Curse* (1929). It was in his next novel, *The Maltese Falcon* (1930), that Dashiel Hammett mastered his own line of country in the province of detective fiction, following it with his equally popular *The Glass Key* (1931) and *The Thin Man* (1934), the last named showing more humanity in its character drawing and becoming better known as a film than in its original form. In Dashiell Hammett's work there is a brutal realism of subject, treatment, and especially of dialogue, devised to keep the reader in a state of shock. His typical characters are cold, self-seeking, licentious and treacherous. His Sam Spade is the blueprint for the tough, 'hard-boiled' private investigator who works alone on a dangerous assignment, using his fists and his gun as readily as his brain; who always has a bottle of whisky handy and a beautiful blonde or redhead needing his help. His exploits, invariably successful despite the hazards of his unpredictable methods, are mystery thrillers rather than detective novels.

Several writers followed Dashiell Hammett's lead, notably Erle Stanley Gardner and Raymond Chandler, both of whom surpassed him in output and introduced their individual changes in the pattern. Erle Stanley Gardner (1889——)[28] shows immense fertility of imagination, and though writing represents for him a commercial rather than a literary enterprise, his work is of a quality to be read with pleasure. His best-known detective figure is a young, forceful criminal lawyer, Perry Mason, introduced in *The Case of the Sulky Girl* (1933), while in a separate series the investigator is a country district attorney, Douglas Selby, as in *The D.A. Holds a Candle* (1938). Under the pseudonym of "A. A. Fair," Mr. Gardner has produced a third series with Donald Lam and Bertha Cool in the role of detectives, as in *Lam To The Slaughter* (1939), and *Some Slips Don't Show* (1957). Of Gardner's recent work, *The Case of the Fan Dancer's Horse* (1952) deserves notice for its clever plot.

Raymond Thornton Chandler (190?——)[29] follows the Dashiell Hammett technique of piling violence on violence—"When in doubt, bring a man through the door with a gun!"—but Chandler wears his toughness with a difference, and tends to embellish his writing with short passages of quasi prose-poetry, not invariably congenial in their context. His first best-seller, *The Big Sleep* (1939), has a particularly good plot (used again with modifications in later novels) and Chandler shows his mastery of a difficult technique in *The High Window* (1942), related in the first person by the detective himself, Philip Marlowe. Chandler's typical detective-hero, usually investigating crime in millionaire play-boy circles, is not presented as a dominating, all-knowing figure, but is often caught up in the sweep of events, regaining control only towards the end. *The Long Good-bye* (1953) is perhaps his most characteristic work in the present decade.

Among the many other American writers who in recent years have produced detective novels with an individual *cachet* and have given pleasure to readers on both sides of the Atlantic, the following names come instantly to mind: Rex Stout,[30] who in *Fer-de-Lance* created the elephantine detective, Nero Wolfe, and his unusually bright 'Watson,' Archie Goodwin, and whose later works, in particular *The Golden Spiders* (1953), show his powers unimpaired; Stuart Palmer,[31] for his unexpected settings and the 'team' of Miss Hildegarde Withers and Inspector Oscar Piper, whose investigations swing from farce to successful detection; Fulton Oursler, "Anthony Abbott," for his Thatcher Colt, Police Commissioner for the City of New York, the best of the very few convincingly competent police detectives in American fiction. Phoebe Attwood Taylor, "Alice Tilton,"[32] created an original detective in Asey Mayo, the shrewd hero of her Cape Cod *Mystery* (1931). Of her recent novels *Diplomatic Corpse* (1951) attracted much favourable comment. "Craig Rice,"[33] (Georgiana Ann Randolph, who died in 1957) followed the 'tough' Dashiell Hammett tradition, the only notable woman writer to do so. She will be long remembered for her 'little lawyer,' John J. Malone, and for her *Trial By Fury*, which was well received on both sides of the Atlantic. Two other popular characters who appeared in several of her novels, Bingo and Handsome, those entertaining and intelligent street photographers, were engaged in solving another detective mystery, *The April Robin Murders*,

THE DEVELOPMENT OF THE DETECTIVE NOVEL

at the time of the author's sudden death. The novel, thus interrupted when three parts finished, has been completed by Ed McBain, himself a well-known writer of detective fiction. Mignon G. Eberhart,[34] often adopting the detective methods of Miss Green's Amelia Butterworth, brought a gentle, romantic approach and a hospital setting to *The Patient in Room 13* (1929) and *From This Dark Stairway* (1931). In later novels she has employed analytical psychological techniques as in *Another Man's Murder* (1957). Among other writers who have successfully woven a detective plot into novels of social life, we must notice Constance and Gwyneth Little, collaborating as "Conyth Little,"[35] who can sometimes introduce a vein of humour quite harmoniously as in *The Black House* (1950); and Mabel Seeley,[36] who brings a refreshing Minnesota background to her soundly constructed mystery novels, such as *The Listening House* (1938), *The Beckoning Door* (1950) and *The Stranger Beside Me* (1951).

Detective fiction, not only in America, owes a great deal to the work of "Ellery Queen,"[37] a pseudonym adopted by two cousins, Frederic Dannay and Manfred B. Lee, both born in Brooklyn in 1905. Their well-known detective 'team,' Inspector Richard Queen and his son Ellery, private investigator, first became popular in *The Roman Hat Mystery* (1929), reached new heights in *The Egyptian Cross Mystery* (1932), and have continued their career for two decades. In 1941, "Ellery Queen" produced a fresh anthology of short detective stories, selected after exhaustive research into hitherto little known sources, and in the same year *Ellery Queen's Mystery Magazine,* now circulating internationally, commenced publication. Between 1945 and 1957, this magazine organised an annual contest for short stories of crime, mystery and detection which stimulated wide interest among established as well as new writers, and did much to foster standards of technique.

This encouragement for the short story form has to some extent been complemented by the 'Edgar Allan Poe Awards' offered annually for mystery novels, as well as for other 'categories of mystery writing,' by the Mystery Writers of America, an organisation somewhat analogous to the Detection Club of

London. The difference in title is significant, underlining the distinction that whereas in England the detective interest remains dominant, in America the essential element is Mystery, whether or not detection is also involved, a return in spirit to the tradition inherited from Poe (and, indeed, from Brockden Brown) whose works ranged beyond detective themes to 'mystery and imagination,' horror and fantasy. In *The Soft Talkers* (1957) by Margaret Millar[38] (the present President of the Mystery Writers of America, and already celebrated for her *Beast in View* (1955)), the mystification intrigues and baffles, the social and geographical setting, the subtly drawn characters, are all entirely credible, suspense is cleverly fostered from the first page to the last, but there is very little detection in the English interpretation of the term.

As an offshoot of this trend towards mystery, horror and fantasy in American fiction, recent years have shown remarkable developments in the type of story loosely classified as 'science fiction,' which is in general outside our purview. Two writers, however, have succeeded admirably in merging 'science fiction' with detective themes, Fredric Brown[39] and Isaac Asimov,[40] whose work has attracted attention on both sides of the Atlantic, and who may inspire a vogue for this specialised variation of the *genre*. Nothing of quite the same quality has yet appeared in England, though it is by no means improbable that the attempt will be made, and that English writers will continue to borrow or adapt American patterns in the future, as they have in the past.

Twenty years ago, the American 'hard-boiled' detective hero was introduced into English fiction by Peter Cheyney (1896—1951) in his tales of Lemmy Caution and Slim Callaghan, who in their separate spheres perpetuated the Sam Spade tradition with meteoric success. Cheyney used Dashiel Hammett's technique of quick-fire dialogue and diamond-sharp action full of unexpected twists, changed the setting to London and the Home counties, adding a slangy or topical title. But his novels, bestsellers though many of them were in their day, brought nothing new to the *genre*. Many of his contemporaries were doing better work.

American-born John Dickson Carr (1905———),[41] who has lived for many years in England, is one of today's most notable writers of detective fiction. Under his own name or as "Carter Dickson," sometimes as "Carr Dickson," he has, during the last quarter of a century, written a great number of novels and short stories as remarkable for the craftsmanship of their plot and their well-sustained interest, as for their literary quality and their atmosphere of effortless ease. His stature as a writer has steadily improved through the years, but even his first novel, *It Walks By Night* (1930) deserves to be remembered. In it, Carr introduced one of the best known French detectives in contemporary English fiction, Bercolin, and experimented with a technique which he employed in later novels with even better effect, the trick of building up suspense by implying that the mystery must be due to supernatural agency. There is nothing supernatural about the eventual explanation, however, and Carr has a talent for making the ingenious mechanism of his solutions seem entirely credible as presented, whether actually feasible or not. In Carr's hands, even that well-worn theme, murder in a 'sealed room,' entered upon a new lease of life, notably in *The Hollow Man* (1935), in which that massive figure, Doctor Gideon Fell, foreshadowed the success he gained later in such novels as *The Arabian Nights Murders* (1936) and *The Problem of the Wire Cage* (1939). As "Carter Dickson," Carr created yet a third memorable detective in Sir Henry Merrivale, better known as "H.M.," or "the old man," in *The Plague Court Murders* (1934). Character drawing in Carr's work is well defined and convincing, his grasp of psychology sound, and his settings, whether in London, Chartres, Scotland, or the New Forest, aboard the liner *Queen Victoria*, or deep in the old Waxworks Museum in Paris, all have the atmosphere of reality.

Besides producing excellent examples of traditional detective stories, Dickson Carr has struck out upon new lines. In *The Reader Is Warned* (1939), he brings a new interpretation to the 'fair play' convention, giving the reader footnote 'warnings' which still do not help him to escape bewilderment, so subtle is the misdirection. A contemporary setting has long been customary in detective fiction, but several times in recent years Carr has given his work a historical background. *The Bride of Newgate* (1950) recreates London in the 1800's; *The Devil In Velvet* (1951) takes us back to the days of Charles II; his recent novel, *Fire Burn!* (1957) is set in the Regency period; and his clever short story, *The Gentleman From Paris*, brings to life the New York waterfront in 1849, and conjures up an imaginary incident in the life of Edgar Allan Poe so realistically that it seems actually true.

In addition to his own fictional works, John Dickson Carr has compiled with sympathetic insight a biography of the creator of Sherlock Holmes, *The Life of Sir Arthur Conan Doyle*, and has collaborated with that distinguished author's son, Adrian Conan Doyle, to produce an apocryphal, nostalgic group of short stories, *The Exploits of Sherlock Holmes* (1954).

Among the few writers who, like John Dickson Carr, can successfully combine a historical setting with a detective plot, we must include Lillian de la Torre,[42] an American author who reproduces the life and times of a great Englishman with remarkable effect in her *Dr. Sam. Johnson, detector* (1946), with James Boswell as the Watsonlike biographer who relates the investigations performed by his illustrious companion. Notable among her other novels are *Villainy Detected* (1947) and *Heir of Douglas* (1952).

Ngaio Marsh (1899———),[43] born in New Zealand of an English family, worked between 1928 and 1932 in London, where she wrote her first detective novel, *A Man Lay Dead*, not published until 1934. Many of her stories have an English setting, often, as in *Enter A Murderer* (1935), *Overture to Death* (1939), *Final Curtain* (1947) and *Opening Night* (1951), linked with the world of the theatre which she knows so well from her experience as an actress and, latterly, as a producer. Her detective, Inspector Roderick Alleyn, "Lady Alleyn's son," singularly fortunate in the way his official and social activities complement and occasionally overlap each other, is an essentially English figure, a 'gentleman policeman,' efficient, unobtrusive, given to understatement, conventional in that his successes depend upon routine police methods. In Miss Marsh's work the detective theme sometimes tends to slip into second place, eclipsed by the interest of the 'slice of life' the novel portrays. This is noticeable in *Died In The Wool* (1945), which gives a vivid picture of life, work and death on a New Zealand sheep farm, and the ramifications of the wool trade, with the local vernacular perhaps a little too much in evidence, but adding its quota to the verisimilitude of the whole. Some of Miss Marsh's other novels are better known, notably *Artists in Crime* (1938), which made her name in America as well as in England, but *Died In The Wool* has the merit of bringing a new setting to a *genre* in which such novelty is rare.

Originality of setting and treatment also distinguishes the work of A. E. Martin,[44] an Australian writer whose reputation is growing in America and England. His remarkable short story, *The Power of The Leaf* (1948), tells of aboriginal tribes living in the Bush more than a century ago, with "Ooloo of the Narranyeri" exercising his natural talent for observation and deduction on a puzzle that baffles the medicine man. Mr. Martin's *The Chinese Bed Mysteries* (1955) has another unconventional setting, a Freak Show touring Australia in more modern times.

Among the English writers who began producing detective fiction in the 1930's we must notice Gladys Mitchell[45] for her authentic pictures of middle-class suburban life in such novels as *The Mystery of a Butcher's Shop* (1929) and *The Saltmarsh Murders* (1932), and for creating at least one unforgettable character, Mrs. Bradley. Georgette Heyer,[46] now perhaps better known for her many light historical romances, has written entertaining detective novels, from *Merely Murder* (1935) to *Detection Unlimited* (1953). *A Blunt Instrument* (1938) with its well-differentiated character drawing and an unorthodox murderer in its Bible-quoting police constable, is one of her most popular stories.

Margery Allingham,[47] born in London in 1904, began writing in 1928, but her success in the *genre* dates from the first appearance of her mild-seeming amateur detective, Albert Campion, in *Death of a Ghost* (1934). Mr. Campion, bespectacled, unobtrusive, quietly aware of his own intelligence, is a master of the casual conversational phrase that carries a shattering implication. Margery Allingham's novels, especially those written in the 'thirties when social satire had its own vogue, are largely *romans de moeurs*, and her writing is more studied, more 'precious,' than in detective fiction generally, but the detective interest is so well-contrived, so subtly maintained and developed, that they must be included in this category. From the world of artists and critics in *Death of a Ghost*, the scene moves to a London publishing house in *Flowers For The Judge* (1936), and in *The Fashion in Shrouds* (1938) to a Mayfair dressmaking business. In *Black Plumes* (1940) Miss Allingham created a new detective, Inspector Bridie, as canny a Scot as Dr. James Bell himself, but less popular than her earlier hero, who, in *Traitor's Purse* (1941) returned to undertake counter-espionage in war-time London and continue his career on the same lines as before.

John Creasy, a sound, prolific writer, uses three conventional types of investigator; an amateur, "The Toff"; a policeman, Inspector West; and a 'scientist', Dr. Palfrey; each with a long series of cases to his credit.

"Anthony Gilbert's"[48] (Lucy Malleson's) first detective heroes, Scott Egerton and M. Dupuy, have been eclipsed by her most popular character, Arthur Crook, the jaunty, chatty lawyer whose highly original detective methods are particularly successful in *Something Nasty in the Woodshed* (1942) and *A Nice Cup of Tea* (1951). "Anthony Gilbert" is still adding to her laurels with *And Death Came Too* (1956), notable for its skilful handling of an unusually gripping theme, a threat to a child, and with *Give Death a Name* (1957).

"Josephine Bell"[49] (Dr. Doris Bell Ball) struck a new note in her early novels, writing refreshingly and with an atmosphere of authenticity about hospital procedure, discussions in medical lecture rooms, or the daily routine of a busy East End doctor as in *The Port of London* Murders (1938). Her amateur detective, Dr. David Wintringham, first interrupted his professional duties to investigate a mysterious crime in *Murder in Hospital* (1937) and was called in again to other cases, notably *Fall Over Cliff*

(1938) and *From Natural Causes* (1939). The war understandably caused a break in "Josephine Bell's" literary work, but she returned to popularity with *Summer School Mystery* (1950) and continues to gain prestige with *China Roundabout* (1956) and *Double Doom* (1957).

Christopher Bush,[50] one of many schoolmasters who have left that profession to write detective fiction, gained wide recognition for his first book, *The Perfect Murder Case* (1929) and has added to his reputation with a long series, notably *The Case of the Platinum Blonde* (1944). His speciality (as it was Freeman Wills Crofts') is breaking the 'unbreakable alibi,' and his frequent subject is murder on a seaside holiday, though *The Case of the Dead Shepherd* (1934) has an entirely convincing background in a secondary grammar school. Mr. Bush has a light, flowing narrative style and his plots are credible as well as intricate, qualities that are especially apparent in *The Case of the Seven Bells* (1949), well-received on both sides of the Atlantic. His later novels, in particular *The Case of the Extra Man* (1957) and *The Case of the Flowery Corpse* (1957) are equally pleasing.

"Richard Hull," (Richard Henry Sampson, 1896————)[51] writes from a very different stand-point, usually relating in the first person the story behind a murder, as planned in the mind of the murderer, a modification of the technique adopted by "Francis Iles," whom "Richard Hull" greatly admired. The first of his many novels in this vein, *Murder of My Aunt* (1935) was an immediate success and remains one of his best.

Edward Grierson[52] reaches an unusually high literary level in his *Reputation for a Song* (1952), which builds up slowly and by natural degrees into a crescendo of violence and crime, and in *The Second Man* (1956), in which a woman barrister, defending a difficult, reticent client charged with murder, succeeds in penetrating the deceits of a lying witness. Particularly well-presented are the court scenes and the interplay of professional jealousy and loyalty, written with the inside knowledge at Mr. Grierson's command. Accuracy in legal matters also distinguishes the detective novels of Michael Gilbert,[53] a London solicitor, whose stories range over a wide variety of subjects and settings.

His first, *Close Quarters* (1947) deals with a 'sealed room' problem in the precincts of a cathedral. Organised crime in London, routine police work and judicial procedure are the subjects of *They Never Looked Inside* (1947) and *The Doors Open* (1949). *Smallbone Deceased* (1950), set in the office of a London lawyer, is less striking, but *Death in Captivity* (1952) shows originality in its presentation of a murder mystery in an Italian prisoner-of-war camp. His next novel, *Fear To Tread* (1953) is outstanding and gives an alarming, authentic-seeming picture of the gangster violence behind large-scale pilfering on the railways. Mr. Gilbert has not yet surpassed this achievement, and of his later works perhaps the most entertaining is *The Claimant* (1957), an ingenious reconstruction of the Tichborne Case.

John Innes Mackintosh Stewart,[54] born near Edinburgh in 1906, distinguished himself in the world of letters while still at Oxford, and after a period as lecturer at Leeds University accepted an appointment in Australia, as Professor of English at Adelaide University. As "Michael Innes" he has written many novels and short stories of his Scotland Yard detective, Inspector John Appleby (later Sir John), a scholarly sleuth with a "weakness for cultivated reverie" and a habit of overfrequent conversational references to the classics and the lesser-known poets. The first in the series, *Death at the President's Lodging* (1936), with its very complicated plot, is set in a provincial university, described with satirical humour and a wealth of detail. *Hamlet, Revenge!* (1937) brings a detective drama to complicate an amateur Shakespearean performance in an English country house. In his third novel, *Lament For A Maker* (1938), Michael Innes came to full stature in the *genre*, and produced one of the most memorable detective novels of recent years. The title itself is derived from a fifteenth century historical poem, William Dunbar's *Lament For The Makaris*, the setting is Scotland, gloriously portrayed, while the method of presentation and the plot itself are cleverly modernised from Wilkie Collins's *The Moonstone*. The literary quality of this novel has not been reached again in Michael Innes's later work, though his popular detective, erudite as ever, has continued to appear in a long series of slight tales, with his name in the title of each volume, and has regained something of his former stature in *The Long Farewell* (1958), which shows Sir John grappling with a complicated mystery that calls for his own special blend of scholarship and detective skill.

A younger author belonging to this same donnish school of detective story-writers is "Edmund Crispin" (Robert Bruce Montgomery),[55] also an Oxford man and an educationalist, as devoted as Michael Innes to the polysyllabic adjective, the abstruse noun, and whimsical proper names. His amateur investigator, Dr. Gervase Fen, is himself an Oxford don who writes detective stories, when not distracted from his literary labours by mysterious crimes affecting his personal friends, the headmaster of a public school, for instance, in *Love Lies Bleeding* (1948), where the plot turns on the discovery of the original manuscript of a 'lost' Shakespeare play. To offset his somewhat 'precious' literary style, "Edmund Crispin" has a vein of original humour, a talent for vivid description, unusual settings and intriguing titles—*Frequent Hearses, The Moving Toyshop, Beware of the Trains*—and is one of the most promising English writers of the *genre* to come to the fore in recent years.

The early crime novels of Julian Symons,[56] historian, biographer, poet and literary critic, have somewhat the same scholarly atmosphere, though to a less marked degree, as in *The Immaterial Murder Case* (1945) and *A Man Called Jones* (1947). But a change towards realism became apparent in *The Thirty-first of February* (1950) and reached completion in *The Narrowing Circle* (1954), a terse account of crime and personal relationships in a third-rate publishing business, with ruthlessly factual descriptions of London night life and of the chief characters. His latest, *The Colour of Murder* (1957) is exceptionally entertaining, despite the somewhat arbitrary solution to the detective problem, and has received the Crime Writers' Association's special award as the best Crime Novel of the year.

A contrasting 'realistic' or 'naturalistic' school is well represented by Raymond Postgate[57] (brother of Mrs. M. I. Cole whom we have noticed earlier) who, in addition to his works on economics and social studies has written three murder mysteries, *Verdict of Twelve* (1940), *Somebody at the Door* (1943) and *The Ledger is Kept* (1953). In them the detective interest, though well sustained, is less convincing than his sharply etched settings and his analysis of the psychological causes of the crime.

Another exponent of straightforward detection, Roy Vickers,[58] shines in short stories, grouped in volume form. His *Department of Dead Ends* (1949) adopts an interesting inverse technique, somewhat in the manner of J. Austin Freeman's *The Singing Bone*, giving the reader full information as the crime is committed, and then showing how "dead ends," odd items of rubbish, trifles disregarded by the criminal or left behind by the victim, eventually lead the police to the truth. His *Eight Murders in the Suburbs* (1956) is in the same vein.

In his many detective novels, "Nicholas Blake"[59] makes no parade of erudition, but everything he writes shows the same sense of drama in everyday life, the same sensitive choice of language, which distinguishes the poetry he has published under his own name of Cecil Day Lewis. His first novel as "Nicholas Blake", *A Question of Proof* (1935), set in a preparatory school, was followed by *Thou Shell of Death* (1936) which made his name known in America. His detective, Nigel Strangeways, first appeared in *The Beast Must Die* (1938), a gripping study of criminal psychology. *Malice in Wonderland* (1940), set in a popular seaside summer holiday camp, shows acute observation in its varied characterisation, and his more recent novels, *The Dreadful Hollow* (1953) and *The Whisper in the Gloom* (1954) display a masterful handling of tension and suspense. Margaret Erskine[60] shows her grasp of the same technique in *The Whispering House* (1947), in which her Scotland Yard detective, Inspector Septimus Finch, finds himself in a rambling mansion on a lonely moor where violent storms rage and murder follows murder. Similar themes are exploited in a sequence of tales such as *Give Up The Ghost* (1949) and *The Voice of Murder* (1956). Suspense is also the keynote of Christianna Brand's[61] novels, but shorn of such theatrical trappings. *Death in High Heels* (1941) is set in a dress shop, with murder no less terrifying in a prosaic background. *Cat and Mouse* (1955), and *The Three-Cornered Halo* (1957) display Miss Brand's increasing skill in this technique.

Quite a different atmosphere characterises the novels of C. E. Vulliamy,[62] biographer, archeologist and historian, one of the very few English writers who can, without offence, blend humour with a detective theme, as in *Body in the Boudoir* (1956). For originality of setting and treatment we must notice an American writer, Clayton Rawson,[63] whose detective, Merlini, is a professional conjurer, and employs his art as an illusionist in three novels, *Footprints on the Ceiling* (1939), *Death From a Top Hat* (1940) and *The Headless Lady* (1941), all of them fantastic, but remarkably entertaining. An equally original idea, but much less bizarre, inspired Leonard Gribble,[64] who began writing detective stories as long ago as 1928 and now has an immense range of literary interests in addition to a prolific output under several pseudonyms. In *The Arsenal Stadium Mystery* (1939), he introduced the world of professional football as the setting for a detective mystery, continuing the same pattern with an additional topical twist in *They Kidnapped Stanley Matthews* (1950).

William Wiegand[65] has to his credit one really clever detective mystery with an original technique, *At Last, Mr. Tolliver* (1950) which immediately attracted attention not only in the States but also in Great Britain. The setting is convincing, the characters typically American. It is the mystery which is so unusual, and concerns the motive for the crime, not the crime itself. Murder takes place quite early in the story, and the detection, or, rather, the assembling and interpretation of clues, is concerned with discovering the hidden reasons for the apparently inexplicable "Why?" not "How?" or "By Whom?" the crime was committed.

An English writer of unusual promise, Winston Graham,[66] has adopted the technique of presenting an absorbing detective problem in the form of a personal problem urgently affecting the chief character in the story. In *The Little Walls* (1955) the hero, investigating the alleged suicide of his brother, finds himself involved in a net of mystery and danger that stretches from

Amsterdam to Italy. In *The Sleeping Partner* (1956) a husband hunts for the murderer of his estranged wife. This method of presentation dispenses with any advantage to be gained from the over-sized personality of a recurring detective-hero, and has instead the force of genuine delineation of character. *The Little Walls* has the additional merit of richly varied geographical backgrounds, and it is not surprising that this English novel at once attracted interest in the States.

For years there has been a quick interchange of fiction of this type across the Atlantic. There are, and will probably remain, certain national differences between English and American detective stories, but to an increasing extent writers find readers in both countries. Publishers' organisations, such as the 'Crime Club,' here and in the States, keep the public directly informed of the best work currently produced in the *genre*. Periodicals devote considerable space to reviews of new detective novels, and in England, particularly, the standard of reviewing is remarkably high, the work of specialists in this field. The Detection Club of London, the Mystery Writers of America, Crime Writers Associations in England and America, exist to maintain and improve standards of writing, plot construction and technical accuracy, stimulating new writers who seek the prestige of membership. The writing of detective fiction, in contrast to all other literary *genres*, has in fact now become an intensively organised, highly competitive business.

The ultimate effect of these developments cannot yet be foreseen. Will the detective novel become stereotyped, like so many other forms of entertainment in modern times, ingeniously devised, cleverly produced, its mechanism functioning with polished precision, but still a stereotype? Or will it find ways to retain its individuality, remembering that its ancient roots lie not in puzzles merely, but in puzzles as they affect people, and drawing from that original source the vitality to make new growth? At the moment, these probabilities seem evenly balanced.

CHAPTER
XIII

THE DETECTIVE STORY IN
FRANCE, AMERICA AND ENGLAND

It is difficult to determine exactly when the term 'detective novel' first came into general use. It was recognised in France, earlier than elsewhere, that such stories constituted a new *genre* requiring a new descriptive phrase, and when Gaboriau produced his novels of Monsieur Lecoq his publisher, Dentu, gave them the name of *romans judiciaires*. Public usage quickly modified this into the more apt *romans policiers*, which has been used ever since for French tales of crime and detection, whether with a police hero or not. When the novels of Gaboriau and his successors became popular in English translation the French description was retained, no English equivalent having as yet been devised. America, however, coined the term 'detective story,' a description which Anna Katharine Green used in 1878 on the title page of *The Leavenworth Case*. Though this novel became as popular here as in America, England was slow to adopt the descriptive term, and current periodicals, the *Athenaeum* for instance, still continued to employ such cumbersome phrases as "a sensation novel in the Gaboriau style," or "a tale of crime and detection of the school of Du Boisgobey." By 1888 the description "police novel" had become generally accepted—Stevenson used it freely in *The Wrong Box* and *The Wrecker*—and as soon as that great amateur, Sherlock Holmes, began to dominate the field in the 1890's, the term 'detective novel' or 'detective story' came into use in England as well as in America.

It must be recognised that in France the *roman policier*, notwithstanding its profuse growth and its influence on detective fiction generally, has never attained the status that the detective novel enjoys in England and America. The causes for this wide divergence of opinion lie partly in the general historical and social backgrounds of these countries, and partly in their national differences in questions of literary taste. Detective fiction, from its very nature, is so largely affected by the way in which each country regards its police, and by its system of retributive justice, that some consideration of these matters seems called for, before going on to discuss certain qualities that French, American and English readers, respectively, find congenial in fiction.

An essential feature of detective fiction in any language is that the sympathy of writer and reader lies with the investigator. If, as is generally the case, the plot deals with a crime that would normally call for police action, the reader, enjoying in imagination the search for the criminal or for the evidence that proves him guilty, is to that extent sharing the function of the police. Even when the detective is an amateur, police ·organisation is in the offing, ready to play its part at the appropriate moment, and Sherlock Holmes spoke for others beside himself when he said: "I go into a case to help the ends of justice and the work of the police."[1] Because of the very different relations between police and public in France and England (leaving for a moment the American attitude to this question) it was far more difficult for a Frenchman than for an Englishman to ally himself, even only in imagination, with the affairs of the police during the years when detective fiction was coming into existence as a separate *genre*.

When Buonaparte reorganised the French police in the early nineteenth century, his purpose was to create a powerful instrument of internal government, and the first duty of the men who composed this force, from Fouché downwards, was not so much to protect the public from criminals as to keep close watch on any subversive factions that might threaten the newly established *régime*.[2] In so far as they concerned themselves with trying to catch thieves or murderers, they delegated the investigations to *agents*, who, more often than not, were ex-convicts, as Vidocq himself was, for the plausible reason that such men were familiar

---

[1] Sir Arthur Conan Doyle, *The Valley of Fear*, L. 492.
[2] In politically troubled times, under the Consulate, for example, there were several separate sections of the police, all fully occupied in spying on each other. Cf. ' Mémoires de Mme de Rémusat', *Revue des Deux Mondes*, 1.8.1879; pp. 54-69.

with the ways of criminals, and thus more likely to bring in dependable information. This long-continued practice gave the public good cause for further misgiving and distrust, and the scathing comments that occur so frequently in French literature throughout the nineteenth century, particularly in the novels of Balzac and Victor Hugo, leave no doubt as to what Frenchmen of the times thought of their police. Even Gaboriau, much as he admired the efficiency of police organisation, described the typical *agent* of the 1860's as a shady customer, treacherous and cunning, as false as his flashy jewellery, hated by the common people even while they poked fun at his shabby overcoat, buttoned up to the neck to hide his complete lack of underwear.[1] Monsieur Lecoq, of course, was a vastly different figure whose personal elegance, theatrical successes and masterly command of logic made him a popular hero of fiction, *policier* though he was, without, however, overcoming the people's mistrust of the police in real life.

The *Mémoires* of M. C. Macé, *ex-Chef de la Sûreté*, published in 1884, show how extensive were the powers of the police, how far they could at that time intrude upon the private lives of French citizens, particularly of those who worked for their living. Anyone suspected of even a minor offence had little chance of avoiding arrest, whether innocent or guilty, and the police were not only allowed but compelled to question and cross-question a suspect with extreme severity. Yves Guyot, a member of the *Conseil Municipal de Paris*, gave even more illuminating details in *La Police*,[2] reviewing the whole history and organisation of the *Préfecture*. For the individual *gardien de la paix* Guyot expressed sympathy. His work was thankless and difficult, often dangerous, always poorly paid. But he was a member of a powerful organisation that would, for its own sake, cover up any delinquency on the part of one of its own men, and if, as sometimes happened, an *agent* augmented his income by robbery, even with violence, the policy of the *préfecture* was to conceal the matter.[3] The promotion of an *agent de police* depended

[1] Cf. Gaboriau, *Le Crime d'Orcival*, Ch. 5.
[2] Yves Guyot, *La Police*, Paris, Charpentier, 1884.
[3] *Ibid.*, p. 387.

chiefly upon the number of arrests he made, irrespective of the seriousness of the charge, and more than forty thousand Parisians were taken into custody in 1882, mostly for trivial offences, while crimes of violence too often went unpunished.[1]

Guyot stressed the contrast between the methods of the French police and those of their more kindly English counterparts, urging his fellow-countrymen to adopt less brutal, more modern and scientific ways of conducting their investigations.[2] Such changes came about only gradually, however, and it is plain from articles which continued to appear in authoritative journals[3] that although the French police became more reputable and more efficient, they did not become more popular with the general public, at least until the twentieth century was well advanced. Hack writers continued to produce quantities of *romans policiers* for uncritical readers (often showing the police flouted by rogue heroes) but it is hardly surprising that French authors of good literary standing held themselves aloof from subjects involving police affairs or the detection of crime, despite the notable example set by Conan Doyle and his contemporaries in England at the turn of the century. Not until Simenon's stories began to appear in the 1930's was there in France any appreciable recognition of detective fiction as a literary or quasi-literary *genre,* and even then the popularity of these tales was due rather to Simenon's skill in depicting the French scene, his psychological interpretations of motives, actions, human relationships, than to the personality and activities of Inspector Maigret, excellent police officer though he was.

In England, Londoners reserved judgment when the New Police Force was inaugurated in 1829, but by the middle of the century the police, including the more recently established Detective Branch, had won respect and esteem throughout the country. The public grew interested in their work and enjoyed reading of their methods. The police-officer became a familiar figure in melodrama, and appeared to still better advantage in the novels

[1] *Ibid.*, pp. 387-389.
[2] *Ibid.*, pp. 420-423.
[3] Cf. *inter alia,* Paul Allard, ' L'anarchie de la police ', *Revue de Paris,* 15.3.1934. Ernest Raynaud, ' La police des moeurs ', *Mercure de France,* I.X.1934.

of Charles Dickens and Wilkie Collins, Detective-Inspector Bucket and Sergeant Cuff creating a popular conception of the typical English policeman that endured for half a century.

In England the police are un-armed, non-political, and (with the exception of the Metropolitan Police) are not direct servants of the Government but are administered locally, often being local men. They are, in fact, civilians whose job is to protect and assist their fellow citizens, and to see that the law is kept. The basic conception is plain in the Instructions issued in 1830 by Sir Richard Mayne, one of the first two Police Commissioners:

'Every member of the Force, . . . whilst prompt to prevent crime and to arrest criminals, must look upon himself as a servant and guardian of the general public and treat all law-abiding citizens, irrespective of their social position, with unfailing patience and courtesy.'

Wise administration on these lines has given the English police a unique advantage. In contrast to the police of France, and, indeed, of most other nations, the English policeman is regarded by the public as their safeguard against any threat to their personal rights and liberties, their ready helper in any emergency. In turn, they will assist the police whenever they can. The average Englishman is interested in the details of police work, particularly in detective investigations, and when reading of such matters in fiction he can happily range himself on the side of the investigator. If there have been more amateur than professional detectives in English fiction, this may be because we admire an enterprising individualist more spontaneously than a member of an organisation, no matter how respected that organisation may be. But every detective of fiction, private or official, works towards the same objective, and it is taken for granted that once the criminal is identified, police organisation will bring him to trial.

The position of a prisoner in an English court is vastly different from that of a prisoner before a French court because of the wide disparity between the legal systems of the two countries. In England a prisoner is fortunate in that his personal rights are scrupulously respected; he suffers no violence; he cannot be forced or even induced to make a statement that might incriminate him. Even when the charge is murder, the accused is presumed innocent until his guilt has been clearly established. He will be convicted only if the police can produce such incontrovertible proofs that a jury of twelve ordinary men and women can entertain no reasonable doubt of his guilt, and their verdict must be unanimous. Not till sentence has been passed can the accused be referred to, in the Press or anywhere else, as a murderer. The average Englishman takes a strong pride in this interpretation of Justice, unperturbed by the fact that our legal system seems strange and illogical to French minds.

France is equally proud of her own judicial system, and her 'Code' has been drawn up with the most scrupulous care to specify precisely the application of the law in respect of every conceivable set of circumstances. In a French court, everything depends, in principle, upon the written word of the Code. In practice, however, the administration of the Code, perhaps because of an anxiety to make it impossible for the guilty to escape punishment, often seems to operate to the prejudice of the accused and to permit police abuses. Consequently, a fairly general impression exists that in France the accused is presumed guilty unless he can prove his innocence. Indeed, Francois Fosca not only states this as being true, but regards it as one of the chief causes for the contrast between the *roman policier* and the Detective Novel in France and England respectively.[1]

How has this impression gained credence? Why does French justice provoke the assertion that it assumes guilt, when, in literal fact, it is committed to assume the contrary? Some consideration of the following points, necessarily presented in a simplified form, may help to show why this has come about.

English readers, accustomed to a system in which a barrister acts sometimes for the defence, sometimes for the prosecution, find it difficult to understand why this can never occur in the French Courts. An *avocat,* who acts as counsel for the defence, belongs to one branch of the legal profession, while the *juge* and the *procureur* leading the prosecution both belong to a

[1] Cf. *Op. cit.,* p. 16.

different group. They are both *magistrats*, members of a special body of state officials whose experience is gained in judging or in prosecuting, perhaps alternately, but never in defending. In their qualifications and their interests they are linked with each other, not with the *avocat*. Rightly or wrongly, the impression begins to form in an English mind that such a system may lend more weight to the prosecution than to the defence.

A *juge d'instruction*, to whom we have no equivalent, is intended to be a safeguard for the innocent. The arrested man is placed in his charge, and should he decide there is no case to answer he can set him free. The *juge*, however, is responsible for establishing the facts of the case; he must use the police as his agents; and it is generally easier to conduct the enquiry if the accused is kept in custody. Thus, instead of protecting a possibly innocent man, the *juge d'instruction* may open the door to police abuses. Further, when the *juge d'instruction* declares there is a case against the prisoner, it is a judge who has said so, and this already creates an assumption of guilt in the public mind, an assumption often fostered by the tone of Press reporting.

As to the methods of interrogation practised by the French police, the authorities and the public alike have come to accept that there may be justification for 'ruthless repression' of crime or of subversive activities in a country where violent disturbances are by no means unknown. While the accused is in custody, waiting for the case against him to be completed in meticulous detail—a lengthy process—the police may obtain his confession which then becomes part of the evidence, making 'incontrovertible proofs' less essential. When the public trial opens, what remains is for the *avocat* to establish the moral factors in the case, the 'extenuating circumstances,' which may materially affect the severity of the sentence. An indulgent jury can often be swayed by such a plea, put forward by an eloquent *avocat*, to a degree quite unknown in England, but the argument has weight only if the prisoner is guilty, not if he is unjustly accused. The hazardous position of a prisoner facing trial in a French court cannot be denied. It is not precisely true that the law considers him guilty unless he can acquit himself, but he is in

jeopardy even if innocent, and if guilty he certainly faces conviction and sentence. As far as the Press and general public are
concerned, he may well be considered guilty even before his
public trial begins, virtually condemned by the fact that a trial
is to take place.

This, then, is the background that colours so distinctively
the French detective stories of Simenon and his imitators. The
question of 'proof'; the dove-tailing of time, place, detail,
material clues; the mechanism of the puzzle device; all these are
given far less importance than in English crime fiction. In any
case, French readers attach less value to these impersonal things
than to the personal characteristics of the human actors in the
drama. The detective must have patience, untiring watchfulness,
an intuitive flair. His job is not so much to collect and marshal
evidence for use at the trial—that is largely the province of
others—as to succeed in arresting the right man. The reader
looks beyond "How?" to "Who?" and on with even greater
interest to "Why?" To know the identity of the criminal is not
the end, as it so often is in English fiction, but to understand
him, possibly to sympathize with him. Hence the emphasis upon
his psychological history, the influences that brought him to
commit the crime, the *motif* of 'extenuating circumstances.' As a
result, the tale may become a study of criminal psychology rather
than of detection, a development that is apparent in some of
Simenon's work. Occasionally he shows the criminal, still free
and possibly unsuspected, throwing himself repeatedly in
Maigret's way, driven by remorse or by some uncontrollable
impulse, hovering around danger like a moth around a flame.
Here is a modern interpretation of the old Greek idea that a
criminal, by his own action, sets in train a process of retribution
that he is powerless to escape. A detective, in that event, would
have no function to perform, and development along those lines
could bring detective fiction to an end.

It is, in any case, unlikely that detective fiction will develop as
extensively in France as it has in England and America, or gain
comparable acceptance among well educated people. One reason
is the prejudice that still exists in cultured circles (though it has

become less in recent decades) against the old over-sensational *romans policiers* and their fictional descendants. But the fundamental cause seems to lie in the French attitude of mind towards literature in general and popular fiction in particular.

The French expect to derive something of value from their reading, some information about life or some commentary upon it. Fiction should broaden their knowledge of mankind, help them to gain a clearer understanding of realities and an insight into the minds of others, or inspire them with new lines of thought. Such themes are outside the scope of detective fiction, whose purpose is seldom more than to entertain its readers, generally by distracting their thoughts from 'real life.' French readers are not accustomed to read solely for diversion, as a means of occupying their leisure with no particular purpose in mind, and the disfavour, or lack of favour, so long expressed by the French for detective fiction may be only a part of their general attitude towards books they regard as having only entertainment value.

English-speaking peoples take a very different view of the purpose of fiction. They have long been in the habit of reading primarily for relaxation, often seeking a panacea for the mental stress of their daily work or their own real-life problems. Like Mrs. Battle, they 'unbend their mind over a book,' and the fact that the detective story offers such an 'escape' more readily and more completely than almost any other type of fiction would of itself go far to account for its long popularity in England and America. Readers in these countries also share a certain liking for facts and details, and can enjoy watching the jigsaw puzzle of clues being pieced together to form a complete and perhaps unexpected picture.

Since American legal procedure has some basis in the English systems that early settlers brought with them across the Atlantic, it is not surprising that similarities still exist, for example an accused man's right to be regarded as innocent until proved guilty. There are, on the other hand, radical differences. The vast geographical area of America, its division into States, each with its own laws, makes impossible anything approaching the uniformity and coherence that characterise English administration. There is not the same public attitude towards law-breaking or the same friendly regard for the police. America has her own exceptional problems and her own methods of coping with them. In addition to the activities of individual criminals there are highly organised crime rackets; the police are as well armed and as quick on the draw as the gangsters they fight; violence is taken for granted, and the general public does its best to keep out of range of both sides, often cultivating a detached attitude of mind. The known prevalence of third degree methods of interrogation, and the influence that local politics can exert on police administration, are matters which do not encourage confidence. American detective fiction makes a great deal out of such sensational elements as it can find to hand;—'big time crooks,' gangster warfare, the insidious corruption of graft, the experienced criminal, confident that his defence lawyer will find some hole in the legal net for his client to slip through, working with all the chicanery depicted by Davisson Post in *The Strange Schemes of Randolph Mason* as long ago as 1896.

In American fiction it is the amateur who flourishes, rather than the police detective, and there are sound reasons for this choice of hero. In the States the professional private detective, licensed by the police, working sometimes with them, sometimes in defence of their suspect, has a prestige and a position that his English counterpart does not possess outside the pages of fiction. (England has nothing comparable to the Pinkerton National Detective Agency, famous throughout America for more than a hundred years). In the comparatively rare cases when American stories give a recurring role to a police official he is usually supported by an unofficial investigator, as Inspector Queen is by his celebrated son, Ellery.[1]

For the rest, the American detective story dwells less on material clues and itemised evidence, more upon exciting action and a multiplicity of crimes. Mystery, sometimes intensified by horror, may play a larger part than 'pure' detection. Several

[1] The one notable exception is ' Anthony Abbott's ' Thatcher Colt, Police Commissioner of New York.

attempts have been made to extend the *genre* by incorporating studies of criminal psychology, but developments in this direction are likely to be limited. Few subjects lend themselves to treatment on these lines, and few writers have the knowledge or skill to do it well. It is, moreover, a very different subject, bearing little relation to detection.

There is, in fact, little room in the detective story for special consideration of psychological issues. To give more than fleeting attention to these questions would be to change the nature of the novel, and to cross the narrow boundary that divides the detective story from other types of fiction which may concern a mysterious crime. Trollope's *The Last Chronicle of Barset*, for example, is a wonderful psychological study of the poor, proud vicar, Joseph Crawley, accused of theft. The growing suspicion and suspense, the evidence of motive and opportunity, the official investigations and the trial, the efforts of his friends to discover the truth and prove his innocence, all these would be quite in keeping with a detective story. But this novel is of a different kind, because the central interest lies in the drama taking place in the mind of the accused man, not in the steps whereby the mystery is at last solved.

The detective novel has maintained its separate identity more clearly in England, where everything favoured its growth. It was soundly rooted in the work of important literary figures, while from Charles Dickens and Wilkie Collins in particular it learned to concentrate on 'pure' detection, rather than on horror. We have a friendly interest in our police, a lively interest in their detective work, and a fondness for a hero who can mingle dependability with 'infinite resource and sagacity.' Because of our legal code with its tradition of fair play for the accused and no victimisation, it is not enough for the detective to identify and arrest the criminal. He must support the charge with evidence obtained legitimately by intelligence and diligence, evidence strong enough to stand up under cross-examination. This insistence upon proof is mirrored in our detective fiction, and readers have from long experience become skilled in assessing the implications of the clues given by the author. One result has been to maintain the standard of accuracy in detective fiction, and no twentieth century writer could afford to make such a mistake about a scientific fact as Gaboriau did when he spoke of a body continuing to bleed after death. The plot of a detective story may, indeed often does, tell of events unlikely to occur in real life, but once those events are accepted as stated, all the evidence and the conclusions drawn from it must be entirely credible, or the novel will fail in its appeal to an English reader, no matter what attractions it offers in other respects.

One other characteristic that marks the typically English detective story is its remarkably unsensational treatment of murder, compared with the way in which this subject is handled by American writers from Dashiell Hammett to Raymond Chandler, even by Poe himself. It is, of course, a frequent theme, since there are more motives and methods for murder than for any other crime, but the English detective story merely postulates murder as a start for the argument, treating it like a point in geometry, having position but no magnitude, in no way dwelling on its morbid aspects, as novels of violence, 'thrillers,' and, indeed, psychological novels so often do.

In England the detective novel still bears, perhaps indelibly, the marks of its Victorian adolescence in its adherence to traditional techniques of construction and presentation, its uncompromising classification of people into 'good' and 'bad,' its rigid morality and its precept "Be sure your sin will find you out," its exclusion of sex and of 'the soul' as subjects for fiction. Yet despite these conventional restrictions it continues to achieve an atmosphere of modernity, even of novelty, because of the facility with which it can introduce fresh subject matter drawn from the most diverse sources.

The detective novel has acquired an identity of its own, but not, as yet, the status of a literary art form, even among English-speaking peoples. The idea that any work of fiction could be regarded as 'art' has gained acceptance only in comparatively recent times, and the conception may possibly be extended in the future. It is, however, more difficult for detective novels than for novels of another kind to attain a level of artistic quality because of the emphasis necessarily given to the mechanics of the plot, too often at the expense of that portrayal of character and social background which is the true purpose of literature. A few outstanding writers have succeeded in maintaining a harmonious balance between these two differing themes, but it must be acknowledged that most detective novels, born as they are of ingenuity rather than of inspiration or true imagination, are neither art nor literature. Yet they must be accorded some recognition in any survey of modern literature, in view of their long and sometimes distinguished history, their appeal to readers of almost every type, the breadth and scope of their influence, their potential excellence in the hands of writers of literary calibre.

The detective story, in essence fantasy, is a highly-finished product of the story-teller's craft. Even at its most pedestrian level it must have a good tale to tell and tell it well. It is devised as a game of skill, a game that has for generations been played with remarkable enthusiasm by writers and readers alike. Of late, it is sometimes said that this enthusiasm has begun to wane, that the rigour of the game has been lost, that its future is in doubt.

Somerset Maugham made his opinion plain in the very title of his essay on *The Decline and Fall of the Detective Story* (1952), and it is true that the last decade or so has seen a slackening of standards, with little to equal the achievements of the 1930's and early 1940's. The demand remains enormous, so does the output, but less of it bears the hallmark of quality, and originality is rare. Prophecies foreshadowing its eclipse may, however, prove to be mistaken, as has so often happened in the past. As long ago as 1890, *Blackwood's* said of crime fiction: "Considering the difficulty of hitting upon any fancies that are decently fresh, . . . surely this sensational business must soon come to an end,"[1] yet even at that moment a new era was dawning, and the detective story was on the point of rising to unprecedented heights in the adventures of Sherlock Holmes and his contemporaries. Who can say that this same pattern of

[1] *Blackwood's Edinburgh Magazine*, Dec., 1890 (Vol. CXLVIII, p. 189).

events will not occur again? It may well be that the Detective Novel is now lying fallow in preparation for new growth. Having reviewed the vicissitudes of its history so far, we can feel confident that so sturdy a *genre* has not yet exhausted its vitality or its capacity to surprise, and as long as readers seek in their fiction for entertainment that exercises their wits, so long will new writers of talent, perhaps brilliance, come forward to take up the challenge.

GENERAL BIBLIOGRAPHY

In addition to critical studies of the principles of fiction; histories of the novel; books and articles on individual authors; and English, French and American periodicals for the relevant period; the chief sources consulted are as follows:—

HISTORICAL AND SOCIAL BACKGROUND

(a) Autobiographies, Memoirs, Essays and Letters:
E. C. Bentley, *Those Days*, Constable, 1940.
G. K. Chesterton, *Autobiography*, Hutchinson, 1949.
Sir Arthur Conan Doyle, *Memories and Adventures*, Hodder and Stoughton, 1924.
Charles Dickens, *Letters*, Macmillan, 1893.
Baroness Orczy, *Links in the Chain of Life*, Hutchinson, 1947.
R. L. G. Ritchie, *France*, Methuen, 1937.
Frederick C. Roe, *Modern France*, Longmans, 1955.
M. Lincoln Schuster, *The World's Great Letters*, Heinemann, 1941.
William Tinsley, *Random Recollections of an Old Publisher*, Simpkin, Marshall, 1900.

(b) Works on Police History and Organisation:
S. Theodore Felshead, *Shades of Scotland Yard*, Long, 1950.
Joseph Gollomb, *Scotland Yard*, Hutchinson, 1926.
Maître Yves Guyot, *La Police*, Paris, Charpentier, 1884.
Richard Harrison, *C.I.D. and F.B.I.*, Muller, 1956.
Anthony Martienssen, *Crime and the Police*, Penguin Books, 1951.
Sir John Moylan, *Scotland Yard and the Metropolitan Police*, Putnam, 1930.
Quentin Reynolds, *Police Headquarters*, Cassell, 1956.
Henry Morton Robinson, *Science versus Crime*, Bell, 1937.
Alwyn Solmes, *The English Policeman*, 1871-1935, Allen & Unwin, 1935.
Sir Basil Thomson, *The Story of Scotland Yard*, Grayson, 1935.

(c) Judicial Administration:
R. C. K. Ensor, *Courts and Judges in France, Germany and England*, O.U.P., 1933.
Maître Maurice Carçon *La Justice Contemporaine*, Paris, Grasset, 1933.
R. M. Jackson, *The Machinery of Justice in England*, C.U.P. 1940.
F. C. Roe. 'French Institutions', R. L. G. Ritchie, *France*, Methuen, 1937.

WORKS ON DETECTIVE FICTION

(a) Studies published in volume form:
François Fosca, *Histoire et technique du roman policier*, Paris, Nouvelle revue critique, 1937.
Howard Haycraft, *Murder for Pleasure*, Davies, 1942.
Régis Messac, *Le "detective novel" et l'influence de la pensée scientifique*, Paris, Champion, 1929.
Marie Rodell, *Mystery Fiction: Theory and Technique*, Hammond, 1954.
Sutherland Scott, *Blood in their Ink*, Kegan Paul, 1953.
H. Douglas Thomson, *Masters of Mystery*, Collins, 1931.

(b) Introductions to Anthologies and critical studies:
Nicholas Blake, (Cecil Day Lewis), to Howard Haycraft, *Murder for Pleasure*, Davies, 1942.
S.S. Van Dine, (Willard Huntington Wright), to *The Great Detective Stories*, New York, Scribners, 1927.
John Gawsworth, to *Thrills, Crimes and Mysteries*, Assoc. Newspapers, 1936.
E. V. Knox, to *The Best Detective Stories of 1928*, Faber, 1929.
Dorothy L. Sayers, to *Great Short Stories of Detection, Mystery and Horror*, Gollancz. Series 1, 1928; Series 3, 1934.
E. M. Wrong, to *Crime and Detection*, O.U.P., 1921.

(c) Articles on Detective Fiction:
Anon, 'Detectives', *Saturday Review*, May 5th, 1883.
Anon, 'Crime in Fiction', *Blackwood's Edinburgh Magazine*, Aug. 1890.
Anon, 'Emile Gaboriau', *Times Literary Supplement*, Nov. 2nd, 1935.
John Carter, 'Detective Stories', *New Paths in Book Collecting*, Constable, 1934.
G. K. Chesterton, 'A Defence of Detective Stories', *The Defendant*, Brimley Johnson, 1901.
Jean Hankiss, 'Littérature populaire et roman-policier', *Revue de Littérature Comparée*, 1928.
Léon Lemonnier, Edgar Poe et les origines du roman-policier', *Mercure de France*, Nov. 15th, 1925.
A. E. W. Mason, 'Detective Novels', *Nation and Athenaeum*, Feb. 7th, 1925.
W. Somerset Maugham, 'The Decline and Fall of the Detective Story', *The Vagrant Mood*, Heinemann, 1952.
Paul Morand, 'Reflexions sur le roman-policier', *Revue de Paris*, I. IV. 1934.
H. T. F. Rhodes, 'The Detective in Fiction and in Fact', *Cornhill*, Jan. 1938.

BIBLIOGRAPHY AND NOTES
TO CHAPTER XII

[1] N.Y. Knopf, also Grosset & Dunlap, 1919.

[2] N.Y., Grosset & Dunlap, also Putnam, 1923; London, Putnam, 1923.

[3] N.Y., Appleton, 1918; London, Putnam, 1923.

[4] Freeman Wills Crofts:
The Cask, London, Collins, 1920; New York, Boni, 1924.
Inspector French's Greatest Case, London, Collins, 1925; New York, Boni, 1925; also Burt, 1927.

[5] Agatha Christie: —
The Mysterious Affair at Styles, London, Lane, 1921; New York, Dodd, Mead, 1927. Mrs. Christie's later novels have been published simultaneously in London by Collins and in New York by Dodd, Mead.

[6] H. C. Bailey: —
Call Mr. Fortune, London, Methuen, 1920.
Garstons, London, Methuen, 1930; U.S. Title: *The Garston Murder Case*, New York, Doubleday, 1930.
Black Land, White Land, London, Gollancz, 1937; New York, Doubleday, 1937.
The Life Sentence, London, Macdonald, 1946; New York, Doubleday, 1946; Toronto, Nelson, 1946.
Shrouded Death, London, Macdonald, 1950.

[7] Dorothy L. Sayers: —
Whose Body, London, Fisher, Unwin, 1923.
Clouds of Witness, London, Fisher, Unwin, 1926; N.Y., Dial Press, 1926.
Unnatural Death, London, Benn, 1927.
The Unpleasantness at the Bellona Club, London, Benn, 1928; N.Y., Harpers, 1957.
Lord Peter Views The Body, London, Gollancz, 1928; N.Y., Brewer, 1928.
Miss Sayers's Anthologies, *Great Short Stories of Detection, Mystery and Horror*, all published in London by Gollancz, Series 1 (1928); series 2 (1931); series 3 (1934). U.S. titles: —
The Omnibus of Crime, New York, Harcourt, 1928.
The Second Omnibus of Crime, New York, Coward, McCann, 1931.
The Third Omnibus of Crime, New York, Coward, McCann, 1934.
Her later novels appeared simultaneously in England and

America, published in London by Gollancz, and in New York by Harcourt. *The Nine Tailors* (1934), *Gaudy Night* (1935) and *Busman's Honeymoon* (1937) were also published in Toronto by the Ryerson Press.
In *Titles To Fame*, Edited by D. K. Roberts (London, Nelson, 1937) Miss Sayers gave an account of how *Gaudy Night* was conceived and constructed.

[8] George and Margaret Cole: —
The Brooklyn Murders, London, Collins, 1923; N.Y., Boni, 1924.
The Death of a Millionaire, London, Collins, 1925; re-issued 1926.

[9] Philip Macdonald: —
The Rasp, London, Collins, 1924; N.Y., Burt, 1927.
Later novels published simultaneously in London by Collins, and in New York by Doubleday & Doran. (*The Nursemaid who Disappeared* issued with the U.S. title, *Warrant for X*).
Short Story, *The Green and Gold String*, published in *The Queen's Awards: Third Series*, Boston, Little, Brown, 1948; London, Gollancz, 1950.

[10] A. E. W. Mason: —
At The Villa Rose, London, Hodder & Stoughton, 1910; New York, Scribner, 1929.
The House of the Arrow, London, Hodder & Stoughton, 1924; New York, Doubleday & Doran, 1924.
The Prisoner in the Opal, London, Hodder & Stoughton, 1929; New York, Doubleday & Doran, 1928.

[11] Published in the Famous Trials series.

[12] "John Rhode's" novels were all published in London by Geoffrey Bles.
The Ellerby Case was published in New York by Dodd, Mead, 1927; also by Burt, 1928.
The Murders in Praed Street, N.Y., Dodd, Mead, 1928.

[13] Ronald A. Knox: —
The Viaduct Murder, London, Methuen, 1925; New York, Simon & Schuster, 1928.
The Body in the Silo, London, Hodder & Stoughton, 1933.
Still Dead, London, Hodder & Stoughton, 1934; N.Y., Dutton, 1934.
Double Cross Purposes, London, Hodder & Stoughton, 1937; U.S. title, *Settled Out of Court*, New York, Dutton, 1934.
Essays in Satire, London, Sheed & Ward, 1928.
The Best Detective Stories of 1928 (in collab. with H. Harrington) London, Faber, 1929.

[14] Willard Huntington Wright: —
World's Great Detective Stories, New York, Scribners, 1927.
As "S. S. Van Dine": —
The Benson Murder Case, Serialised in New York, Scribner's
Magazine, 1925; Re-issued, New York, Burt, 1928.
The Greene Murder Case, N.Y. Scribners, 1928; London, Benn,
1928.
The Bishop Murder Case, N.Y. Scribners, 1929; London,
Cassell, 1929.
The Dragon Murder Case, N.Y. Scribners, 1933; London,
Cassell, 1934.

[15] Cf. *inter alia,* Agatha Christie's *Ten Little Niggers* (1940), published in the U.S. with the title *And Then There Were None.*

[16] Based largely on an actual murder case, that of Joseph Bowne
Elwell, the bridge expert.

[17] Earl Derr Biggers: —
The House Without a Key, Serialised in New York, *Saturday
Evening Post,* 1925. London, Harrap, 1931.
The Chinese Parrot, New York, Bobbs, 1926; also Grosset,
1927.
Behind That Curtain, New York, Bobbs, 1928; London,
Harrap, 1928.
Charlie Chan Carries On, New York, Bobbs, 1930; also Grosset,
1931.

[18] J. P. Marquand: —
Thank You, Mr. Moto, New York, Little, Brown, & Co., 1936.
London, Jenkins, 1937.
Think Fast, Mr. Moto, New York, Little, Brown, 1937; London,
Hale, 1938.
Mr. Moto Is So Sorry, New York, Little, Brown, 1938; London,
Hale, 1939.
Last Laugh, Mr. Moto, New York, Little, Brown, 1942;
London, Hale, 1943.

[19] Frances Noyes Hart: —
The Bellamy Trial, New York, Doubleday & Doran, 1928.
London, Heinemann, 1928.
Hide In The Dark, New York, Doubleday & Doran, 1929.
London, Heinemann, 1929.
The Crooked Lane, New York, Doubleday & Doran, 1934;
London, Heinemann, 1936.

[20] Georges Simenon's novels are published in Paris by Presses de
la Cité.

[21] Between 1932 and 1934 by Hurst & Blackett. Later by
Routledge.

[22] N.Y., Harcourt.

[23] Edgar Wallace: —
The Mind of Mr. J. G. Reeder, London, Hodder & Stoughton, 1925; Toronto, Musson, 1927; As *The Murder Book of J. G. Reeder*, New York, Doubleday, 1927.
Red Aces, London, Hodder & Stoughton, 1930; New York, Doubleday & Doran, 1930.
Mr. J. G. Reeder Returns, London, Collins, 1933 (posthumously). As *Mr. Reeder Returns*, New York, Burt, 1933.

[24] "Francis Beeding" (the pseudonym used by John Leslie Palmer and Hilary Aiden St. George Saunders, working in collaboration) has produced a long series of 'Spy Thrillers' from 1925 onwards, and also a few bona fide detective novels, notably *Death Walks in Eastrepps*, London, Hodder & Stoughton, 1931; New York, Mystery League, Inc.

[25] Leslie Charteris: —
The "Saint" series, published London, Hodder & Stoughton, 1930 on; New York, Doubleday; Toronto, Musson.

[26] Anthony Berkeley Cox: —
As "Anthony Berkeley": —
The Layton Court Mystery, published anonymously in London, 1925, later by Herbert Jenkins; New York, Doubleday & Doran.
The Second Shot, London, Hodder & Stoughton, 1930; New York, Doubleday & Doran, 1931.
As "Francis Iles": —
Malice Aforethought, London, Gollancz, 1931; New York, Harper, 1931.
Before the Fact, London, Gollancz, 1932; N.Y. Doubleday & Doran.
As For The Woman, London, Jarrolds, 1939; N.Y., Doubleday & Doran.

[27] S. Dashiell Hammett: —
Red Harvest, New York, Knopf, 1929; London, Cassell, 1929.
The Dain Curse, N.Y., Knopf, 1929; London, Cassell, 1929.
The Maltese Falcon, New York, Knopf, 1930; London, Cassell, 1931.
The Glass Key, New York, Knopf, 1931; London, Cassell, 1931.
The Thin Man, New York, Knopf, 1934; London, Barker, 1934.

[28] Erle Stanley Gardner: —
The Case of the Sulky Girl, New York, Morrow, 1933; London, Harrap, 1933.
The D.A. Holds a Candle, New York, Morrow, 1938; London, Cassell, 1939.

The Case of the Fan-Dancer's Horse, New York, Morrow, 1952; London, Heinemann, 1952.
As "A. A. Fair": —
Lam To The Slaughter, London, Hamilton, 1939.
Some Slips Don't Show, New York, Morrow, 1957.

[29] Raymond Chandler: —
The Big Sleep, New York, Knopf, 1939; London, Hamilton, 1939.
The High Window, New York, Knopf, 1942; London, Hamilton, 1943; (also Ryerson Press).
The Long Goodbye, New York, Knopf, 1953; London, Hamilton, 1953; also Toronto, T. Allen, 1953.

[30] Rex Stout: —
Fer-de-Lance, London, Cassell, 1934.
The Golden Spiders, New York, Viking Press, 1953; London, Collins, 1954.

[31] Stuart Palmer: —
Cf. *inter alia,* his *Exit Laughing,* London, Collins, 1954; (U.S. title, *Cold Poison,* New York, M. S. Mill, 1954.

[32] Phoebe Attwood Taylor, "Alice Tilton": —
Cape Cod Mystery, Indianapolis, Bobbs-Merrill, 1931.
Diplomatic Corpse, New York, Little, Brown, 1951; also McClelland, London, Collins, 1951.

[33] "Craig Rice": —
Trial By Fury, New York, Simon & Schuster, 1941; London, Hammond, 1951.
The April Robin Murders (completed by Ed McBain) published posthumously, Random House, 1958.

[34] Mignon Eberhart: —
The Patient in Room 13, New York, Doubleday, 1929; London, Crime Club, 1929.
From This Dark Stairway, New York, Doubleday, 1931; London, Crime Club, 1931; Heinemann, 1932.
Another Man's Murder, New York, Random House, 1957.

[35] "Conyth Little": —
The Black House, New York, Doubleday, 1950; London, Collins, 1950.

[36] Mabel Seeley: —
The Listening House, New York, Doubleday & Doran, 1938; London, Collins, 1940.
The Beckoning Door, New York, Doubleday & Doran, 1950; London, Collins, 1950.
The Stranger Beside Me, New York, Doubleday & Doran, 1951; London, Muller, 1953.

[37] "Ellery Queen": —
The Roman Hat Mystery, New York, Stokes, 1929; London, Gollancz, 1929.
The Egyptian Cross Mystery, New York, Stokes, 1932; London, Gollancz, 1933.
101 years' Entertainment: The Great Detective Stories, 1841—1941.

[38] Margaret Millar's novels mentioned here are both published in New York by Random House, and in London by Gollancz. *Beast in View* published in French translation as *Mortellement Votre*, Paris, Presses de la Cité, 1957.

[39] Fredric Brown, Cf, *inter alia*: —
Death Has Many Doors, New York, Dutton, 1951; London, Boardman, 1952.
We all Killed Grandma, New York, Dutton, 1952; London, Boardman, 1953.

[40] Isaac Asimov: —
Cf. *I, Robot*, New York, The Gnome Press, 1950; London, Grayson, 1952.

[41] John Dickson Carr: —
It Walks by Night, London & New York, Harper, 1930.
The Hollow Man, London, Hamish Hamilton, 1935; U.S. title: *The Three Coffins*, New York, Harper, 1935.
The Arabian Nights Murders, London, Hamilton, 1936; New York, Harper, 1936.
The Problem of the Wire Cage, London, Hamilton, 1939; New York, Harper, 1939.
The Plague Court Murders (as "Carter Dickson"), London, Heinemann, 1934; New York, Morrow, 1934.
The Reader is Warned (as "Carter Dickson"), London, Heinemann, 1939; New York, Morrow, 1939.
The Bride of Newgate, London, Hamilton, 1950; New York, Harper; also Musson, 1950.
The Devil in Velvet, London, Hamilton, 1951; New York, Harper, 1951.
Fire, Burn! London, Hamilton, 1957; New York, Harpers, 1957.
The Gentleman From Paris, included in *The Queen's Awards: Fifth Series:* New York, Little, Brown, 1950; London, Gollancz, 1952.
The Life of Sir Arthur Conan Doyle, London, Murray, 1949; New York, Harper; also Musson, 1949.
The Exploits of Sherlock Holmes (in collaboration with Adrian Conan Doyle), London, Murray, 1954; New York, Random House, 1954.

[42] Lillian de la Torre: —
Dr. Sam: Johnson, detector, New York, Knopf, 1946; London, Joseph, 1948.
Villainy Detected, New York, Appleton-Century-Crofts, 1947.
Heir of Douglas, New York, Knopf, 1952.
The above titles are the abbreviations normally accepted. The actual titles are very lengthy, in the eighteenth century manner.

[43] Ngaio Marsh: —
A Man Lay Dead, London, Bles, 1934.
Enter a Murderer, London, Bles, 1935.
Overture to Death, London, Crime Club, 1939; New York, Little, Brown, 1939.
Final Curtain, London, Crime Club, 1947; New York, Little, Brown, 1947; Toronto, Collins & Collins, 1947.
Opening Night, London, Crime Club, 1951; Toronto, Collins & Collins, 1951: U.S. title: *Night At The Vulcan,* New York, Little, Brown, 1951.
Died In the Wool, New York, Little, Brown, 1945; London, Crime Club, 1947.
Artists in Crime, London, Bles, 1938; New York, Furman, 1938; Toronto, Saunders, 1938; New York, Grosset, 1940.

[44] A. E. Martin: —
The Power of The Leaf, included in *The Queen's Awards: Third Series,* New York, Little, Brown, 1948; London, Gollancz, 1950.
The Chinese Bed Mysteries, New York, Reinhardt, 1955.

[45] Gladys Mitchell: —
The Mystery of a Butcher's Shop, London, Gollancz, 1929; New York, Dial Press, 1930.
The Saltmarsh Murders, London, Gollancz, 1932; Philadelphia, Macrae, Smith, 1933; New York, Grosset, 1934.

[46] Georgette Heyer: —
Merely Murder, London, Crime Club, 1935; New York, Doubleday, 1935.
A Blunt Instrument, London, Hodder & Stoughton, and Crime Club, 1938 (re-issued, Heinemann, 1954); New York, Doubleday, 1938.

[47] Margery Allingham: —
Death of a Ghost, London, Heinemann, 1934; New York, Doubleday, 1934.
Flowers For The Judge, London, Heinemann, 1936; New York, Doubleday, 1936.
The Fashion in Shrouds, London, Heinemann, 1938; New York, Doubleday, 1938.

Black Plumes, London, Crime Club; also Heinemann, 1940; New York, Doubleday, 1940.
Traitor's Purse, London, Crime Club; also Heinemann, 1941; New York, Doubleday, 1941.

[48] "Anthony Gilbert": —
Death at Four Corners, London, Collins, 1929.
Something Nasty in the Woodshed, London, Collins, 1942; U.S. title: *Mystery in the Woodshed*, New York, Smith & Durrell, 1942.
A Nice Cup of Tea, London, Collins, 1951; U.S. title: *Wrong Body*, New York, Random House, 1951.
And Death Came Too, London, Collins, 1956; New York, Random House, 1956.
Give Death a Name, London, Collins, 1957.

[49] "Josephine Bell": —
Murder in Hospital, London & Toronto, Longmans, 1937.
The Port of London Murders, London & Toronto, Longmans, 1938.
Fall Over Cliff, London & Toronto, Longmans, 1938.
From Natural Causes, London & Toronto, Longmans, 1939.
Summer School Mystery, London, Methuen, 1950.
China Roundabout, London, Hodder & Stoughton, 1956.
Double Doom, London, Hodder & Stoughton, 1957.

[50] Christopher Bush: —
The Perfect Murder Case, London, Crime Club, 1929; New York, Doubleday, 1929; Grosset, 1930.
The Case of the Dead Shepherd, London, Cassell, 1934; U.S. Title: *Tea Tray Murders*, New York, Morrow.
The Case of the Platinum Blonde, London, Cassell, 1944; Macmillan, 1949.
The Case of the Seven Bells, London, Macdonald, 1949; Toronto, Nelson, 1949; New York, Macmillan, 1950.
The Case of the Extra Man, London, Macmillan, 1957.
The Case of the Flowery Corpse, London, Macmillan, 1957.

[51] "Richard Hull" (R. H. Sampson): —
Murder of My Aunt, London, Putnam, 1935.

[52] Edward Grierson: —
Reputation for a Song, London, Chatto & Windus, 1952.
The Second Man, London, Chatto & Windus, 1956.

[53] Michael Gilbert: —
Close Quarters, London, Hodder & Stoughton, 1947.
They Never Looked Inside, London, Hodder & Stoughton, 1947; U.S. Title: *He Didn't Mind Danger*, New York, Harper, 1948.

The Doors Open, London, Hodder & Stoughton, 1949; New York, Musson, 1949.
Smallbone Deceased, London, Hodder & Stoughton, 1950; New York, Harper, 1950; also Musson.
Death in Captivity, London, Hodder & Stoughton, 1952; U.S. Title: *Danger Within,* New York, Harper, 1952.
Fear To Tread, London. Hodder & Stoughton, 1953; New York, Harper, 1953.

[54] "Michael Innes" (John Innes Mackintosh Stewart): —
Death at the President's Lodging, London, Gollancz, 1936; U.S. Title: *Seven Suspects,* New York, Dodd, Mead, 1937.
Hamlet, Revenge! London, Gollancz, 1937; New York, Dodd, Mead, 1937; Toronto, Ryerson Press, 1937.
Lament For a Maker, London, Gollancz, 1938; New York, Dodd, Mead, 1938; Toronto, Ryerson Press, 1938.
The Long Farewell, London, Gollancz, 1958.

[55] "Edmund Crispin" (Robert Bruce Montgomery): —
Love Lies Bleeding, London, Gollancz, 1948; New York, Lippincott, 1948.
Frequent Hearses, London, Gollancz, 1950; Toronto, Longmans, 1950; U.S. Title: *Sudden Vengeance,* New York, Dodd, Mead, 1950.
The Moving Toyshop, London, Gollancz, 1951.
Beware of the Trains, London, Gollancz, 1953.

[56] Julian Symons: —
The Immaterial Murder Case, London, Gollancz, 1945.
A Man Called Jones, London, Gollancz, 1947.
The Thirty-first of February, London, Gollancz, 1950.
The Narrowing Circle, London, Gollancz, 1954.
The Colour of Murder, London, Collins, 1957.

[57] Raymond Postgate: —
Verdict of Twelve, London. Crime Club, 1940; New York, Doubleday, 1940; Toronto, Collins & Collins, 1940.
Somebody at the Door, London, Joseph, 1943.
The Ledger is Kept, London, Joseph, 1953.

[58] Roy Vickers: —
Department of Dead Ends, London, Faber, 1949.
Eight Murders in the Suburbs, London, Jenkins, 1956.

[59] "Nicholas Blake" (Cecil Day Lewis): —
A Question of Proof, London, Collins, 1935.
Thou Shell of Death; U.S. Title: *Shell of Death,* Collins, 1936.
The Beast Must Die, London, Lehmann, 1938.
Malice in Wonderland, London, Collins, 1940; U.S. Title: *The Summer Camp Mystery.*

The Dreadful Hollow, London, Collins, 1953.
The Whisper in the Gloom, London, Collins, 1954.
[60] Margaret Erskine: —
The Whispering House, London, Hammond, 1947.
Give Up The Ghost, London, Hammond, 1949
The Voice of Murder, London, Hodder & Stoughton, 1956.
[61] Christianna Brand: —
Death in High Heels, London, John Lane, 1941; New York, Scribners.
Cat and Mouse, London, Joseph, 1950; New York, Scribners.
The Three-Cornered Halo, London, Joseph, 1957; New York, Scribners, 1957.
[62] C. E. Vulliamy: —
Body in the Boudoir, London, Joseph, 1956.
[63] Clayton Rawson: —
Footprints on the Ceiling, New York; London, Collins, 1939.
Death From a Top Hat, New York; London, Collins, 1940.
The Headless Lady, London, Collins, 1941.
[64] Leonard Gribble: —
The Arsenal Stadium Mystery, London, Harrap, 1939; Jenkins, 1950.
They Kidnapped Stanley Matthews, London, Jenkins, 1950.
[65] William Wiegand: —
At Last, Mr. Tolliver, New York. Rinehart, 1950; London, Hodder & Stoughton, 1951.
[66] Winston Graham: —
The Little Walls, London, Hodder & Stoughton, 1955; New York, Doubleday, 1955.
The Sleeping Partner, London, Hodder & Stoughton, 1956.

INDEX

(In order to facilitate reference, the names of famous fictional detectives are in capitals, and all book titles italicised).